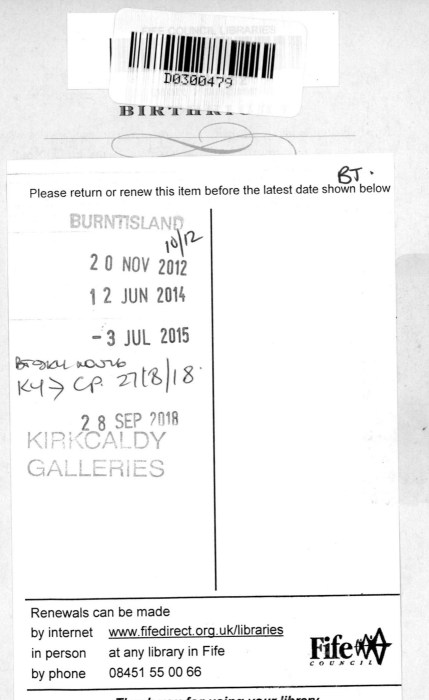

"A perfect mix of true crime and real-life adventure."
—*Booklist*, starred review

"Roger Ekirch expertly illumines eighteenth-century societies in the British colonies and the seedy underside of Georgian Dublin."
—Toby Barnard, author of *Making the Grand Figure: Lives and Possessions in Ireland, 1641–1770*

"Ekirch penetrates the cloud of witnesses at the various legal proceedings to create a fascinating picture of Ireland under its Protestant aristocracy. . . . An engrossing familial and legal tale told with dash and clarity."
—*Kirkus Reviews*

"It was the *Da Vinci Code* of the 19th century—a rollicking adventure story about a young nobleman abducted and sold into slavery in America. But now it has been revealed that Robert Louis Stevenson's classic novel *Kidnapped* was not fiction at all, but a loosely based version of a shocking real life tale involving the cream of Dublin society. And amazingly, Stevenson even toned down the drama in his novel, according to historian Roger Ekirch, who has now written up the true story behind the famous fiction."
—Jim Clarke, *Irish Sunday Mirror*

" [A] fascinating read."
—*Publishers Weekly*

"If you like edge-of-the-seat courtroom drama with a dash of kidnapping, revenge and murder thrown in, then this is the book for you."
—*Practical Family History*

"Ekirch does a masterful job . . . in this meticulously researched and highly readable narrative."
—*Library Journal*

ALSO BY A. ROGER EKIRCH

At Day's Close: Night in Times Past

John Brooks after J. Pope-Stevens,
James Annesley, ca. 1744

BIRTHRIGHT

The True Story
That Inspired *Kidnapped*

A. ROGER EKIRCH

W. W. NORTON & COMPANY

New York · London

For information about permission to reproduce selections from this book,
write to Permissions, W. W. Norton & Company, Inc.,
500 Fifth Avenue, New York, NY 10110

For information about special discounts for bulk purchases, please contact
W. W. Norton Special Sales at specialsales@wwnorton.com or 800-233-4830

Manufacturing by RR Donnelley, Bloomsburg
Book design by JAM Design
Production manager: Julia Druskin

Library of Congress Cataloging-in-Publication Data

Ekirch, A. Roger, 1950–
Birthright : the true story that inspired *Kidnapped* / A. Roger Ekirch.
p. cm.
Includes bibliographical references and index.
ISBN 978-0-393-06615-9 (hbk.)
1. Annesley, James, 1715–1760. 2. Kidnapping victims—Ireland—Biography.
3. Kidnapping—Ireland—History—18th century. 4. Trials (Kidnapping)—
Ireland—History—18th century. I. Title.
HV6604.I72A564 2010
364.15'4092—dc22
[B]
2009033194

ISBN 978-0-393-34001-3 pbk.

W. W. Norton & Company, Inc.
500 Fifth Avenue, New York, N.Y. 10110
www.wwnorton.com

W. W. Norton & Company Ltd.
Castle House, 75/76 Wells Street, London W1T 3QT

1 2 3 4 5 6 7 8 9 0

For Alice,

Alexandra, Sheldon, and Christian,

but for whom . . .

The neglect of one child may be the destruction

of a long succession of families.

"A.M.," *Dublin Weekly Journal,*
October 16, 1725[1]

CONTENTS

MAPS

ILLUSTRATIONS

ACKNOWLEDGMENTS

In the course of my research, I became indebted to numerous institutions and their staffs on both sides of the Atlantic. In Dublin, I wish to thank the National Library of Ireland; the Library of Trinity College, Dublin; the Pearse Street Library; and Philomena Brant at the Registry of Deeds. Deirdre O'Connell performed preliminary research for me at the National Library of Ireland, and Stuart Kinsella, a historian at Christ Church, graciously answered my questions about the Cathedral. I am grateful to the Public Record Office of Northern Ireland in Belfast; the Record Offices of Oxfordshire, Cheshire and Chester, Lancashire, North Devon, and Devon; Jennie Lynch at the Parliamentary Archives in Westminster (formerly the House of Lords Record Office); the Senate House Library at the University of London; the National Archives at Kew (in particular James Ross and Ian Strawbridge); and the Manuscripts Department of the British Library in London. In the United States, thanks are due to the staffs of the Houghton and Widener Libraries at Harvard University; the Library of Congress; Alderman Library at the University of Virginia; the Delaware State Archives; and Newman Library at Virginia Tech, most of all the staff of the Interlibrary Loan Department for their unfailing perseverance on my behalf. For supporting this project with both grants and academic leave, I am indebted to the Department of History and the College of Liberal Arts and Human Sciences at Virginia Tech.

For assistance in providing access to the book's maps and illustrations, I wish to express my gratitude to Máire Ní Chonalláin and Colette Dayly at the National Library of Ireland; Paul Ferguson and Rachel Moss at the Library of Trinity College, Dublin; Camille Lynch at the National Gallery of Ireland; Donnacha O'Maille of Old Irish Maps; Matthew Bailey at the National Portrait Gallery in London; Stephanie Fawcett at the Victoria and Albert Museum; Gudrun Muller at the National Maritime Museum; Jane Cunningham at the Courtauld Institute of Art; William Laffan; and Susan I. Newton at the Winterthur Museum. The Rev. David Gatliffe, rector of St. Margaret's, Lee, kindly photographed the old churchyard where James Annesley and his son are buried. He has my deep appreciation.

I would like to pay special tribute to the Conway family of Dunmain House, who warmly invited me into their historic home. It was a grand pleasure to spend an afternoon with James and Ann, their daughter Elizabeth, and her children, Charlotte and John Robert. Thanks also to Thomas O'Connor for showing me the surrounding countryside and to the boys of Ringsend with whom I shared a Zodiac in Dublin Bay on a brilliant July day.

For reading an early draft of the manuscript, I am grateful to Kevin Whelan, Toby Barnard, Sean Connolly, and Neal Garnham. All were extremely generous in sharing their deep understanding of Irish history and culture. My nephew Jason Chung took time from the campaign trail to help with proofreading. Jackie Hill supplied important information on the Giffard family manuscripts. I am also indebted to Lord Wilson of Tillyorn and Lord Lloyd of Berwick for their valuable counsel. The assistance of Linda Fountaine, Janet Francis, Susan Archer, Jesse Sherman, Kathy McIntyre, Clara Enriquez, and Shenna Stamper was greatly appreciated. "Lucky" Garvin and my two brothers-in-law, David and Don Lee, contributed their medical knowledge, whereas my sister Caryl, besides lending her advice, was good enough to accompany me on a hike through patches of Mill Creek Hundred in northern Delaware.

I could not wish for a more splendid agent than Georges Borchardt, who together with Anne and Valerie Borchardt has been unflagging in his support. My editor, Alane Salierno Mason, has, as always, been an exceptional source of wisdom and good sense. She and so many others at Norton, including Denise Scarfi and Alex Cuadros, have my profound gratitude—as does Allegra Huston for her sensitive reading of the manuscript.

PREFACE

"Wicked uncle, kidnapped heir, bastards, sudden death. Very gratifying," pronounced the young novelist Patrick O'Brian in 1945 on reading a contemporary sketch of James Annesley's life.[1] The presumptive heir to five aristocratic titles and sprawling estates in Ireland, England, and Wales, Annesley was kidnapped from Dublin in 1728 at the age of twelve and shipped by his uncle to America. Only after twelve more years, as a servant in the backwoods of northern Delaware, did he successfully return to Ireland to bring his uncle, the Earl of Anglesea, to justice in one of the most sensational trials of the eighteenth century.

But was Jemmy, in fact, scion of the house of Annesley or, as his enemies insisted, the bastard son of a common house servant? And how, in an age bereft of paternity tests, fingerprint records, and DNA laboratories, could a prodigal who had been missing for over a decade hope to reclaim his birthright in a court of law?

This extraordinary tale has over the centuries inspired at least five novels, including *Kidnapped* (1886) by Robert Louis Stevenson and Sir Walter Scott's *Guy Mannering* (1815). Set either in Ireland or Scotland, these narratives have invariably revolved around the dramatic abduction of a young heir for the purpose not of extorting ransom but of usurping the lad's patrimony.[2]

The real-life ordeal of Jemmy Annesley is even more incredible, though historians, curiously, have all but ignored his strange saga.

Memoirs of an Unfortunate Young Nobleman, Return'd from a Thirteen Years Slavery in America . . . (1743) is easily dismissed as sentimental fiction—which was my instinctive reaction upon first reading it twenty-five years ago. But more recently, a stray reference to Annesley's tribulations in an obscure English diary in Oxford's Bodleian Library caused me to probe further, only to discover transcripts of court proceedings held in London as well as Dublin.[3] And, too, along with newspaper reports, I located nearly four hundred legal depositions, largely pertaining to Jemmy's youth, in the National Library of Ireland in Dublin and the National Archives outside London. Although few scraps of personal correspondence have survived, members of the Annesley family left a vast trove of legal documents in their wake. The sheer density of the depositions, many containing richly detailed recollections of rural Ireland, is stunning. Though of varying quality and length, they speak not only of the minutiae of everyday existence—the clothing, furnishings, and customs of lords and peasants—but also of the cadences of Irish life. More than that, the Dublin trial in 1743 was but one episode in an extraordinary family drama that unfolded on two continents over seven decades, to the fascination of the public on both sides of the Irish Sea. In the rough-and-tumble world of eighteenth-century Ireland, few aristocratic families could match the house of Annesley for venality or violence. "Surely this is melodrama and not history," a distinguished legal scholar has quipped.[4] The truth is that it is both.

The Annesleys, an English family who during the course of the 1600s achieved wealth and fame in Ireland on a grand scale, were scarcely the only noble house in either kingdom racked by internal discord. By the eighteenth century, many family dynasties, once united by bonds of kinship and clientage, had given way to nuclear households comprising parents, children, and a small ring of close relatives. Legal quarrels, especially rival claims over inheritance, were not uncommon among distant relations. "When kinsfolk are

a degree or two removed, they grow perfectly indifferent to each
other, and come to forget all mutual regards," lamented a Dublin
writer in 1734.[5]

But the Annesleys fought the bulk of their battles at close quarters. The ferocity of their clashes—over rank and wealth, rather
than theology or political dogma—cut to the family's very core,
pitting husband against wife, father against son, and brother
against brother. Jemmy's abduction by his Uncle Dick was merely
the most brazen act of treachery, neither the first nor, surely, the
final breach of trust. Ultimately, this is a story about betrayal
and loss—but also about endurance, survival, and redemption.
Despite its English origins, it is, at its heart, an Irish tale.

ROGER EKIRCH
Sugarloaf Mountain
Roanoke, Virginia
February 2009

A NOTE ON THE TEXT

All dates are rendered in new style, with the new year beginning on January 1, and all miles are statute miles. Quotations are in the original spelling except when altered to improve clarity. Capitalization has been modernized, and punctuation added when necessary. I have chosen to adhere to the traditional spelling of "Anglesea," in contrast to "Anglesey," except when the latter appears in quotations or in the titles of artwork and archival collections.

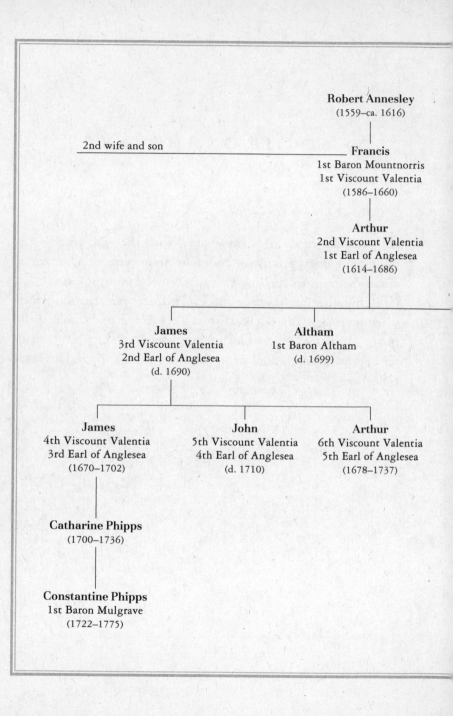

Robert Annesley
(1559–ca. 1616)

2nd wife and son ————— Francis
1st Baron Mountnorris
1st Viscount Valentia
(1586–1660)

Arthur
2nd Viscount Valentia
1st Earl of Anglesea
(1614–1686)

James
3rd Viscount Valentia
2nd Earl of Anglesea
(d. 1690)

Altham
1st Baron Altham
(d. 1699)

James
4th Viscount Valentia
3rd Earl of Anglesea
(1670–1702)

John
5th Viscount Valentia
4th Earl of Anglesea
(d. 1710)

Arthur
6th Viscount Valentia
5th Earl of Anglesea
(1678–1737)

Catharine Phipps
(1700–1736)

Constantine Phipps
1st Baron Mulgrave
(1722–1775)

ANNESLEY

FAMILY

PEDIGREE*

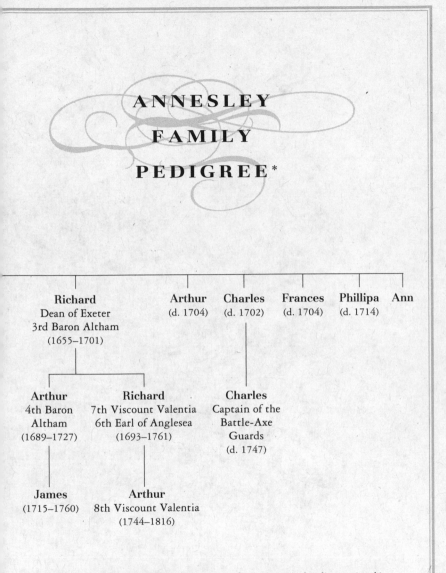

Richard	Arthur	Charles	Frances	Phillipa	Ann
Dean of Exeter	(d. 1704)	(d. 1702)	(d. 1704)	(d. 1714)	
3rd Baron Altham					
(1655–1701)					

Arthur	Richard	Charles
4th Baron	7th Viscount Valentia	Captain of the
Altham	6th Earl of Anglesea	Battle-Axe
(1689–1727)	(1693–1761)	Guards
		(d. 1747)

James	Arthur
(1715–1760)	8th Viscount Valentia
	(1744–1816)

*Modified to include chiefly the family's main stem, from the original pedigree printed in
1817 (Richard Annesley Correspondence, 1741–1766, Additional Manuscripts 31889,
British Library, London). Just the highest titles in Ireland and England for each peer have
been listed.

Charles Brooking, *A Map of the City and Suburbs of Dublin*, 1728. A view of the capital looking from north to south in the year of Annesley's kidnapping.

BIRTHRIGHT

PROLOGUE

To commit the care of a minor to him who is the
next in succession to him is like committing the lamb
to be devoured by the wolf.
SIR JOHN FORTESCUE, 1471[1]

he crier's elegy echoes in the bleak evening air, as the bare-
foot boy darts off in the direction of Christ Church. Across
Ormond Bridge, where fluttering oil lamps cast a feeble glow, to
Wood Quay on the south bank of the River Liffey. Damp cob-
blestones likely slow his pace ahead of Pudding Row. No street
urchin knows the waterside better, its wide quays, market stalls,
and gabbard-men. A winding passage, strewn with rubbish, emp-
ties past the sign of the Palm-Tree into Winetavern Street, the
heart of Dublin's old city. Catching his breath, Jemmy climbs
Cock Hill to reach the cathedral grounds, anxiously pushing past
a sparse crowd that has gathered for his father's funeral.[2]

On the night of November 16, 1727, less than twenty-four
hours after his sudden death, mourners inter the remains of Arthur
Annesley, fourth Baron Altham. Only thirty-eight, he died, with
his mistress by his side, early that morning in bed. Coughing
uncontrollably and unable to stand, he began to lose his sight
while a servant cradled his head. "Lord have mercy on my soul,"
he at last muttered, "I am going into another world."[3]

The ceremony bears little resemblance to a traditional Irish wake. No fiddles or ballads or whiskey to lighten hearts. Instead, somber footmen with torches lead the bereaved, draped in mourning scarves, from a still column of coaches. In recent years, the city's Protestant aristocracy has adopted the English fashion of staging nocturnal funerals. These occasions are smaller and more private, and, as such, have the virtue of being less expensive. A lone chaplain, attended by a verger, presides. The darkness lends an element of solemnity absent from much of the baron's life.[4]

A massive Romanesque edifice dating from the high Middle Ages, the Church of the Holy Trinity, popularly known as Christ Church, sits atop a summit overlooking the Liffey as it flows through the city toward the sea. "A venerable Gothic pile," in the words of an eighteenth-century writer. The cathedral, a favorite place of worship for the country's lord lieutenant, the king's preeminent representative in Ireland, has become a bastion of the Anglo-Irish establishment. That alone, however derelict Altham's own attendance, makes the church a natural resting place.[5]

It is not Jemmy's young age—twelve years—that gives him away, nor his dress. Long ago, his feathered hat and scarlet jacket were abandoned for tattered breeches and a soiled coat—not unlike the ragtag garb of "blackguard boys" drawn that night by curiosity to the church. More revealing is the youth's weeping, rare among others in attendance, including the baron's younger brother, Richard. "My father, my father," Jemmy finally blurts out as pallbearers descend narrow steps to place the coffin inside the church's ancient crypt. So stunned is a mourner that she quickly spins the boy around, begging to know his identity. Lord Altham's son, he declares; and with that, he is off, tears streaming from his eyes all the way to Phoenix Street and the abode of John Purcell the butcher.[6]

For more than three years, Jemmy Annesley has roamed old Dublin's maze of by-lanes and crooked streets, with their rows of red brick houses capped by roofs of blue slate. Although Ireland is

George Grattan, *South View of Christ Church Dublin*, ca. 1805. Christ
Church Lane passes before the nave of the cathedral, with the ruins of the
Four Courts on the right.

predominantly Catholic, the capital is two-thirds Protestant and
the stronghold of the country's ruling elite. It is also a flourish-
ing port, boasting ninety-two thousand residents in 1725, second
in the British Isles only to the population of London. Dublin,
nonetheless, still has the physical appearance of a large European
town. Its area, a contemporary estimates, comprises just one-third
of London's vast expanse. And unlike the broad swath cut by the
Thames, the Liffey, whose shallow channel does not permit ships
with freight beyond the customs house at Essex Bridge, measures
fewer than 170 feet in breadth. With some exaggeration, a visitor
observes, "Dublin is like a large market town in England where
everyone knows and is known by everybody."[7]

This intimate, bustling metropolis—its familiar ways and customs—Jemmy has come to know firsthand after being turned out, at age eight, by his father in the spring of 1724. For several months, father and son dwelled north of the Liffey on Phrapper Lane, just to the west of Green Market. A neighborhood school offered instruction in English and Latin. But once the baron, together with Miss Gregory, removed to the suburban village of Inchicore, the boy was put to board on the south side of the river. "Over the water," as a person later says. In the shadow of Dublin Castle, the residence of the lord lieutenant, Jemmy lives on Little Ship Street, just the first of several stops in coming months.[8]

No one spot keeps him for long. Once, he makes the short

Crypt of Christ Church, n.d., photograph by Peter O'Toole. Dating to the twelfth century, the crypt remains Dublin's oldest surviving architectural structure.

journey on foot to Inchicore, only to be turned away at his father's door. By Christmastime, Jemmy has returned to Phrapper Lane, where he occasionally sleeps in the hayloft of a playfellow's home. Then, for nearly two years, he works as a shoeboy along Inns Quay, employing a mixture of lampblack and eggs for polish and a rag or tattered wig for a cloth. He also runs errands as a "scull" for students at Trinity College, despite his rumored notoriety as a nobleman's son. "You little rogue, you often say you are Lord Altham's son," a young scholar scolds one day. "Now you tell me [the] truth—are you, or are you not?" "Indeed, indeed, I am my Lord and Lady Altham's son," Jemmy protests. Nights find him sleeping in a doorway or curled beneath a vendor's stall, like hundreds of other destitute children in Dublin's streets. "Whole swarms of bastards," rails a writer, that "should be shipped off to the wildest of our plantations abroad."[9]

When taxed for his gross neglect, Altham blames his mistress, to whom the profligate baron has become indebted in the amount of £500. "That bitch will not suffer me to do any thing for him," he protests to a confidant. In the spring of 1727, three years after leaving Phrapper Lane, he does, at last, arrange for Jemmy to lodge with an old acquaintance, Dominick Farrell, a humble linen dealer. Within two months, however, Jemmy again is forced to fend for himself. The peddler's wife cares little for the baron, who owes Farrell a debt, or, consequently, for his boy.[10]

So it is fortunate that Dominick should encounter his friend John Purcell one Wednesday afternoon three weeks later. The butcher resides with his wife two blocks north of Arran Quay; and though they already have a son, the couple is anxious for another. The two men find Jemmy in Smithfield cattle market—"all in rags and tatters" with a *sugán* (straw rope) around his waist as he leads a horse for sale. Asked his name, he responds, "James Annesley, son to Lord and Lady Altham." Once Purcell invites him to join his household, the boy drops to his knees in gratitude.

Hugh Douglas Hamilton, *A Shoeboy at Customs House Gate*, 1760.
Standing by a gate leading to the Liffey and Essex Bridge, a youth
cradles a pot of black polish, with rags wrapped round his waist, as a
younger shoeboy, to the right, tends to a customer.

"I'm almost lost," he mumbles. Taking the boy's hand, the burly
butcher replies, "Well, Sir, have a good heart."[11]

Home lies a short distance away. "There is a present for you,"
Purcell announces to his wife. "I desire you will take care of him, for

he has no friends to do it." That evening, on being scrubbed "head to foot" in a kitchen tub with a wedge of soap, water, and bran, Jemmy is put to bed in a clean shirt. "While I have a bit of bread for my own child," Mrs. Purcell promises, "you shall never want."[12]

An affable man, Purcell follows a rough trade. Butchers are a stout lot, whose ranks dominate the neighborhood bordering the slaughterhouses of Ormond Market. Mostly Catholic, they frequently battle the city's Protestant weavers. Only constables and bailiffs, with whom both butchers and weavers scuffle, inspire greater hatred.[13]

On a fall afternoon, barely three weeks before Lord Altham's death, a gentleman pays the Purcells a visit. To augment their modest living, the couple keep a tippling house, and the stranger, who arrives with a fusil and a setting dog, requests a pot of beer. Do you, he asks the butcher, have a boy in the house named James Annesley? Yes, replies Purcell, calling the boy, hesitantly, from the fireside, once and then a second time. Stricken with fear, his eyes beginning to moisten, Jemmy whispers to "Mammy," Purcell's wife, "That is my Uncle Dick."[14]

"So, Jemmy," questions Captain Richard Annesley, "how do ye do?" Bowing, the boy replies, "Thank God, very well." In fact, he has just recovered from smallpox, and his face still bears a red rash. "Don't you know me?" inquires the gentleman. "Yes" comes the reply, "you are my Uncle Annesley." "Jemmy," continues Richard, "I think Providence was very good to you to put you into such hands to take care of you." More questions follow. Does Purcell intend to keep Jemmy as an apprentice? No, the butcher replies. Being "bred to such a slavish business himself," he does not think it proper "to take a gentleman's son" to "make a butcher." Instead, he expresses the wish that father and son might be reunited. (On a separate occasion, Jemmy himself has told Purcell that he yet hopes to succeed his father.)[15]

Nor, in response to Richard's query, will Purcell accept money for the boy's board. Finally, after pledging to inform Lord Altham of Jemmy's circumstances, Uncle Dick departs. What if anything is reported, we do not know. Tempted himself to visit Altham, Purcell is strongly discouraged by friends. "They told me he was a passionate little man, and by reason of the whore he kept in his house, he would not matter to shoot me."[16]

It does not appear that Jemmy and his uncle speak at the baron's funeral. No eyewitness reports even a cursory exchange. Clearly, however, the boy's sudden appearance at Christ Church makes a deep impression on the small gathering of mourners, not least on Richard Annesley himself—who, not incidentally, seeks to be enrolled in his brother's place as Baron Altham. Afterward, during a heated meeting in Dublin Castle, the king at arms, the country's senior herald, initially refuses to certify the title, an essential step before the lord chancellor can grant a writ of summons to the House of Lords. Owing to the boy's "great noise" at the funeral, it seems to many that the late lord has left a son, and a legitimate heir at that. Over the next few days, any mention of the funeral elicits a torrent of invective from Richard, who rails that the boy is a vagabond and an impostor. Ever since, Richard complains, he cannot "make his appearance at the Castle, or anywhere, but that he was insulted." An attorney counsels forbearance. If the boy is a bastard, he will be found out. If a vagrant, he might be shipped as a servant to America.[17]

Except for a few patches of sunlight, December brings gray skies, rain, and fog. It is during the first week that an unfamiliar servant appears one morning on Phoenix Street. Jemmy, he says, is summoned to Ormond Market by his uncle. Can he come right away? A cudgel in one hand, John Purcell hoists the lad by the other. A short walk brings them to the George, a tavern in Bow Lane, where Richard, newly titled Baron Altham, stands inside with the owner, Mr. Jones. Joining them in the cramped alehouse are a constable and several "odd-looking fellows." Removing his hat, the butcher bids them good morning. "How do you do, Mr. Purcell," replies the uncle. Still in mourning, he is dressed totally in black. Then, pointing to Jemmy, he instructs a figure by the door, "Hark you sir, take that thieving son of a whore!"[18]

Before anyone can act, Purcell presses Jemmy between his legs. Striking the constable with the cudgel, he vows, "Whosoever suffers to do him mischief, by all that's good, I'll knock his brains out." Furious, Richard insists that the boy will be transported to the colonies. "By God he shall not stay in the kingdom, I will send him to the devil." But no one dares test the butcher's mettle. Then, with his eyes fixed on the baron, Purcell declares, "You make a good appearance of a gentleman, and I am surprised that you should show so much revenge and so much malice as to say that you will destroy this poor creature." It is a remarkable outburst for a humble tradesman. Grasping his sword, Richard swears that he will "stick" Purcell "to the wall," but a band of butchers, hearing the fracas, arrives outside, scattering the baron and his men. "I have more friends here than you have," warns Purcell.[19]

This first skirmish ends in a draw; but Annesley's business is not done. Jemmy's anxiety only deepens over the winter. Before, he ran errands, but on most days he now lingers inside the Purcells' home. More than once, strangers are seen lurking outdoors. One even attempts to enter the tiny yard, only to bolt "like a buck" upon the butcher's approach. In early February, nearly nine months after his arrival, Jemmy makes off, increasingly fearful of being abducted. For a short spell, he resides as a servant at the nearby home of Richard Tighe, a prominent attorney. Perhaps the boy gambles that Tighe's home will afford the safer haven. If so, he miscalculates.[20]

The early days of spring see strong gusts, hail, and drenching rains. The swollen Liffey tops its banks, flooding homes and workshops. Mud, tree limbs, and animal carcasses lie everywhere. But brightening skies in April draw Jemmy outdoors, prompted by his master's inattention. For more than a month, Annesley's servants have scoured likely haunts, including Smithfield on the north side of the Liffey and College Green and Newmarket to the south. Then, on April 30, a Monday, the boy is sighted in Ormond Market not far from John Purcell's empty "shambles" (butcher's stall), nabbed, and brought, once again, to the George.[21]

The baron has left little to chance. Along with servants, he commands two constables, each promised half a guinea. Richard alleges that the boy has stolen a silver spoon. Neither constable bears a warrant, but their presence gives the abduction a whiff of legality. "Do this job for me," Richard promises one, "and I will make a man of you all the days of your life." Even so, the market is unfriendly terrain, and by now Jemmy is crying uncontrollably, certain that he will be either murdered or transported. As they force their way on foot toward the quay, a crowd of people has formed in the bright sunlight, their numbers growing by the minute. This is "the mob"—laborers, tradesmen, and servants—that so frightens Dublin's respectable classes. Nor do such folk have any fondness for kidnapping, an occasional expedient employed by ship captains to fill their holds.[22]

It is a short walk to the north end of Essex Bridge, where, in front of a dilapidated watchhouse, the constables bundle the boy into a coach. Still the curious throng follows, across the Liffey to Custom House Quay and Temple Bar, ultimately as far as George's Quay, over half a mile downriver, where convicts and indentured servants customarily embark for the colonies. "What is the matter?" ask several persons in the crowd.[23]

For all of the commotion, none, in the end, interferes; nor does anyone in a position of authority step forward. These, after all, are deeply troubled times, the impetus for Jonathan Swift's sardonic proposal to cannibalize the babies of starving paupers. The economy lies in ruins, and Dublin all of a sudden faces an influx of vagabonds, with boys no older than Jemmy already transported for their poverty. Housebreakings and street robberies are spreading. Recent crop failures across much of the country have triggered fresh fears of famine, never far from an Irishman's mind. Given the presence of constables, the commotion on George's Quay, at least to some onlookers, must appear less like a kidnapping than punishment sanctioned by a court—probably none too soon.[24]

Uncle Dick is the first to descend the stone steps of the slip to the longboat, followed by the two constables and Jemmy. Exhausted from crying, the boy falls silent as the men begin to row toward Ringsend, a tiny fishing village perched on a tongue of land barely a mile to the east. There, riding at anchor, where the Liffey enters Dublin Bay, is the *James*, a ship of one hundred tons, loaded with servants. Once abreast, Jemmy's uncle escorts him aboard and returns, minutes later, to the waiting boat. A large buoy bobs in the distance, with mighty Howth Head lying just to the northeast. As night comes on, the *James* prepares to make its way over the bar with the shifting tide.[25]

1

FAMILY

If you come to live with me you shall never want a shilling
in your pocket, a gun to fowl, a horse to ride, or a whore.
ARTHUR ANNESLEY,
fourth Baron Altham, n.d.[1]

At the time of his abduction, Jemmy Annesley was the putative heir to one of the greatest family fortunes in Ireland. Other than his father's properties and peerage, he stood to receive extensive estates in Ireland, England, and Wales as well as four aristocratic titles, including the treasured earldom of Anglesea, one of two English peerages. By one estimate, the annual income from the lands approached the princely sum of £10,000, roughly comparable in today's prices to more than £1,000,000. By contrast, in Stevenson's *Kidnapped*, set in Scotland in the year 1751, the young protagonist, David Balfour, is due to inherit, following his father's death, no more than an estate west of Edinburgh that includes the house of Shaws, a large but decrepit mansion.[2]

Just a century earlier in Ireland, the Annesleys had been newcomers—aspiring Englishmen with neither titles nor substantial riches. Apart from personal tenacity and ambition, their rise owed much to Ireland's dramatically transformed social order. Following a new wave of Elizabethan conquest in the late sixteenth century, Protestant adventurers laid claim to confiscated estates, displacing the native Irish with English and Scottish tenants. Colonization, the English monarchy hoped, promised to relieve Britain of its impoverished masses and subdue the indigenous Catholic population—"that rude and barbarous nation," remarked Elizabeth.[3]

In the "plantation" of Munster in southwestern Ireland, among the thirty-five grantees, or "undertakers," seeking to better their fortunes was an army officer fresh from the fighting, Captain Robert Annesley of Newport Pagnell, Buckinghamshire. The younger son of a gentry family, he obtained in 1589, at thirty years of age, 2,600 acres in County Limerick. The grant was smaller than most. Another military man, Sir Walter Raleigh, a courtier, topped the beneficiaries with 42,000 acres in Cork and Waterford. But Annesley's tract was a start, and, for an ambitious squire, a promising one.[4]

Greater glory awaited his son Francis, a favorite of James I, who became vice-treasurer of Ireland in 1625 and the recipient of two Irish titles: Baron Mountnorris, for the fort of Mountnorris that he had garnered in County Armagh, and Viscount Valentia, after an island once allegedly settled by the Spanish off Ireland's southwestern coast. Those honors, however, paled next to the achievements of Arthur, his eldest son. After serving in the English House of Commons for a brief period during the Civil War, Arthur helped to choreograph the return in 1660 of Charles II. For his loyalty, he became not only a privy counsillor but also an English peer, the first Earl of Anglesea as well as Baron Newport Pagnell. Displaying a shrewd aptitude for political advancement, he was appointed lord privy seal in 1673, a traditional font of patronage.[5]

Already one of Ireland's most powerful men, Arthur became, with the acquisition of fresh estates, one of its largest landowners. He was a figure of considerable learning and culture, adopting the motto, from Horace, of *Virtutis Amore* (With Love of Virtue) for the family's coat of arms. Dinner guests at his London mansion in

John Michael Wright, *Arthur Annesley*, 1st Earl of Anglesey, 1676.

Drury Lane, lying just south of St-Giles-in-the-Fields, included
the likes of John Locke and the Earl of Salisbury. A patron of the
poet Andrew Marvell, the earl boasted the largest private library
in England, some thirty thousand volumes, which he regularly
consulted until his death from quinsy, a severe inflammation of
the throat, in 1686.[6]

Such were the heights attained by the house of Annesley over
just three generations. Along with other "New English" families arriving after the Reformation, the Annesleys were charter
members of Ireland's Protestant Ascendancy, the Anglo-Irish
elite that dominated the kingdom until the nineteenth century.

Fundamental to the family's success was its deepening involvement in court politics, coupled with a willingness to subordinate political principles and personal loyalties in pursuit of preferment and private gain. Although they were not men devoid of convictions, neither religion nor ideology hampered their quest. According to his diary, the Earl of Anglesea was a devout Calvinist, though he attended Anglican services, occasionally with the king. Nor did his nonconformist beliefs prevent the marriages of two of his daughters to prominent Irish Catholic nobles. Above all, the Annesleys, as responsible aristocrats, remained committed to furthering the family's fortunes. Eager to establish titled

Annesley Coat of Arms, n.d. The crest displays a shield bordered by a Roman centurion on the left and a Moorish prince, a popular heraldic symbol, on the right. The profile of a Moor's head crowns the shield, beneath which is the maxim *Virtutis Amore* (With Love of Virtue).

households in both Ireland and England, Anglesea persuaded the
king in 1673 to create an Irish barony for Altham, his second son.
In the meantime, his eldest son, James, stood poised to inherit not
only his father's English and Irish titles but also the bulk of his
estates, which, one observer later claimed, "far exceed any other"
in Ireland.[7]

If the Annesleys spent much of the seventeenth century advancing their fortunes, only the rapidity and scale of their ascent set
them apart. After all, the Ascendancy was an imported Protestant elite imposed upon a predominantly Catholic population; in
no sense was it a traditional aristocracy animated by an ancestral
attachment to its lands. By the 1700s, only a small remnant of the
leading families possessed either Old Gaelic or Old English roots
(originating before the reign of Henry VIII). Most eighteenth-
century grandees descended from families who had arrived in Ireland between the 1530s and the outbreak of the English Civil
War in 1642. With conquest and colonization came the elimi-
nation of ancient peerages, if not by the mid-seventeenth century then in the aftermath of the Battle of the Boyne in 1690, in
which a larger Protestant army under William III defeated Irish
and French forces commanded by James II, prompting Catholic
Jacobite families, such as the Dillons, MacCarthys, and O'Briens,
to begin leaving the country. The few remaining Catholic peers
were forbidden to sit in the House of Lords, and by 1749, only six
"Popish" lords, like the Earl of Westmeath and Viscount Mount-
garrett, still resided in the kingdom.[8]

The influx of Protestant adventurers resulted, during the early
Stuart monarchies, in a rapid inflation of fresh titles available from
the Crown. A sizable number were put up for sale, regardless of
the buyer's personal qualifications. Whereas an English barony
during the reign of James I cost as much as £10,000, an Irish
title could be had for £1,500. More than two-thirds of new Irish
peers bore no prior connection to the island, including some with

no interest in ever residing there. One aspiring earl, Sir William Pope, could not decide the best town in Ireland for the name of his title. Having narrowed the choice to Granard or Lucan, he received a letter from his puzzled son: "[I] am certain that there is such towns as Lucan and Granard, but can not find it in the map. . . . If it is possible, we will change Granard for a whole county." For his troubles, along with the sum of £2,744, Pope in 1628 took the name of an Ulster county and became the Earl of Downe.[9]

Although the Irish peerage during the eighteenth century was small, with slightly more than one hundred members, its recent origins had resulted in considerable fluidity. For many Protestant nobles, their primary identification with Ireland was one of material fulfillment and social advancement. Often, in fact, the wealthiest peers became absentee landlords, with titles and estates not just in Ireland but also in England. In 1704, at age twenty-one, John Perceval, the future Earl of Egmont, inherited 22,000 acres of land in Cork and Tipperary but spent the bulk of his life in London. As late as the 1720s, from one-sixth to one-fourth of Irish rents was annually remitted to absentees. In England, these lords intermarried with privileged families, only returning to their Irish estates for short spells.[10]

By contrast, the island's resident peerage, along with greater numbers of knights and squires, lacked the cultivated gentility of England's aristocracy. Like the American colonies, Ireland remained a borderland of the British Empire; the advance of metropolitan manners and values, even in Dublin, progressed slowly. "Till their situation or their manners are altered," wrote John Boyle, fifth Earl of Orrery, an English native with extensive lands in Ireland, "I hope it will not be my ill fortune to live amongst them."[11]

Absent from the upper ranks was a strong sense of self-discipline; excess and intemperance set the standard. Cards and gaming, cockfights, hurling matches, and hunting parties filled idle hours.

"A kennel of dogs is the *summum bonum* of many a rural squire," wrote "Hibernicus" in the *Dublin Weekly Journal*. Entertainments were extravagant. Sumptuous dinners, larded with rumps of beef and saddles of venison, flowed with claret and whiskey punch. "The whole business of the day," an essayist complained in 1729, "is to course down a hare, or some other worthy purchase; to get over a most enormous and immoderate dinner; and guzzle down a proportionable quantity of wine."[12]

Still, their improvidence masked a deeper insecurity. A visiting Englishman hinted as much in describing dinner parties: "They always praise the dishes at their own tables and expect that the company should spare no words in their commendation." Another traveler commented upon the vanity of grandees "even from indifferent families."[13]

Many wellsprings fed the insecurity of the Irish aristocracy, including its ambivalent status within both Ireland and the empire. First and foremost, members of the Ascendancy preened themselves as loyal Englishmen, tied by language and law, faith, and blood to the land of their ancestors. In an essay intended for an English audience, Francis Annesley, an influential member of the Irish House of Commons, declared in 1698 that his fellow Protestants were "Englishmen sent over to conquer Ireland, your countrymen, your brothers, your sons, your relations, your acquaintance." And yet, time and again the English parliament enacted legislation counter to Irish interests. Widespread poverty and economic instability only added to the elite's want of self-confidence, as did the country's turbulent heritage. In 1725, a Dublin newspaper reflected, "To be born in IRELAND is usually looked upon as a misfortune." English commentators lost few opportunities to lampoon Irish "backwardness." Jestbooks like *Bogg-Witticisms*, first published in 1682, popularized the comic figure of "Teague" (an English corruption of the Gaelic name Tadhg), a favorite target for years to come on the London stage. Of absentee landlords, a Dublin writer moaned "that many of our gentlemen bring home with them a scorn for our poverty and obscurity."[14]

Long after the last spasms of rebellion and conquest, brute force remained central to the Ascendancy character, not unlike the propensity for bloodshed characteristic of the English aristocracy during much of the sixteenth and seventeenth centuries. "Their long intestine wars, their constant and slavish dependence upon another kingdom, and their just dread of popery are some sort of excuses for the fire of their brains and the fury of their hearts," observed Orrery.[15]

Quick to take offense, Protestant gentlemen in Ireland routinely dangled swords at their sides, whether in town or in the country. Nor was it uncommon for a neighborhood feud to end in violence. Gentry sons grew notorious for abducting young heiresses to wed and ravish at the point of a sword. Few of the perpetrators were prosecuted, much less punished. Indeed, laws often went unenforced owing to the connivance of landed magnates. Always vulnerable to abuse were social inferiors. Overcharged at a Cork inn for wine, a young Englishman gave the waiter a "hearty drubbing." "It is some satisfaction in this country," he marveled, "that a man has it in his power to punish, with his own hand, the insolence of the lower class of people, without being afraid of a crown-office[r], or a process at law."[16]

Dueling was the most obvious manifestation of this violent ethos. At a time when upper-class violence in England had given way to litigation as the preferred mode of combat, duels remained customary, especially in Dublin. Then, too, many adversaries fought not to uphold personal honor but to exact retribution. These were not set pieces of ritualized violence but bloody clashes more often waged on the spot with short swords than with pistols at a dignified distance. A County Cork combatant in 1733 was stabbed in the back as he lay floundering in the grass. Rarely was eighteenth-century etiquette observed or quarter shown. At a private party, two gentlemen fired pistols at one another in a bedchamber. "It is safer to kill a man, than steal a sheep or a cow," complained Dr. Samuel Madden, the author of *Reflections and Resolutions Proper for the Gentlemen of Ireland* . . . (1738).[17]

The first obligation of every aristocrat, instilled from childhood, was to transfer to the succeeding generation his titles and estates in a condition equal if not superior to that in which they had been received. The head of a noble house more nearly resembled a caretaker or trustee than a proprietor free to dispose of his property at will. Estates were not to be squandered or sold, but kept intact and improved to preserve family continuity. To do otherwise, owing to improvidence or negligence, was an act of betrayal to the line. As Lord Delvin, a County Westmeath grandee, observed, it was "a glorious thing to save an estate for a family, and eternize your name."[18]

Just as critical to the family, of course, was a sufficient supply of male heirs to keep the house and its honors from extinction. The Gaelic tradition of partible inheritance had been one in which estates were divided among male descendants; but upon Ireland's conquest, primogeniture in tail male, whereby titles and the bulk of one's property fell to the eldest son, became the established system in order to protect estates from subdivision and dispersion. With infant mortality a persistent danger, most families, nonetheless, favored an adequate number of sons—"an heir and a spare," as the saying went. The more the better, in fact, so long as each understood his place in the chain of succession. The eldest son, in turn, was expected to provide lands for his male siblings until each had entered a profession.[19]

By any measure—honor, wealth, power—the first generations of Annesleys laid a formidable foundation both in Ireland and England for the family's future success. No aristocratic house could have expected more from its forebears. Equally important, there was no apparent shortage of male heirs. In fact, besides James and Altham, the Earl of Anglesea and his wife were blessed with four additional boys, only one of whom died in infancy. By the close of the 1600s, James, who had become second Earl of Anglesea on his father's death, had sired three sons of his own.[20]

All the same, it was the fortunate family that could sustain a direct line of male descent over several generations. The demographic vagaries of life, marriage, and death, even in the best of times, posed a continual threat to family continuity. As fate would have it, the period from 1650 to 1740 in Britain was one of declining marital fertility and rising mortality. Precise reasons are hard to find, though heightened exposure to diseases, via shipping from the New World, Africa, and Asia, might help to explain the mounting toll of deaths.[21]

Among the Annesleys, early signs of trouble arose soon enough within the households of James's three sons, the family's fifth Irish generation. Born in 1670, the eldest, also named James, became third Earl of Anglesea and fourth Viscount Valentia on his father's precipitous death in 1690. At thirty years of age, he wed Lady Catharine Darnley, the illegitimate daughter of James II, well known for her prickly disposition. The unhappy couple had one daughter. Shortly before the earl died from consumption in 1702, Catharine claimed to the English House of Lords that he had tried to murder her.[22]

Waiting in the wings was John, who acquired his elder brother's titles and most of his property. Although married, he, too, fathered no children other than a single daughter before his own death in 1710. That left the all-important business of producing an heir to the family's lands and titles to the youngest of the three brothers, Arthur (b. 1678), who now became fifth Earl of Anglesea and sixth Viscount Valentia, with an annual income estimated at £6,000 from his Irish estates alone, which in County Wexford approached 20,000 acres. Already a leading Tory politician with influence both in Dublin and London, he had been a gentleman of the privy chamber and selected in 1702 to carry the canopy at the funeral of William III. An esteemed scholar of Latin poetry at Cambridge, he represented the university in the House of Commons for eight years, even defeating Sir Isaac Newton for the post in 1705. Arthur was the preeminent figure in an extended family of nearly two dozen households scattered across Ireland and England.[23]

Wedded in 1702 to his English cousin Mary, daughter of Sir John Thompson, Baron Haversham, Arthur was the family's last hope to preserve a line of descent from his father James, great-grandson of the adventurer Robert Annesley. If, on the other hand, he and Mary failed to conceive a male heir, the family's hereditary honors might still endure, including the Annesleys' most esteemed title, the earldom of Anglesea; but rather than descending directly on the main stem of the genealogical tree, the line would instead fork sideways to an uncle or a cousin. Either path was problematic, depending upon the heir's age, character, and upbringing. For an idle relation not trained from infancy to assume the family honors, the acquisition of a peerage could be both dizzying and dangerous. The risk was that the new lord might prove indifferent to customary constraints and put his own well-being above the long-term interests of the family. Still, for the time being at least, the catastrophic loss of one or more peerages would be averted.[24]

Arthur's uncle, first Baron Altham, would have received precedence had he not expired in 1699, as did his infant son soon afterward. In their stead, occupying one of the tree's few remaining branches, was yet another uncle, Richard Annesley, dean of Exeter cathedral. Although Richard died two years later in London at the age of forty-six, his wife, Dorothea, had given birth, years earlier, to not one boy but two, Arthur and Richard. If no son was born to the fifth earl, the fate of the mighty house of Annesley lay with them: the future father and uncle, respectively, of Jemmy Annesley.[25]

One might have expected more from this remote bough of the family tree. Richard Annesley the elder, after all, was no scoundrel. He had received an enviable education, attending, like his father Arthur, Magdalen College, Oxford, where in 1671 he took the degree of Master of Arts. Later, he returned to the university to earn his Doctor of Divinity degree, serving in the interim in a succession of church offices, including that of a prebendary (clergyman) at Westminster Abbey (his final resting place in 1701). Following in the path of his deceased brother, Richard inherited the baronetcy of Altham. Not that his life always stayed above the fray. After a fracas in a London tavern, he was chastised for swearing obscenely at another clergyman. Consequently, only because of his father's intervention as lord privy seal did Richard in 1681 obtain his deanship.[26]

Arthur, his eldest son, was born eight years later. Little is known of his childhood in Exeter, other than the painful impact, at age twelve, that his father's death must have had. Autobiographies from the period bear witness to the trauma of the loss of a parent, as do descriptions of funerals. "The cries of the children at the funeral moved most that were present," noted a Lancashire clergyman at the burial of a widower in 1659.[27]

Worsening mortality rates meant that numerous sons became fatherless at a tender age, with all the attendant opportunities and responsibilities. Many young men stood to inherit their father's property sooner in life. By the late 1600s, the median age of male heirs had plummeted from twenty-nine a century earlier to just nineteen. Barely an adolescent, Arthur became fourth Baron Altham, bereft of the strong guidance that his father might have provided. Nor would parental approval now be necessary in Arthur's choice of a wife.[28]

Had consent been required, Altham might have been spared years of unhappiness. In April 1703, at just fourteen, he wed a cousin, Phillipa Thompson, another daughter of Lord Haversham, in St. Margaret's Church, next to Westminster Abbey. Among the aristocracy, early marriages were promoted in order to secure a suitable partner. Arthur's match enjoyed the family's blessing, but after Phillipa's death one year later, he wed again in July 1707, this time over the angry protests of his mother. His new wife was Mary Sheffield, tall in stature, with dark brown hair and an olive complexion. A pleasing young woman, she may have been an impulsive choice. Mary was the illegitimate daughter of the Duke of Buckingham, so more than love alone, quite possibly, played a role in the baron's decision.[29]

In general, by the early 1700s, members of the English aristocracy, in the selection of mates, proved more open than earlier generations to affairs of the heart, though increasing one's income or status still remained an important consideration. "Who marries for love without money has good nights and sorry days," averred an English proverb. Aside from the bride's "natural" birth, opposition from the Annesleys probably arose over Buckingham's recent marriage to the widow of James Annesley, whose allegation of attempted murder before the House of Lords, just a few years earlier, still irked the family (as Buckingham's third wife, the duchess was thirty-four years his junior). It did not help that the duke had already attracted the enmity of his fellow High Tory, Arthur, the future Earl of Anglesea. This was an era of intense political strife, within as well as between parties, and Arthur desperately tried to thwart his young cousin's wedding.[30]

Whatever his own misgivings, Buckingham, a grand lion of court politics, not only consented to the union but also promised a generous dowry of £2,000 once his son-in-law turned twenty-one, the age of majority (the father of several illegitimate children, the duke faithfully supported them all). According to custom, the groom, in turn, pledged a jointure that would afford his wife an annuity of £400 in the event of his death. A more immediate source of income for the young lord consisted of property, leased by tenants, in two Leinster counties. Besides 1,800 acres in Meath, he possessed in Wexford a prominent portion of the town of New Ross, a prosperous inland port on the River Barrow some seventy miles southwest of Dublin. In 1701, only days after the death of Richard Annesley, Altham's cousin James had bequeathed these properties to him, to the dismay of others in the family. Then, also, according to his father's own will, Altham, on his twenty-first birthday, stood to receive additional lands in Ireland and England.[31]

But those estates, like his wife's dowry, lay in the future. In the meantime, expenses at the couple's London home rapidly mounted. A short, homely man of slight build with gray eyes and black eyebrows, the baron delighted in low pleasures. He was not one to stand on ceremony. A favorite haunt, to judge from an unpaid debt of nearly £20, was a Chelsea alehouse. Like other budding blades, he also seems to have enjoyed gambling, including the fashionable card game basset, first introduced in Venice during the fifteenth century. In 1706, a popular London comedy, *The Basset-Table*, was dedicated in his honor, though the playwright, Susanna Centilivre, declined to expound upon her patron's "personal virtues," a task, she wrote (perhaps ironically), "to which I freely own my ability is unequal."[32]

Larger financial obligations ensued, including, by the terms of the original marriage contract, £800 drawn against his wife's dowry, now mostly squandered. Quarrels erupted at home, which the couple shared with Altham's mother and sister. By the following year, he was heavily in debt. Adopting a frugal lifestyle appears to have been out of the question, as was the likelihood of entering a profession. By definition, a nobleman born to inherited privilege was a gentleman of leisure with neither the need nor the taste for the pursuit of worldly success. "It was the essence of a gentleman's character," wrote Samuel Johnson, "to bear the

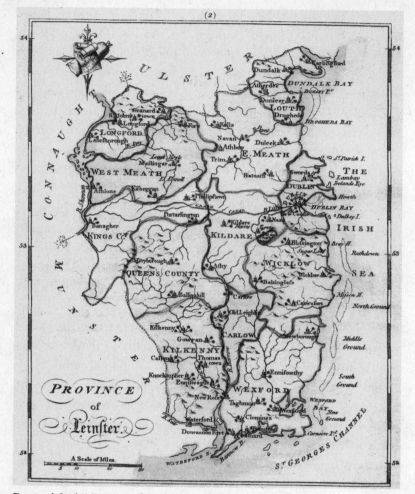

Bernard Scalé, *Province of Leinster*, 1776.

visible mark of no profession whatsoever." In the end, the baron followed the one path open to an impoverished young rake. He deserted his wife and fled London.[33]

That Altham should take up residence in Ireland, in which he had not previously set foot, testified both to his poverty and to his troubled marriage. In recent decades, the wealthiest Annesleys had become absentee landlords. For the first Earl of Anglesea and many of his lineal descendants, court society in London exerted a powerful pull, as did membership in the House of Lords. And, too, many Annesley men married into aristocratic English families, as did a number of the women.[34]

With property in New Ross, Altham removed to County Wexford. Bounded by St. George's Channel and the Irish Sea on the east and the Atlantic to the south, much of the countryside consisted of lowlands with scattered hills and ridges stretching north from the coast to the Blackstairs Mountains. Hedgerows and groves of trees helped to break the uniformity of the undulating landscape. In the south and east, the rich soil commanded some of the highest rents in Ireland, producing oats, wheat, and barley as well as providing grazing land for cattle and sheep. Contrary to popular thought, potatoes, while common, did not dominate the Irish diet. A seasonal foodstuff, unlike bread for instance, they were limited mostly to winter and spring.[35]

With the seaport of Wexford twenty miles to the east, New Ross lay on the county's far western border, separated from the county of Kilkenny by the Barrow. Unusually deep, the river permitted large ships to dock beside a small quay. Major exports included wool, butter, and beef. The town sat on a sloping hillside, with steps descending to the water's edge. Although called New Ross (in contrast to nearby Old Ross), crumbling battlements bore witness to the community's medieval origins. When Oliver Cromwell laid siege in 1649, the inhabitants wisely surrendered after the Aldgate received three blasts of cannonfire (it now bears the name of the Three Bullet Gate). As for "society or amusement," observed an eighteenth-century writer, New Ross was "no place for either."[36]

Just seven miles south of the town along a "very indifferent road" lay Dunmain, which Altham chose for a country home. The estate belonged to the Colcloughs, an ancient Catholic family with

George Holmes, *New Ross, Co. Wexford*, 1791. Long after the arrival of Baron Altham, New Ross remained a modest inland port.

extensive property in the county. Containing nearly 400 acres of mostly arable land amid small knolls and bogs, Dunmain was let to a tenant, Aaron Lambert, for the yearly sum of £17, plus "a fat hog, a summer sheep, and a couple of fat hens." Lambert, in turn, sublet the estate to the baron. Far from making a profit, however, he would lend Altham £500 in coming months, a testament to the clout of even a poor nobleman.[37]

The house, which still stands, was no turf cottage. Constructed in the late seventeenth century, the two-story gray structure boasted a formidable stone façade with a steeply pitched gable roof. Massive granite steps thrust forward from double doors in the center. Like sentries, twin turrets with conical roofs stood watch, one on either side of the main edifice, which contained a dining room, kitchen, parlors, and several bedchambers. Along with basement quarters for servants, the turrets themselves contained small rooms on each floor. In the rear of the house, a high

Anonymous, *Dunmain House*, n.d. The exterior of Dunmain still appears much as it did three hundred years ago, except for the addition of the front portico.

wall enclosed the yard and stables, suggesting lingering fears of military conflict at the time of the manse's construction.

Though a newcomer, the young lord quickly embraced the full-blooded life of a country squire. Although appointed a justice of the peace in 1712, he had little enthusiasm for the office's duties, much less any interest in pursuing a higher post in Dublin other than attending the House of Lords. Unlike justices who faithfully frequented sessions to hear cases and tend to administrative matters, he regarded the office more as a sinecure than a stepping stone. Power was not Altham's abiding passion, as it had been for others in the family. Nor, like some country magnates, did he feel a paternalistic need, through public service, to justify his privileged status. It is telling, as a sign of his isolation, that he barely knew Nicholas Loftus, scion of one of the most politically prominent families in the county, despite the proximity of Loftus Hall, just ten miles south of Dunmain on the Hook peninsula (not once did Altham or Loftus ever visit the other's seat). Instead, the baron's priorities were more mundane, best expressed perhaps upon offering a servant employment. "If you come to live with me," he promised, "you shall never want a shilling in your pocket, a gun to fowl, a horse to ride, or a whore" (the offer was accepted).[38]

Rural sports occupied Altham's days, especially hunting, for which he kept a half-dozen horses and a kennel of prized hounds along with a huntsman and a dog-boy named Smutty. By law, as in England, blood sports remained the preserve of the landed elite. Favorite game included deer, fowl, and hares. He also relished the ancient sport of hurling. The variety known as *báire* or *ioman* was native to southern Ireland and played during the spring and summer. Players wielded wooden sticks (hurls) to strike or carry a soft ball of animal hair, a *sliothar*, to score goals at opposing ends of an immense green. It was a fast-paced, skillful, and, at times, violent contest requiring agility, speed, and strength. A Wexford critic claimed, "I've heard of several persons being killed on the spot, and others never recovering from the bruises." Drawing large crowds, matches were fought between teams representing local magnates. Players for Caesar Colclough of Tintern Abbey wore yellow sashes, for which they were called "yellow bellies," a term still used today for residents of County Wexford. Lord Altham, in addition to recruiting players, typically sponsored a match on St. George's Day, celebrated every April in honor of England's patron saint. Foot races and dancing accompanied the contest.[39]

Such "merriments" showcased the baron's generosity. Clearly, he delighted in the unaffected camaraderie of country folk, Catholics and Protestants alike. A critic later remarked that "he was naturally inclined to low company." "He was a very free man," attested the keeper of a drinking house, close to the soil in both speech and manner. Often, after a day's hunt, Altham would visit the home of a Catholic priest for a cup of whiskey punch. Alcohol lubricated most social gatherings, including occasional dinners at Dunmain where toasts were the order of the night. Guests might include farmers along with a handful of landed gentlemen. The lord bore a reputation for suffering no one to depart before dawn. Stragglers might linger for a breakfast of mulled wine in a nook nicknamed "Sot's Hole."[40]

And Lady Altham? The baron's wife remained marooned in London with modest assistance from her father, the duke. Lord Altham seems to have entertained the thought of divorce after receiving dubious tales from his mother of Mary's infidelity. That, however, would have been difficult to obtain, for the Anglican church only sanctioned formal separations, which did not permit parties to remarry, even in instances of adultery or physical abuse, unless a spouse disappeared for a span of seven years and was presumed dead (should the spouse reappear, however, the original marriage resumed precedence). For a divorce, the sole expedient was a private act of Parliament, though these were rare and expensive. Between 1670 and 1750, only seventeen such acts were passed.[41]

By 1713, Altham was willing to attempt reconciliation, promoted at the time by Buckingham. Whatever the baron's regard for Mary, he had reason to expect, having attained the age of majority, the remainder of her dowry. Still more critical, reconciliation held out the hope of a male heir, placing not only Altham but his son in line to inherit four additional titles, including the earldom of Anglesea. The incumbent, his older cousin Arthur, remained childless, even though he and his wife had been married for eleven years.[42]

Early December ushered in Dublin's "dirty days"—cold, wet, and short. At Buckingham's urging, Lord and Lady Altham agreed to meet, in the city, for the first time in five years. Just south of Christ Church, they reunited at the home of Captain Temple Brisco and his wife. Brisco was the duke's man in

Dublin; there, in Brides Alley, Mary had resided for the past six weeks. The reunion was a happy one, as the captain could report to Buckingham—the entire family having seen the couple to bed one evening. After several days, lord and lady took lodgings in Temple Bar, close to the Liffey, until, finally, on Christmas Eve, they returned by coach to Dunmain as bonfires lit the darkness and servants turned out in welcome.[43]

Within aristocratic circles, the institution of marriage underwent a gradual transition in the eighteenth century. With greater allowance for personal preference, no longer were adolescents invariably consigned to unhappy unions by hopes of preferment and financial advantage. Companionship became more common between couples, with wives performing a valued role in managing the household. The drawbacks of traditional matrimony, in turn, were vividly portrayed in the popular play *The Beaux' Stratagem* by the Irishman George Farquhar, first performed in 1707, the year of the Annesleys' wedding. Among the central characters were Squire Sullen and his wife, whose marriage portion of £10,000 only produced indifference and neglect from her sodden husband. In the end, they were formally separated, though not before the squire was forced to forfeit the handsome dowry.[44]

Of course, many "companionate marriages" also ended in failure, especially when embarked upon at a young age. Nor, in the case of Lord and Lady Altham, is it clear that mutual affection was the original basis of their marriage. And yet during the winter prospects for a successful union were encouraging. Rarely in the past had Altham been so attentive to his wife's wishes. Though a proud woman, Mary seemed determined to make the best of life at Dunmain, joining her husband at hurling matches and entertaining local landowners over dinner. On Sundays, she frequented a nearby church at Kilmokea. Despite their isolation from London, she betrayed no evident sign of homesickness or regret. Besides her maidservant, Mary Heath, a slight woman with black hair, the baroness enjoyed a staff of more than a dozen servants, from the housekeeper Mrs. Settright to "little black Nell," the so-called weeding wench known for her swarthy complexion.[45]

A hopeful start, but just that. There were limits to Altham's gallantry, which did not come naturally. As more than one person noted, he was a highly-strung man with a sharp temper. In the spring, Mrs. Brisco and her daughter Henrietta visited from Dublin. Having befriended the young couple, the captain's wife may have felt an obligation to stay informed, if only for the sake of Mary's father.[46] But at dinner one evening, the lord erupted in fury over the housekeeper's choice of saucers on which to serve sweetmeats. The china, acquired years earlier by Altham, was decorated with a series of obscene images, and, following Mary's arrival, he had issued orders never again to use it. Altham hurled the saucers into a fireplace, barely missing his wife at the opposite end of the table. One senses in his anger a glimmer of embarrassment for Mary, who, erupting into tears, retreated to the bedchamber. Worse, having only recently become pregnant, she miscarried later that night.[47]

This misfortune was not the last. In July, she again miscarried, this time following the baron's return late one night from a drunken rout, when he threw a bed stool in the direction of her maidservant. "You have done a fine thing, my lady has miscarried," Mary Heath later scolded him, adding that her mistress "would be as fruitful a woman as any in the kingdom," were it not for his "ill-usage." It was only that autumn, after his wife became pregnant for a third time, that Altham attempted to make amends by curbing his nights at a nearby alehouse. Among other small acts of kindness, he purchased for Mary a pair of low-heeled slippers to prevent an accidental fall and yet another miscarriage. A cane lent added support. Without doubt, the baron was anxious for a son, or, as he liked to predict, "an Irish bull." "By God," he exclaimed, clapping a servant on the back in November, "Moll's with child!"[48]

Spring brought the birth of a baby boy, just days after the spectacular solar eclipse in late April of 1715. If any in the house thought it an ill omen, like other celestial marvels, no one seems to have said so. Brought to bed at dusk in the upstairs chamber called the Yellow Room, Mary, who felt ill, was first bled by a surgeon, in keeping with common medical procedure, to relieve a harmful build-up of blood, the supposed source of myriad maladies. Once the vein was lanced, a narrow stream of blood trickled from her arm onto a pewter plate. Later, kneeling on a sheet, she endured a relatively brief labor of three hours with the aid of a seasoned midwife, Mrs. Shiels, from New Ross. Bathed in a mixture of water and brandy, the infant was given the name of James in honor of Altham's late cousin and benefactor. "That is a strong boy," remarked an attendant, "hear how strongly he cries."[49]

The following night, dinner guests celebrated the heir apparent to the Earl of Anglesea with wine and whiskey. Milk pails brimming with ale were carried outside. To the joyful sound of fiddles and uileann pipes, laborers and servants drank, danced, and frolicked by a large bonfire in a clearing beyond the house. Five cartloads of furze and timber fueled the blaze. They drank, recalled the servant Patrick Closey, "to the safe uprising of . . . Lady Altham and long life to her new born son." The baron was seen to toss his hat in the air. Strangely—probably he was drunk—he ordered that all bottles and glasses be broken, an act that in Gaelic tradition portended ill fortune. Before the night was out, more than a few revelers lay intoxicated in ditches, one of whom was found dead the next morning.[50]

Three weeks later, the parish minister christened the baby in the large parlor at Dunmain amid plum cake and wine. From landowners and substantial tenants, there were gifts of money, and from others, eggs and live chickens, symbols of childbirth and motherhood. In attendance were three "gossips," the traditional term for godparents. Selected for their friendship and loyalty were the county squire Anthony Colclough, Anthony Cliff, a New Ross lawyer, and Mary's confidante, Mrs. Piggot. At dinner, healths were drunk, a British custom popular after the Restoration, whereby mother and son—the "lady in the straw" and the "young Christian"—were each toasted. Outdoors, servants and laborers drank from piggins and pails of punch.[51]

Among the island's ranking families, it was common to enlist a wet-nurse for a newborn's care. As in England, aristocratic women found breastfeeding inconvenient and degrading. Some feared that it aged one's appearance. Equally important, as contemporaries recognized, lactation ordinarily delays the onset of ovulation. Despite the risk to their health, wives were repeatedly encouraged to augment the family's male line, with often just eighteen months separating one birth from the next. As one historian has written, "Rich women [were] tied to perpetual pregnancy and poor mothers to perpetual suckling"—sometimes resulting in insufficient nourishment for their own infants.[52]

Finding an experienced wet-nurse of good character was a time-consuming task. With the help of a doctor, Lady Altham interviewed several candidates from the neighborhood, including one in poor health and another whose milk tasted bitter. Proximity to the great house was essential. One nurse declined interest on learning of the lord's "very bad character"—for which "she would gain no credit being in his service"—only to be upbraided later for her foolish judgment. "It would have been worth a hundred pounds a year to her," insisted a friend. "Though Lord Altham's fortune was but small, yet if his son lived till after the death of Arthur . . . Lord Anglesea, he would have a very large one."[53]

The choice fell on a young kitchen-maid on the estate named Joan, or "Juggy," Landy, known for bearing some of the "best milk" in the parish of Tintern. A single mother, Landy and her son lived with her parents just two fields from Dunmain, a short distance beyond the dog kennels. There, in a small thatched cottage—

partitioned for privacy and freshly whitewashed for cleanliness—
she cared for the infant for a year, nursing, bathing, and dressing
him "in the English way," according to Lady Altham's instructions (probably in keeping with the growing prejudice against
swaddling in order to permit babies greater freedom of movement). A stone chimney was constructed for added warmth, and a
plain looking glass hung on a wall. Servants also laid a new coach
road, made of gravel with drains on either side, which ran from
the cottage across a bog, called the Currah, to permit easy visits
back and forth, including deliveries of jellies to sweeten Landy's
whey (the liquid residue, rich in protein, from curdled milk). Not
permitted were greens, potatoes, or roots. Afternoons often found
Lady Altham having tea at the cabin. On returning to Dunmain
for good, Jemmy, with leading straps fastened to his clothing and
his mother's help, learned to walk on the bowling green out front.
He also joined her on occasional jaunts to New Ross. Playmates at
home included the children of servants, one of whom—the son of
a coachman—recollected years later how "very fond" Mary was of
her young son.[54]

2

BETRAYAL

Matrimony, according to Bernard de Mandeville, "gives a man's fancy a distaste to the particular dish, but leaves his palate as luxurious as ever." Despite the marked rise in companionate marriages, more and more men drifted from their domestic moorings. Sexual mores relaxed dramatically during the Restoration era, following harsh decades of Puritan asceticism. In the forefront of this transformation were Charles II and his courtiers, who freely consorted with prostitutes, mistresses, and, on occasion, one another's wives—"gay rakes and libertines," they were called. Ironically, the same change in moral standards that encouraged rising numbers of couples to marry for love and sexual satisfaction also led numerous men, once married, to pursue adulterous relationships, a trend that persisted well beyond 1700. "Those things grow more fashionable every day," Lady Mary Wortley Montagu wrote her sister in 1725.[2]

Marital relations were equally carefree among Ireland's landed elite, especially in the middle and southern sections of the country, where Puritan values had never taken hold. There was a kernel of truth in Jonathan Swift's observation that most aristocratic marriages dissolved by the second month, with lords and ladies afterward rarely seen together. Unlike wealthier peers, Lord Altham lacked the resources to maintain a mistress, so serving-maids and tenants' daughters became fair game. When over a convivial dinner he informed a Dublin acquaintance, Tom Barns, of his son's birth by "Moll Sheffield," Barns shook his head in disapproval, not recalling Lady Altham's maiden name. "Zounds, man," exclaimed Altham, "she is my wife!" Apologizing for the error, Barns wished him well but took the opportunity to urge the baron "to turn off all his whores." Mary's fidelity, by contrast, appears to have been steadfast, in keeping with the double standard for men and women—one stemming from concerns over inheritance as much as moral purity. According to the prevailing rationale, a wife's adulterous relationship, by producing a bastard, ran the risk of breaking the chain of succession and polluting the family bloodline. "There is no offence deemed more unpardonable," noted an Irish commentator.[3]

All the more remarkable, then, was the drama that unfolded at Dunmain on a Sunday in early 1717. Were the incident and its consequences not so serious, it would have all the makings of a bad farce. On the morning of February 3, just after Candlemas, Lord Altham left the estate, against Mary's wishes, to dine out. Within minutes, he returned, shouting to servants that a houseguest by the name of Tom Palliser had violated his wife's bedchamber. Rushing upstairs and throwing open the door of the Yellow Room, Altham made a thrust with his sword, but the younger man darted out of the way, only to be forced by servants into the adjoining dining room where they beat him with clubs. The fracas was over quickly. Not yet two years old, Jemmy watched from a short distance as the estate huntsman cut off one of Palliser's earlobes with a large case knife, leaving a lasting mark of infamy (Altham ordered that his nose be spared). Kicked down the stairs, Palliser was turned out of the house. In the meantime, the baron dragged Mary from bed over her frantic protests. That evening toward dusk, after Lord Altham had pulled Jemmy from the arms of his distraught mother, she was put in a chaise for the short ride to New Ross. And there the affair ended. Never would Lady Altham return to Dunmain.[4]

Long afterward, it became clear that Altham had contrived the scandal with the aid of servants who had taken a dislike to Palliser, a hunting companion of the baron. Besides complaining of their conduct, the young squire, as a practical joke, had once put horse jallop, a purgative, into their tea. The morning of the scuffle, Altham had requested that Palliser keep the baroness company over breakfast in her room. Or such, at least, was the explanation later proffered by Palliser. Despite Lord Altham's many faults, it is difficult to imagine Mary committing such a foolhardy indiscretion, particularly at Dunmain. Whatever the exact truth, it is indubitable that at the time of the incident Altham lay stationed nearby, waiting for a servant's signal to snare the unwitting couple.[5]

Reasons for Altham's perfidy are not difficult to find, beginning with his strained relationship with his father-in-law. Ever in debt, the baron repeatedly failed to provide his wife with the promised jointure of £400. Shortly after their reconciliation, he wrote Buckingham a plaintive letter pledging to honor the marriage contract both parties had signed before their wedding. Although, Altham noted, "some should insinuate that I would not make good my wife's jointure," he would obey the duke's "commands," despite his "lessened" estate in Ireland. Altham also requested his interest in obtaining the command of a troop of cavalry, an appointment that "would be an addition of near £400 a year" to his "small fortune." But like the jointure, neither the command, a sinecure, nor the balance of Mary's dowry ever materialized, and by July 1715, Buckingham was refusing fresh requests for credit.[6]

Over the next year and a half, the baron's distress had only deepened, raising the possibility that his treacherous ruse was designed to bring Buckingham to terms. At worst, Altham might have reasoned, should the ploy fail, Lady Altham would be cast out and he would still possess an heir. Such a turn of events could also help to mend his frayed relations with the family patriarch, Arthur, Earl of Anglesea, who had never warmed to the idea of the baron's marriage to Buckingham's daughter. During spells in Ireland, Arthur resided thirty miles northeast of Dunmain at his country seat, Camolin Park. At first, Anglesea's favor had mattered less to Altham than the birth of a son. "I have given him a good deal of trouble already," he boasted to his physician in 1715, "and I have it now in my power to give him a great deal more, for I thank God Lady Altham is delivered of a son." At the time, the earl's death seemed imminent anyway from the complications of a severe bout of gout.[7]

But the "Old Dog," as Altham called him, survived the attack. Nor, as a man of stature and wealth, was Anglesea to be trifled with. Sharp-witted and thin-skinned, he did not shrink from asserting his dignity either in the family or in public life. Twice he served as vice-treasurer of Ireland and twice as a privy counsillor, first to William and Mary and later to George I. "That great peer the Lord Anglesea," wrote Swift in 1721. And though the earl's honors and a majority of his estates were entailed, he still controlled the selection of an heir for his immense personal fortune.[8]

After Mary's banishment, Baron Altham had reason to expect closer ties. Palliser later claimed that Altham had confided in him, barely a week before the tussle at Dunmain, that Anglesea was "very angry" with him "for keeping this woman." "I am determined to put her away," Altham vowed. If, in fact, that was his purpose, relations with the earl remained strained. Family visits were infrequent, if civil. Plainly, Anglesea suffered no illusions about his cousin's affections. "Lord Altham," he told a friend, "longed much for his death."[9]

The baron's financial woes were mainly of his own making—the fruits of an extravagant lifestyle that far exceeded his modest income from tenants' rents, which included, after the death of his mother in

Thomas Roberts, *A Frost Piece* [1769]. A pair of huntsmen and their dogs pass before a small cottage, encrusted with ice, that unlike most dwellings of the rural poor boasts a chimney and a window.

1717, remittances in Devon, England. Even so, some of his pecuniary distress arose from broader problems common to much of the country's landed elite. The Irish peerage was less wealthy than that of England. A number of lords, not just Altham, incurred mounting debts that went unpaid. Credit, a critic wryly noted in the *Dublin Weekly Journal*, was a gentleman's "way of begging."[10]

Much of the problem stemmed from a shortage of solvent tenants. Rather than engage in commercial farming themselves, big landowners were rentier landlords. Tenants in the thinly populated countryside led lives of grinding poverty, eking out a bare existence in mud-walled cottages, some barely seven feet in height, with earthen floors and thatched roofs. In County Wexford, whereas the well-to-do relied on peat, cut in slabs from bogs, for fuel, the poor burned furze, a prickly shrub gathered from wasteland. Except for the dim glow of a hearth, interiors stayed dark from an absence of windows or chimneys to dispel the smoke. "As miserable as they look on the outside," described Samuel Madden, "the family within are full as wretched, half starved and half clad." With few tools, limited labor, and even less capital, the peasantry often turned to tending sheep or cattle rather than tilling the soil, aside from providing for their own subsistence. Pastureland for grazing livestock was widespread in this underdeveloped agricultural economy. Madden complained of "little or nothing but land and great herds of cattle to lay out our little wealth on."[11]

A large landowner in 1737 expressed the dilemma that he and others faced: "I and every other gentleman wou[l]d have good substantial Protestant tenants if we cou[l]d get them, but as they are not to be had, we must take the best we can, or have our land wast[e], w[h]ich is next to having no estate." There was no easy remedy. Typically, resident as well as absentee landowners let substantial tracts to well-to-do tenant farmers, many of them Catholic. They sublet smaller plots of five or fewer acres to cottiers and laborers. By the early eighteenth century, there was extensive reliance upon middlemen willing to take on the burdensome collection of rents from under-tenants as well as to make limited improvements to the property.[12]

Not only did proprietors like Baron Altham receive reduced remittances from these "small country gentlemen," but they were forced to grant long leases as an inducement. Despite the security that these brought, the leases invariably failed to keep pace with rising land values. Most rentals extended in length from twenty-one years for Catholics to as long a period as "three lives" for Protestants. Middlemen, in turn, sublet their plots for shorter intervals at higher rates. Still worse from the landowner's perspective, rents often went uncollected in hard times, falling into arrears for years. In Ireland, a good fortune, a person estimated in 1739, was £1,000 per annum, a modest sum by the standards of

England's upper crust. "The lord is a poor tyrant," a contemporary wrote of the typical Irish aristocrat.[13]

Well, not always. There were, of course, exceptions. The great proprietors continued to prosper by shrewdly investing their capital on both sides of the Irish Sea. Fresh lands continued to be accumulated. In 1724, a Wexford farmer wrote to Judge Michael Ward, apprehensive that the Earl of Anglesea, with his far greater resources, would defeat the farmer's plans to lease a Ward estate in the county. "Lord Anglesea," he protested, "has a mind for it, and the great fish swallow up the little ones."[14]

The morning after his humiliation at Dunmain, Tom Palliser responded as a proper Irish gentleman by challenging Altham to a duel. Palliser's father also volunteered for the right to exact revenge. Refusing to give satisfaction, the baron shortly departed for Dublin, allegedly to attend the House of Lords (years later, the younger Palliser would claim that, pistols in hand, he had given chase as far as New Ross).[15]

At Dunmain, where Altham had left orders forbidding his wife's return, Jemmy stayed with Joan Laffan, his dry-nurse since he had left the care of Juggy Landy. Lady Altham remained nearby in New Ross, lodging at the homes of friends. With little trouble, she bribed servants from Dunmain to bring the boy on short visits. These continued for as much as a year during Altham's absence. Jemmy was her only comfort, other than her father, who, one suspects, was glad to be rid of the baron despite the renewed burden of Mary's support. To listeners, she spoke bluntly of her plight, freely condemning "that barbarous lord of mine" who had "banished" her "from his bed" and taken "her little boy." "I had better be wife to the meanest tradesman in town, than to Lord Altham," she told a shoemaker in New Ross.[16]

Never again did the baron reside at Dunmain. From Dublin he removed with a handful of servants to Ballyshannon in County

Kildare, southwest of the capital, hoping to board with the widow of a cousin. The visit, alas, was brief. Owing to reports of Altham's ill character, Deborah Annesley, a strong-minded matriarch of her branch of the family, rejected his offer of £100 rent; and by early 1718, he had resettled nearby at a modest country house called Kinnea. There, not far from the River Liffey, three-year-old Jemmy joined him, as did the baron's horses and dogs. Kinnea, though, was just the beginning of a rambling odyssey for father and son, ending five years later with their arrival on Phrapper Lane in north Dublin.[17]

Along the way, they paid an early visit to the capital, staying in a small house near St. Stephen's Green, a fashionable quarter south of Trinity College. The following year, 1720, found them back in Wexford at a spot named Mountain Grainge, living in tents over the summer for fishing and buck hunting and in a thatched cottage during the fall. A neighbor later recalled Altham's request for carrion and horse carcasses for his hounds. That winter the baron and Jemmy retreated north to Carrickduff, a sixteenth-century castle in the Blackstairs Mountains just across the Wexford border in County Carlow. Known traditionally as Clonmullen Castle, it had been acquired by the Annesley family in 1690 when its Gaelic owner, Charles Kavanagh, joined James II in France after the Battle of the Boyne. Altham and Jemmy resided at Carrickduff for the next year and a half before returning to Dublin, where they first took lodging north of the Liffey on Cross-Lane.[18]

Irish aristocrats, by nature, were a nomadic lot, alternating seasons between Dublin and the country, just as English peers spent a portion of every year in London. "Parliament winter," when the legislature convened upon the lord lieutenant's biennial arrival from England, always drew numbers to the capital, if only for the social round of assemblies and balls. And, of course, some lords of great wealth kept seats in both kingdoms. Even so, Altham's behavior was unusually peripatetic, more the product of

William Van der Hągen, *State Ball at Dublin Castle, 4 November 1731*,
1739.

financial necessity than personal choice—seeking less costly quarters and refuge from creditors. If anything, his circumstances had
grown more straitened since departing Dunmain. According to
one report, he left Kinnea after a creditor seized his goods and
"stripped the place of all that was in it." Later, at Carrickduff, a
Wexford blacksmith appeared after a tiresome journey to request
payment of a lingering debt, only to be told by Altham that he
was penniless; and, as a peer, he could not be arrested for debt.
The baron, however, did introduce the smith to his son, who, he
declared, would one day become Earl of Anglesea. Taking the
boy by the cheek, he instructed him to remember the man, who
departed none the richer. A less patient creditor, if not an enraged
husband, may have been the aggrieved soul who shot Altham one

night through a window. Escaping death but losing an eye, he wore a black patch for the remainder of his life.[19]

By the second half of the seventeenth century, a marked change had begun to take place in child-rearing among upper-class families. Repressive discipline, rooted in a pessimistic view of early childhood prevalent in the late Middle Ages, gave way to greater parental indulgence, especially during a child's first years. Lending credence to this transformation was John Locke's widely read book *Some Thoughts upon Education* (1693), which cautioned parents against the use of physical coercion. If mothers were thought apt to pamper their children, fathers, too, were encouraged to express their affection. Altham was no exception, though vanity and pride colored his emotions. His son, the baron boasted to a friend, had "pith [strength] in his bones" and "wou'd out live all the family"; whereas to Jemmy himself, he remarked that if he "behaved well, he would one day or other be a great man." He also fondly claimed that the boy bore a closer resemblance to his father than to his mother.[20]

As a nobleman's son, Jemmy certainly looked the part, typically appearing in a scarlet silk coat with silver buttons and a gold-laced hat sporting a white feather. Commoners called the fair-haired boy "An Tiarna Og" (the young lord). Notwithstanding their itinerant life, Altham took pains to enroll him in a succession of day schools, though every so often he enlisted a tutor instead. At one point, the baron pointedly entered him in a small school to display support for its embattled teacher, a Catholic priest whom he liked. To another schoolmaster, he urged that Jemmy be kept from "the lower sort of boys" to "prevent his getting ill habits or getting the itch [scabies]."[21]

For amusement, there were hurling matches and fishing trips. During a birthday celebration at Carrickduff, cottiers, tradesmen, and "all kinds of people" attended to honor the youth, drinking a mixture of freshly churned cream and ale. Later, as bonfires lit the sky, revelers played King and Queen, a favored game whereby in a reversal of roles two servants, young Bridget O'Neal and John Wilson, their names pulled from a hat, each enjoyed the privilege of receiving a cup of wine and sitting at the head of the supper table.[22]

The honor was temporary, as O'Neal knew from personal experience. She occasionally played with Jemmy, once catching an eel that they cooked in straw. Finding his son's face smudged with ashes, Altham objected that he was "not [fit] company for her, he being of the family of the Buckinghams on one side and of his family on the other side."[23]

By age six, Jemmy had a sword and a small sorrel mare named Hanover, in honor of George I. So upset was Altham when the boy fell from the horse that he gave the handler's head a sharp crack with the butt of his whip. "If you will take more care of Master Jemmy hereafter," said the baron, "when he is Earl of Anglesea and you an old man, he will give you a townland [an administrative unit of land, more compact than a parish, comprising multiple farms]." Subsequently, when the young lord at Carrickduff contracted measles, Altham spent days and nights in his room. If Jemmy kept his health, the baron declared with a mixture of pride and envy, "he will be the happyest Annesley that ever was of the name."[24]

That, however, was before Altham's financial ruin, which by 1722 appeared imminent. As if his debts were not onerous enough, a depression had struck the Irish economy, stemming from slumping prices for exports, the collapse of the South Sea Company in 1720, and successive years of disappointing harvests. An agent in County Leitrim warned his landlord of rents "remaining due in the poor tenants' hands for want of markets to convert the cows into money."[25]

Already, in desperation, the baron had joined other debt-ridden lords in selling fraudulent "protections." These were certificates designed to shield the servants of members of the House of Lords from arrest in civil cases while Parliament remained in session, a privilege that peers themselves enjoyed. Meant to defend bearers from creditors, the certificates precluded imprisonment for debt, which was their overriding appeal. Altham's malfeasance came to light during an investigation by the Lords in the autumn of 1721. Among other disclosures, he had sold twenty-one protections, which was nevertheless considerably fewer than the eighty-plus apiece granted by the two leading offenders, Lords Blessington and Roscommon. There were not "three more beggerly Lords in the Kingdom," wrote Philip Perceval to his brother, Baron Perceval of Burton. Altham's character, he remarked, was "the worst in the world."[26]

On October 2, in a resolution of censure, the House of Lords declared that Altham had "obstructed the course of justice" and "prostituted the honour of the House." Owing to the allegation that one certificate, sold for about five pounds, bore the counterfeit signature of an English lord, the baron was committed to the custody of the Gentleman Usher of the Black Rod (the serjeant-at-arms) for more than a month, before being freed on bail. The Lords took the extraordinary step of urging his prosecution by the attorney-general. Not for another year was he acquitted at the Court of King's Bench in Dublin, and then only through the timely intervention of his former father-in-law, Lord Haversham, whose signature, in fact, he had forged.[27]

The likelihood that Baron Altham would inherit the titles and entailed estates of his elder cousin, the Earl of Anglesea, was not lost upon senior members of the family—nor upon responsible leaders of the Protestant Ascendancy. Still childless, Anglesea had become a widower in 1719. At the time, the powerful archbishop of Dublin, William King, wrote to his lawyer, Francis Annesley, a cousin and close confidant of the earl: "I would council him to marry as soon as possible a good wholesome country Lady, and live with her there, till he recruited the family." Three years later, in

the midst of the protections scandal, King again prodded Annesley, but with greater urgency: "Tell his Lordship I shall not be
satisfyed with his conduct till he has done some thing in the grand
affair, which was to do what is in his power to prevent his honour
and estate descending to a person unworthy of them."[28]

We cannot be certain what first drew Lord Altham to Miss
Sally Gregory: whether it was her beauty, her small fortune, or, in
all likelihood, an amalgam of passion and self-preservation. Soon
after their meeting in the summer of 1722 at Carrickduff, she
joined the household as his mistress. And when they and Jemmy
shortly moved to Dublin, Gregory's mother and two brothers
accompanied them to Cross-Lane. More than that, Gregory, having little use for Jemmy, increasingly complained of his misbehav-
ior. Besides other transgressions, he had freed a frog in the house,
allegedly causing Gregory, who was pregnant, to miscarry.[29]

Beatings were regular. Once, to his teacher, Jemmy raised his
shirt to reveal more than thirty stripes received from Gregory
and her mother. Among the servants, rumors were rife that Sally
wished to begin her own family with the baron, notwithstanding
Altham's protestations that his son would succeed him and one
day become Earl of Anglesea. Emotionally and financially dependent upon his mistress, the baron to an increasing extent became
a guest in his own household—so much so that, on moving yet
again, first to Phrapper Lane and then to Inchicore, he consented
to lodging the boy elsewhere.[30]

For the British aristocracy, boarding boys outside the home
was not, in itself, unusual. Around seven years of age, children
were thought to enter a new stage of mental and physical matu-
rity, distinguished by the ability to tell right from wrong. A
proper moral education, preferably by male instructors, was considered imperative. Many boys, never again to reside permanently
at home, faced a program of boarding school and university, followed by a grand tour of the Continent. The son of the first Earl

of Bute did not return home once between age seven and late adolescence. But clearly, Lord Altham's motives were altogether different in removing Jemmy to Little Ship Street. Otherwise, he explained to friends, "I shall have no peace." To one, he promised that once "some little jealousies were over," he "would take him [home] again."[31]

Never was there any chance that Jemmy might rejoin his mother, despite her close proximity. Ever since leaving Dunmain, the baron had rebuffed Lady Altham's efforts to reclaim her son. While still at Kinnea, he had threatened to shoot an emissary from New Ross whom he suspected of trying to kidnap the boy. He even ordered a bricklayer to seal the house's lower windows to forestall future attempts. "It's true she bore him," he stormed at one point, "and that's all the pleasure she shall have of him."[32]

In early 1722, Lady Altham fell seriously ill, losing the use of her arms and legs. Unable to walk, she was said to suffer from "dead palsy," in all likelihood a disorder of the central nervous system. Years of sadness and anxiety had left her mentally and physically exhausted. In March, she and Mary Heath left New Ross for the home of a friend, Charles Kavanagh, in Dublin. They lodged on Stable Lane, while the baron and Jemmy as yet resided on Phrapper Lane just to the north. One of Kavanagh's servants later claimed to have spoken to Jemmy on his mother's behalf, only to be threatened by Altham with imprisonment. The baron's own servants were menaced with "transportation" to America if they should contact her, whereas Jemmy, should he attempt a visit, feared disownment. In mid-1723, her health declining, Lady Altham departed for London where her father lay on his deathbed—not, however, without telling an acquaintance, "I wish I had never seen Ireland, and I wish you better luck in it than I have had." The baroness would not return. Still an invalid, she died at her modest London home five years later.[33]

It would be too easy to blame Jemmy's abandonment upon

Sally Gregory and her naked attempt to undermine his father's affection. The baron appears to have had an additional motive for forsaking his son, if only temporarily. In another desperate gambit to raise money, he had already begun to sell reversionary leases to lands belonging to his cousin, the earl. As drawn, these were designed to take effect less than a year after Anglesea's death, thereby permitting existing tenants a short interval in which to renew their leases at a new rent or find fresh quarters.[34]

In exchange for a down payment, purchasers gambled that Baron Altham would survive his elder cousin. To sweeten the bargain, Altham advertised leases in newspapers for as little as half the sum of a full year's rent, thereby hoping to reap a short-term gain at the expense of more favorable terms. There was, however, one major obstacle, apart from Anglesea's revived health. For the leases to be appealing, they needed to be a sufficient length, which, by law, required not only Altham's agreement but also the consent of his closest male heir, in this case his son. And therein lay the rub, for legally Jemmy was too young to grant his approval.[35]

Initially, this problem was not of evident concern. Thus to Richard Bayly, a Dublin merchant, the baron sold a lease to several Wexford properties for a term of thirty-one years at an annual rent of £365. In exchange, he received payment of £300. After several years, however, Bayly began to have misgivings, especially after Altham confided in 1724 that "he could get no purchasers" for other estates, despite his advertisements. Bayly rashly responded that "no body would treat with him till he had got a divorce from the Lady Altham and bastardized" his son by disavowing his paternity. Enraged by the suggestion, Altham swore that "he would not bastardize his son for the whole estate" and then set his dogs on the poor man. Bayly immediately gave the baron "all the money in his pocket" to make amends and to prevent "being torn to pieces."[36]

For the time being, the baron chose another course, informing potential tenants, when necessary, of the boy's death or, less commonly, denying his birth by Lady Altham. Neither explanation was implausible, especially to those with only passing knowledge of the Annesley family. Nor in an age devoid of maternity tests could the boy's legitimacy be easily determined, short of making a trip to Tintern parish, where Dunmain lay, to discover if a register of births had been kept.[37]

Even so, the decision to deny Jemmy's legitimacy, if only temporarily, was fraught with peril. The allegation might haunt the boy to his grave, destroying any chance of receiving the family's property or titles. Although aristocratic promiscuity had lessened the stigma of bastardy by the first half of the eighteenth century, the law regarding inheritance was unambiguous. Illegitimacy, wrote the author of *Lex Spuriorum; or the Law Relating to Bastardy* (1703), "excludes him that is a bastard from all succession, descending from the father or the mother, as 'tis holden both in the common, civil, and canon laws." In short, in the line of succession, the child was *filius nullius* (a son of nobody). And while some lords openly acknowledged their illegitimate offspring, for many children the tainted circumstances of their birth remained an indelible stain. Even the Duke of Buckingham, Jemmy's maternal grandfather, was heard, late in his life, to lament the birth of his natural progeny. Once blessed with legitimate children, "he wish'd [that] he had never had the others, or at least had not own'd them, it being in private families an ill example."[38]

The baron's hoax raised yet another complication: he had to enlist his younger brother—his new heir—as a co-conspirator. Not that Richard Annesley's scruples precluded his cooperation. No less rapacious, Richard, if anything, was more ruthless, the consequence perhaps of being a younger son with neither rank nor financial security. As the brother of a lowly baron, in contrast to a duke or marquess, he was even denied the coveted title of "lord."[39]

Born in 1693, Richard spent his youth in Exeter as something of a knockabout, joining other boys in stealing dogs. More than Altham, he may have felt the absence of a male authority figure at a young age. As an adult, he was of middling height, and, by one account, had the "clumsy" manner of a country farmer. Unfortunately, no known portrait has survived, nor was Richard (or his brother) the sort to sit for one. Owing to both his appearance and character, a female acquaintance later volunteered, "I would not have had him if I was young, no not [even] to be a countess."[40]

But Richard was nobody's fool. By virtue of his father's will, he received £500 on turning twenty-one to help launch a career. With little taste for trade and even less for the church—two traditional paths for younger sons—he initially followed another well-trod course by purchasing an ensign's commission in the army. His career, however, was short-lived; two years after the close of the War of the Spanish Succession in 1713, he was struck from the service at half pay. By then, Captain Annesley, as he was called, had embarked upon a surer avenue of advancement by marrying that same year Ann Prust, the nineteen-year-old daughter of a wealthy Devon gentleman—"first wive, then thrive," to invert the order of a seventeenth-century adage. After initially renting a home in London, Richard and his wife moved to Ireland and settled in New Ross, hoping perhaps to profit from his brother's proximity. In 1720, however, the couple separated, with Ann returning to Devon.[41]

In Dublin, Richard found quarters along the Liffey, across from the customs house at Essex Bridge, though by 1725 he too had returned to Devon, only to be arrested and jailed for highway robbery along with two accomplices in Wiltshire. At the assize court in Salisbury, the pair were sentenced to hang, though Richard escaped conviction after his attorney paid a prosecution witness two pounds not to appear in court. One year later, in a secret ceremony, the captain acquired a second wife, fifteen-year-old

Ann Simpson, whose father was a prosperous Dublin clothier. First, however, the bride had to sign a certificate, dated December 22, 1726, pledging never to "prosecute" Richard "on account of any marriage contracted to any one formerly"—in short, for bigamy.[42]

Although illegal according to the Anglican church and canon law, bigamy was difficult to curb. Before parliamentary passage of Lord Hardwicke's Marriage Act in 1753, any clergyman, whether invested with a church living or not, could bestow his blessing upon a couple in the absence of a license or written contract. "Every man may privately have a wife in every corner of this city," complained a London resident, "without it being possible for them to know of one another." Only after 1753 did marriages have to be publicly recorded, with husbands and wives required to sign their names in a parish register.[43]

The Annesley brothers, by all accounts, had a contentious relationship, fueled by the envy often felt by younger sons in aristocratic households. Their mother, the principal link in their lives, had been dead for nearly a decade. While his elder brother stood to inherit four additional peerages and lands in Ireland, England, and Wales, Richard had little to show for years of constant striving. Never does he appear to have reconciled himself to his inferior station. Still and all, their enmity may have been avoidable. Unquestionably there were instances of fraternal affection within dynastic families, especially when elder brothers assisted male siblings to obtain gainful employment.[44]

The baron, by contrast, like other high-handed heirs, openly delighted in his brother's subordination. He had welcomed the birth of a son partly to thwart Richard's hopes for an inheritance. Following the blessed event, Altham crowed to friends, "By God, . . . my wife has got a son, which will make my brother's nose swell." Richard, in turn, resented both mother and child. Because of his low "principles," Lady Altham once banished him from Dunmain. Months later, following her own abrupt departure, Richard cursed his brother for not turning out the boy as well. "Damn my blood," he railed, "I would have let her have him, and she might carry him to the devil, for I would keep none of the breed of her."[45]

Were he a reflective man, Richard might have enjoyed the irony of his brother's latest predicament, which he alone, as the younger son, could help to remedy. More likely, he recognized that Altham's scheme threatened to convey, at reduced sums, lands which he himself might one day inherit. Still, in exchange for a portion of the profits, Richard was prepared, at least for the time being, to go along with the ruse.[46]

It was all to no avail. The few reversionary leases granted, in the end, netted very little, notwithstanding Altham's frenzied salesmanship. In one instance, he attempted to pressure a Dublin acquaintance, William Milton, to purchase not one but several leases. But Milton, on learning that the baron had a legitimate son, demanded an explanation on Altham's "honor," in a direct reference to his standing as a peer of the realm. "He is a poor puny boy," the baron protested, "and won't live a year." When Milton insisted that he "could not be safe in purchasing, as his son was under age," Altham vainly promised that he "would procure his brother" to "join in a bond."[47]

Such, by the latter half of 1726, was the baron's poverty that a visitor to Inchicore found his beloved kennel of dogs bone-thin— "one hound was ready to eat the other." Already gone were his horse and carriage. He even tried to pawn his parliamentary robes. One friend never arrived with more than a guinea in his pocket, knowing that Altham would request his aid. Another guest, invited to dinner, had to pay for his meal. Indeed, the baron was even forced to mortgage an annual pension of £200 that he received as an act of royal charity. Most acquaintances simply stayed away. "No body would trust him," one later testified.[48]

Nor, surely, could he expect assistance from his cousin, the earl. The sale of reversionary leases left Altham's remaining ties in tatters. It was not only his impudence, but his heavy-handed manner in conveying the leases. In more than one instance, he attempted to sell the same lease to two different parties. One new leaseholder in 1725 even brought the earl himself to court over the validity of his Wexford deeds. Meanwhile, that March, Altham urged Archbishop King to broker a settlement with Anglesea whereby the baron would forfeit his claims to remaindered estates in exchange for "a present maintenance." The archbishop flatly refused.[49]

Then, in a letter to King dated May 19, Altham recklessly alleged that Anglesea sought to legitimize "two brats [bastards]." This slander the baron more or less threatened to repeat unless his cousin did "something to relieve him"—"which," he hastened to add, "suited his necessitie (tho not his inclination)." Appalled by his "importunity," King again declined to intercede, though he hastily apprised Francis Annesley of Altham's "design." He also promised to "keep the letter, for perhaps some time or other it may be of use." "I heartily wish that I cou'd do any thing that might be serviceable to my Lord and the family," he assured Francis. If the baron's allegation possessed merit, there is no evidence to support it. Very possibly, the earl was sterile, which, if so, was already the main problem anyway.[50]

One day on the road to Inchicore, Richard Bayly, having forgiven Altham for their earlier row, happened to meet Captain Annesley. On hearing Bayly's report of the incident, Richard volunteered that the boy Jemmy "was his own bastard." Shocked, Bayly later related this claim to Altham, who pronounced his brother "a rogue, a villain, and a rapparee" who would never again set foot in his house. "Rapparee," a term common in the south of Ireland in the late seventeenth century for Jacobite rebels and bandits, was an especially grave insult. Jemmy, the baron declared, was his legitimate son and both his successor and the future Earl of Anglesea.[51]

Some time after this, on a Sunday, Bayly returned to Inchicore for a small dinner party. Without warning, Richard appeared, leading the company to break up as the brothers started to quarrel angrily in the garden. At Altham's urging, Bayly pummeled Richard mercilessly. "Beat him well," the baron bellowed, "for he has denied every word that he said to you" and "swore that he would kill you wherever he met you!" And to Richard, by now prostrate on the ground, he cursed, "You have endeavored to make me bastardize that boy James Annesley. He is my son, and [I] will take care of him as such, and you will get no more money upon reversionary leases." Back on his feet and in tears, Richard snorted bitterly as he left, "If you take him home and own him as your son, you will get no more money!"[52]

How soon Altham intended to make good on his threat is unclear, for he died not long afterward. Of his final days, this much is known, according to the testimony of two servant-maids, Mary O'Neal and Bridget Donohue. Three days preceding his death on November 16, the baron went hunting. Despite years of hard drinking, he had never suffered serious illness nor evidently had reason to draft a will (at thirty-eight years of age, he fell well short of the average life expectancy of sixty-two for an adult male). Although Altham complained of a cold on returning from the hunt, he did not take to his bed. The following day, instead, he ingested a "vomit," an emetic designed to purge the stomach. This apparently brought relief, for on the succeeding day he felt well enough to host company from Dublin for dinner. He also spoke of going hunting again in the morning.[53]

But one hour after retiring with Miss Gregory, the baron suddenly cried out for Mary O'Neal. Feeling very ill, he retreated to the privy for a quarter of an hour, while O'Neal, alarmed by his coughing, summoned her husband. By this time, having visibly weakened, Altham had to be helped back to bed. Alternately clearing his throat and gasping for air, his sight now gone, he reportedly asked for God's forgiveness for having "wronged" his son. He also requested Mary's husband to write down his last words but died immediately after another spasm of coughing.[54]

Less than a year earlier, the baron had discussed the possibility of his murder with his old friend, Dominick Farrell. On a visit to Inchicore, the linen peddler had expressed alarm over Jemmy's neglect. "It would be a scandal to him [Altham] and his posterity," Farrell pleaded, "if his son by being neglected in that matter should fall into ill company by which he might come to an ill end." In response, Altham blamed "those bitches," Miss Gregory and her mother. Were the boy brought home, he predicted, "They would either poyson me, cut my throat, or burn my house."[55]

So the bloom was off the rose. Plainly, the Gregorys possessed ample opportunity to administer a poison—if not in the potion meant to induce vomiting, which would seem counterproductive, then in his food or drink. Although, on the one hand, Altham's coughing and shortness of breath might suggest a pulmonary disorder, his urgent use of the privy could signal a sudden attack of vomiting or diarrhea, consistent with internal bleeding and poisoning. Then, too, a sharp drop in blood pressure may have triggered his sudden loss of vision. Available sources of poison in the eighteenth century included fool's parsley (hemlock) and deadly nightshade (belladonna), both capable of producing the symptoms that Altham reportedly exhibited. It is hard, all the same, to see the benefit his death could have brought the Gregorys, even if Jemmy's return had appeared imminent. What motive could have caused one or both to murder a man who, in fact, still owed them a substantial debt?[56]

In contrast, Richard, if lacking opportunity, manifestly possessed motivation, rooted in years of mutual animosity, culminating in his recent humiliation. And with Altham's demise, he would stand much closer in the line of succession to his brother's title and, more significantly, the honors and estates of his cousin, the Earl of Anglesea. A man's status, after all, could improve dramatically upon the death of an elder brother, especially one whose only son, a street waif, might easily be cast aside. "Death at the one door and heirship at the other," in the words of a seventeenth-century proverb.[57]

Particularly suspicious were Richard's actions in the period surrounding his brother's death. Why, just weeks earlier, did he appear at the door of the butcher John Purcell? One plain purpose of the visit was to ascertain Purcell's intentions and whether Jemmy might one day claim his birthright as fifth Baron Altham. If so, the visit succeeded in verifying the boy's whereabouts. Then, too, after Richard's arrival on November 16 at Inchicore between five and six in the morning, he immediately shouted to the servants, "Damn you, you bitches have poisoned my brother!" It was a curious allegation for one happening upon the scene (whether he had been summoned is not clear). What's more, on demanding keys to a closet and bureau, he at once started to rifle through his brother's papers, extracting a large quantity of documents, leases, and letters, all of which he carried off in two tablecloths.[58]

Oddly, Richard did not think to level the charge of murder at either of the Gregorys, who shortly left Inchicore, never, it seems, to reappear. With Jemmy's possible return looming, might they have conspired with Altham's younger brother in exchange for future recompense?

Regardless, no one at the time felt sufficiently concerned by the baron's passing to investigate the circumstances. No coroner's court convened. No autopsy was performed on the corpse. And in less than six months, twelve-year-old Jemmy would be cast for the colonies as a common servant.

3

EXILE

They {the Irish} sell their servants here as they do their horses,
and advertise them as they do their oatmeal and beef.
Anonymous visitor to Philadelphia,
August 5, 1773[1]

Once the *James* unfurled its enormous sails, young Annesley's best hope to remain in Ireland rested on a pile of sand. Three miles beyond the mouth of the Liffey lay a prominent shoal commonly known as the bar, the accumulation of centuries of ocean sediment. At ebb tide, the water's depth fell to just six feet. The bar was the most treacherous in a string of sandbanks in Dublin Bay that menaced shipping; over the years, many lives had been lost. "The sea and the gallows refuse no body," went an old saying. Or, in a sudden squall, a vessel might be violently blown to the north or the south, only to come aground on vast mudflats called "bulls," for the relentless roar of the crashing waves. But on April 30, 1728, both luck and the tides were running in the *James*'s favor. With its course set, a westerly breeze, and a seasoned captain at the wheel, the ship left the bay unimpeded, slowly carrying Jemmy Annesley and scores of servants toward the Irish Sea and out into the Atlantic.[2]

In the servant trade, the boy's abduction was not at all unprecedented. Although orchestrated by his uncle, rather than by a merchant or ship captain, it belonged to a century-old tradition of involuntary servitude common to the British Isles. Coined in the seventeenth century, the term "kidnapping" originally referred to the abduction of a child for the purpose of being transported across the ocean. Victims were auctioned in the colonies as indentured servants, normally for a period of three to five years. In time, not just children but paupers and vagrants also fell prey to "spirits," the recruiting agents enlisted by shipmasters. Kidnapping, along with other illicit techniques, became notorious enough by 1661 to provoke the Council for Foreign Plantations in London to condemn the "many evils which do happen in the forcing, tempting, and seducing of servants, for a more certain and orderly supply." Despite periodic laws requiring the registration of servants, the crime was difficult either to prohibit or to prosecute, with most victims already at sea. Merchants, customs officials, colonial planters, and even the king of England stood to gain from the lax enforcement of regulations. And in an age of rampant crime and widespread poverty, much of the public welcomed the expulsion of urchins and beggars. Hence, kidnapping for many years remained, under the common law, a misdemeanor, while horse theft, a felony, was punishable by death.[3]

By the early 1700s, with the decline of the English servant trade to the southern colonies owing mainly to the growth of African slavery, kidnapping had all but disappeared from the ports of London and Bristol. Notably, the novel by Penelope Aubin, *The Life of Charlotta du Pont* (1723), in which a beautiful young girl is abducted from Bristol, is set during the reign of Charles II. Meanwhile, the servant trade in Irish ports, designed for Pennsylvania and other "middle colonies" where slavery was less prevalent, flourished during the eighteenth century. Merchants eagerly competed to fill empty berths aboard vessels. Although many immigrants from Ulster traveled to America as paying passengers, a majority from the south embarked as indentured servants. In light of the subsequent flood of immigrants during the famine years

William Jones, *View of Dublin Bay*, engraved by G. King, 1745.

of the nineteenth century, one can easily lose sight of the multitudes that emigrated from both the north and south of Ireland in the 1700s—more than 150,000 souls prior to the American Revolution.[4]

In southern Ireland, the late 1720s and early 1730s witnessed a marked surge in the number of servants. Crop failures and famine, followed by poor markets and plunging prices, drove hundreds of laborers and tenants abroad. Most in Dublin boarded ships either at George's Quay or slightly downriver at Rogerson's Quay, the final terminus before the bay. Or, like Jemmy, they were transported in gabbards and longboats to larger vessels anchored off Ringsend. Joined by ships laden with linen and provisions, or coal from England, vessels in the servant trade helped to make Dublin the country's busiest harbor.[5]

There, kidnapping was commonplace. Just six weeks before Jemmy's abduction, two men were confined to the city's Newgate prison for allegedly trying to force "young boys and girls" aboard a ship in the harbor. Another pair, one a "noted Kid-Merchant," faced imprisonment in March 1733 "for illegally sending people over to the West Indies." Years later, a victim was rescued off a "Kid Ship" in Dublin Bay. In all likelihood, such episodes, rather than suggesting the crime's successful prosecution, reflected instead its stubborn persistence.[6]

Bound, too, for America were smaller numbers of convicts sentenced by courts to transportation, the contemporary euphemism for banishment "beyond the seas." Typically the term of exile, coupled with compulsory servitude, was seven years. To these unfortunates, beginning in 1707, were added prostitutes, wastrels, and other "vagabonds." During the eighteenth century, upward of ten thousand men and women were condemned to exile. As in England, banishment promised the best way to help relieve Ireland of its "offensive rubbish" short of consigning hundreds each year to the gallows. Out of sight, out of mind.[7]

Jemmy Annesley embarked not as a convict but as an indentured servant. Despite his uncle's allegation of theft—that the boy had stolen a silver spoon—no charge was ever brought, much less proven in court. In fact, four months earlier, at Christmastime, Richard Annesley had approached a Dublin merchant, James Stephenson, to place Jemmy aboard a ship "bound for America." Reluctant at first, Stephenson finally agreed to the scheme, and on March 26 a city clerk scrawled "James Hennesley" into an indenture book at the Tholsel, Dublin's guildhall on Skinner's Row, lying just across from Christ Church.[8]

Ordinarily, with any prospective servant, a merchant first met with the subject to discuss terms, including the nature and length of service in America in exchange for passage abroad. The negotiation formed the basis of a contract signed by both parties. At least in English indentures, assurances were given in the case of minors of "necessary cloaths, meat, drink, washing and lodging" during one's service. In newspaper advertisements, Stephenson, one of three owners of the *James*, usually invited candidates to his Dublin home, whereas other merchants were known to negotiate in inns by the Liffey. That done, servants next appeared at the Tholsel with a captain or mate before the lord mayor to sign indentures and register their names.[9]

How, in Jemmy's absence, was his name registered? As the misspelling "Hennesley" suggests, someone at the Tholsel, perhaps Stephenson himself, surreptitiously submitted his name to the clerk. Officials were hardly immune to accepting bribes; nor were merchants and shipmasters averse to paying them. "Public officers," complained Sir Richard Cox of County Cork, "are apt to think they have a right to get as much as they can." Then, also, inferior magistrates, rather than the mayor, occasionally oversaw proceedings. A few years earlier, Dublin's magistracy had been roundly condemned by Parliament for acting "in the most irregular and oppressive manner." As for the ship's captain, Thomas Hendry, it was later said that he "turned out a very great rogue." Whatever the precise explanation, Richard Annesley's plot to deport his nephew had plainly been in the works for months.[10]

James Stephenson was a merchant of modest means. With a partial interest in the *James*, he had first traded butter, beef, and other provisions to the West Indies before opting to ship servants to Philadelphia, the busiest entrepôt in the colonies for Irish immigrants. In Dublin, the servant trade attracted men like Stephenson, with high ambitions and limited capital. Other than a vessel's cost, operating expenses were restricted to insurance and port charges, seamen's wages, equipment, and provisions. In contrast to the passenger trade from Belfast, Londonderry, and other northern ports, the enterprise was decentralized. No one company or set of firms dominated shipping arrangements, with most investors sponsoring just a few voyages apiece, often with one or more partners to defray costs. Correspondents in the colonies assisted in the sale of servants following a vessel's arrival.[11]

Nor was the trade highly specialized. Along with indentured

servants, it was common for the same vessel to carry passengers
and convicts. Captains, in fact, became infamous for disguising
convicts as servants in order to enhance their sales appeal. Trading
servants held secondary importance anyway for many shipowners.
It was the return leg of the voyage that increasingly brought the
highest profits, particularly cargoes of flaxseed for the country's
burgeoning linen industry. In addition, barrel staves from the
colonies became critical to the provision trade, as were shipments
of grain and flour during lean periods like the late 1720s. Having
already relieved the island of hungry mouths, the same vessels, on
their return, performed the added service of bringing foodstuffs
to feed the starving. During the first week of April in 1728, ten
vessels arrived in Dublin with four thousand barrels of wheat from
America and Europe "to the great relief and satisfaction of the
inhabitants." Appearing just weeks before Jemmy's abduction,
one of the ships could easily have been the *James*.[12]

Captain Hendry was an experienced mariner. Unlike some
shipmasters—newcomers anxious to profit from the growing
trade—Hendry was well acquainted with the currents of the
"Western Ocean." Originally from Boston, he had spent nearly a
decade navigating the North Atlantic. Given the *James*'s size, he
likely commanded a crew of at least a dozen men.[13]

According to newspaper reports, the vessel was a type of brig
known as a snow. Though, like other brigs, it had two masts with
square sails, immediately behind the main mast was a small trysail,
known as a spanker, for superior maneuverability in high winds.
By virtue of their speed, snows enjoyed wide popularity among
eighteenth-century merchants. The Royal Navy also favored them
for hunting pirates.[14]

More than ever, Jemmy found himself profoundly alone. Notwithstanding his rootless childhood, he had resided in Dublin for
six years, a city whose streets and quays he had come to know

intimately. Still a youth, he faced a prolonged period of exile that he easily might not survive.

The prospect of colonial servitude could only have compounded his anguish. America, for many in Ireland, bore a frightful reputation. If thousands of indigent men and women annually indentured themselves or embarked as passengers, far greater numbers, however desperate their plight, spurned the chance to flee abroad. And while the English were apt to view Ireland and the American colonies through the same lens—as primitive borderlands—most Irishmen, certainly by the eighteenth century, saw little resemblance to their homeland. Although fabled for natural abundance, America sparked fears of barbarism and isolation. "Nothing but dense woods and deep glens resounding with the roar of wild beasts," wrote an eighteenth-century Irish poet—an alien land peopled by savages, slaves, and convicts. A letter from Lisburn to the *Dublin Weekly Journal* in 1729 spoke of "the sickness and seasonings of the country, the fatigue of clearing woods and forests before we can sow our corn, and the incursions and insurrection of the Indians." Many prospective immigrants were ambivalent. In 1736, Alexander Crawford, a tenant in County Donegal, wrote to his landlord complaining of his burdensome rent. "I can not provid for my children but ame obligt to transport my self and my famly to the deserts of America." Apparently, however, he had second thoughts, for eight years later, Crawford was still in Donegal.[15]

Even the climate of the colonies, despite their more southerly location, seemed less inviting. "We are sometimes frying, and others freezing," noted an Irish visitor. "Men," he reported, "often die at their labour in the field by heat." Accounts abounded of the drudgery demanded of fieldworkers. Everyday use in the British Isles of the term "slavery" to describe the fate of servants in the New World amply testified to popular anxiety. In London, a convict, ordered transported to the West Indies, pleaded that "he had rather bear strangling for a minute" than toil at a sugar works. To be sure, unlike slavery, the length of servitude was fixed—though Jemmy's indenture for seven years exceeded the normal term (Uncle Richard evidently preferred to take no chances). Otherwise, living conditions reportedly resembled those of enslaved Africans—not just wretched quarters but constant toil and the loss of personal freedom. What for most servants might offer a way station to propertied independence, for Annesley must have seemed a nightmare more terrifying than all his years as a street urchin.[16]

And there yet loomed a long ocean voyage. Depending upon the weather, especially the winds, the journey could last from four weeks to several months. Even for a vessel like the *James*, with its optimal size for sailing speed, six to eight weeks was customary. Without doubt, the safety of transatlantic travel had improved by the eighteenth century. Currents, winds, shoals, and shorelines all had grown more familiar. Irish vessels enjoyed the advantage of a shorter route than those faced by ships from continental Europe bearing immigrants from the Rhineland, the other major source of colonial servants. And shipmasters, of course, had a stake in the safe arrival of their passengers.[17]

Even so, conditions aboard most vessels in the Irish servant trade were poor. A ship the size of the *James* might have carried close to one hundred passengers and crew. Quarters were cramped, with scant room between decks. Likely, as on other vessels, parcels of servants had to be herded onto the main deck at regular intervals for exercise and fresh air. Rations of food and water were meager. For shipmasters eager to maximize profits, provisions, besides being costly, occupied valuable cargo space. The English servant William Moraley, who embarked from London in 1729 for Philadelphia, received a daily allowance of three biscuits and either dried codfish or a bit of salted beef. A "thimble full of bad brandy" was dispensed each morning and night. To supplement his spare water ration, Moraley struggled to catch rainwater as it slid down the sails.[18]

Disasters at sea remained common enough. In late 1728, a Londonderry vessel, the *Mary*, plagued by contrary winds, took twenty-three weeks to reach land, resulting in more than sixty deaths from a shortage of supplies. The following year, disease, another persistent threat, afflicted Irish passengers aboard the *George and Ann* bound for Philadelphia. Some one hundred persons perished from an outbreak of measles, with many of the corpses pitched overboard. A despondent servant, according to a passenger's journal, "threw himself over deck and drowned." Among other maladies, smallpox and dysentery took a heavy toll on crowded ships suffering from contaminated water, damp lower decks, and inadequate ventilation. The stench of sewage and vomit must have been suffocating. "There will not be much made of them," a merchant wrote of his cargo after more than half of the servants had died en route of the flu.[19]

The only source of information for the voyage of the *James* is a fanciful narrative modeled loosely on the first twenty-eight years of Annesley's life. Entitled *Memoirs of an Unfortunate Young Nobleman* . . . , it appeared in 1743, a time when overblown stories of high adventure were a popular literary genre. Were the protagonist of humble origins and a roguish bent, the style might be labeled picaresque, not unlike that of Defoe's *Moll Flanders* (1722) or Fielding's *Tom Jones* (1749).

If the book's florid style raises doubts about its credibility, so does the partiality of its anonymous author, who, in light of the prose, unquestionably was not Annesley himself. Still and all, only he could have been the author's principal source of information. Once stripped of their sentimental hyperbole, events in the *Memoirs* for the most part ring true. Moreover, references to names and places, when double-checked, usually prove accurate. That the book does not dramatize the ocean passage, other than recounting an early storm, suggests that the crossing was uneventful—unlike in Stevenson's *Kidnapped*, where the *Covenant* is wrecked on the western coast of Scotland, permitting David Balfour to escape being sent to the Carolinas. At one point, Jemmy evidently rejected, out of despair, rations of salted beef and peas, prompting the captain to calm his fears; but there are no mutinies or pirate raids to enliven the prose, or even complaints of conditions aboard ship.[20]

Arriving in the Delaware Bay, the *James* sailed north toward Philadelphia, the hub of the servant trade. First, however, the ship docked forty miles to the south at the town of Newcastle in

MEMOIRS

OF AN.

Unfortunate Young Nobleman,

Return'd from a

Thirteen Years Slavery in *America*

Where he had been sent by the Wicked Contrivances of his Cruel Uncle.

A STORY founded on Truth, and address'd equally to the Head and Heart,

This is the Heir; come, let us kill him, that the Inheritance may be ours.
LUKE XX. 14.

——————*Foul Deeds must rise,*
Tho' all the Earth o'erwhelm 'em, to Mens Eyes.
Spoken by HAMLET of his Uncle.

LONDON,

Printed for J. FREEMAN in *Fleetstreet*; and sold by the Booksellers in Town and Country.
M DCC XLIII.

Memoirs of an Unfortunate Young Nobleman, Return'd from a Thirteen Years Slavery in America, 'Where he had been sent by the Wicked Contrivances of his Cruel Uncle (London, 1743).

the colony of Delaware. Founded by the Dutch in 1651, Newcastle, or "Amstel" as it was first called (in honor of Amsterdam), was the Delaware Valley's oldest settlement, lying on a little rise beside the Delaware River, the great commercial watercourse connecting eastern Pennsylvania to Delaware Bay and the Atlantic. The town, which was said to possess three hundred families in 1708, had lost out, in wealth and prominence, to its celebrated neighbor upriver, though Newcastle was both Delaware's capital and a thriving port. Summers brought "coole and refreshing breezes" unlike "the so much talked of Philadelphia," sniped a local minister. Containing more than a hundred homes, the town surrounded a spacious green originally paced off by Peter Stuyvesant. In one corner stood Emanuel, a handsome Anglican church constructed of cedar and brick.[21]

Newcastle afforded shipmasters a convenient port before pressing on to Philadelphia. Farmers and tradesmen, eager for servants, appeared not only from northern Delaware but also from adjoining counties in Pennsylvania and Maryland. In 1727, nearly one thousand men and women disembarked from Ireland. Two years later, the number of entering vessels in Newcastle jumped sharply when the Pennsylvania assembly, owing to anti-Catholic fears, temporarily imposed a twenty-shilling duty on imported Irish servants. A report later estimated that 4,500 servants and passengers, mostly from Ireland, arrived that year in the town.[22]

Sales ordinarily took place aboard ships over the course of several days, if not longer. Servants were paraded on deck for the inspection of purchasers, a far cry from the hiring fairs in Ireland, where laborers negotiated terms with prospective employers. Captains, who stood to receive up to one-third of the profits, pushed for quick transactions, hoping to minimize the cost of provisions as well as to avert the possibility of disease. Years later, a visitor to Philadelphia wrote that the Irish "sell their servants here as they do their horses, and advertise them as they do their oatmeal and beef." Another contemporary observed that a "peculiar smell" plagued "all servants just coming from ships."[23]

Male laborers were favored over women, and Germans, for their reputed industry, over the Irish. Servants from Ireland, complained a Philadelphia trader, "have such an ill-name, they won't sell for any tolerable price." Carpenters, smiths, and other skilled workers (a minority) fetched the highest sums, owing to the Delaware Valley's growing demand for tradesmen. Alternately, laborers with agricultural backgrounds excited interest among farmers unable to afford the price of a slave, which was more than three times the £14 that the typical servant cost.[24]

On board the *James*, Jemmy must have appeared an unlikely prospect. Young and inexperienced, he possessed no trade or skill. Probably his puny frame was emaciated, his weathered face taut and deeply tanned. According to the *Memoirs*, a "rich planter" named Drumon purchased the boy after first haggling with Captain Hendry over the price. As a farmer and a small-time merchant, Duncan Drummond was not wealthy. All the same, the possession of a freehold of several hundred acres could easily have impressed a youth from Ireland, where most tenant tracts were tiny by comparison.[25]

So much about America must have seemed new and unfamiliar, all the more for a boy accustomed to the bustle and clamor of Dublin. Newcastle, by contrast, resembled a country village, surrounded on three sides by vast stretches of raw wilderness. It was not just the flatness of the coastal plain that caught a newcomer's eye, nor the sparse underbrush in the immense forests. It was also the trees themselves—oak, hickory, chestnut—so tall that a traveler could ride unmolested beneath the bottom branches. America seemed tailor-made for personal mobility and freedom, with its sprawling landscape, uncluttered by towns and villages one after another.[26]

Each day brought new discoveries. In the summer, days were

shorter than in Ireland and nights darker. Along with the heat, there was less rain. Skunks, panthers, and rattlesnakes were all unknown at home, as were many of the plants and wildflowers. Indians, African slaves, and Germans contributed to a strange medley of customs and beliefs, as did myriad religious faiths, including Presbyterians, Quakers, Anabaptists, and Lutherans. "A great mixture of people of all sorts," described the Swedish visitor Peter Kalm.[27]

Most remarkable was the Delaware Valley's abundant natural environment, affording colonists the economic independence to enjoy a free way of life. Nearly every foreign visitor marveled at the prosperity of rural families. "Everything is growing nice, straight, high, and fast," a German immigrant to southeastern Pennsylvania observed in 1724. Along with livestock, farmers raised a variety of grains—wheat, corn, oats, barley, rye—alternating crops during the long growing season. "As great plenty of bread and provisions of all sorts, as beef, pork, veal, mutton and dung hill fowl, as most other parts have in the King's Dominions," a Newcastle minister wrote. Apple, peach, and cherry orchards adorned well-kept farm-steads. "It is the best poor man's country in the world," declared the servant William Moraley.[28]

But not for bound laborers like Moraley himself, whose lot, he lamented, was "very hard." For them, particularly the unskilled, any chance of material success was unlikely. A Newcastle settler reported in 1729, "Those that are poor have but a bad time, being sold as servants to work for the others for a certain season, then for hire." Amid the natural bounty of the Delaware Valley, the exploitation of bound labor was striking. Not just black slaves, consigned by racial prejudice to lives of degradation, but numer-ous white servants confronted working conditions worse than any regimen of labor in the British Isles. Terms for servants in Amer-ica were longer and more rigid, with few legal or social sanctions against ill treatment. A servant's contract could be transferred

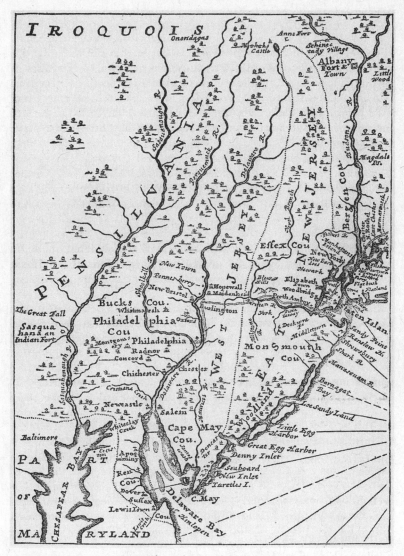

David Humphreys, *The Province of Pennsylvania, 1730.*

from one farmer to another, or bequeathed to an heir. Unlike British servitude, which was more paternalistic due to the gentry's ancient identification with the land and its people, colonial masters often considered laborers mere property, not part of their families. Because of Anglo-Protestant prejudice, Irish servants in all likelihood fared worst of all. The will of one Newcastle farmer prohibited the sale of his lands to "any Irishman whatsoever" and threatened his wife with disinheritance should she marry "an Irishman or any of that extraction." "The negroes in our plantation[s] have a saying," wrote the Irish philosopher George Berkeley: "'if the Negro was not Negro, an Irishman would be Negro.'"[29]

Duncan Drummond, whose own origins were evidently Scottish or Scotch-Irish, lived in northwestern Delaware in Mill Creek Hundred. The hundred, an administrative subdivision of Newcastle County, was bounded on the south by White Clay Creek and on the east by Red Clay Creek. To the north and west lay the "circle," the twelve-mile border, in the shape of an arc, separating Delaware from Pennsylvania. Mill Creek threaded its way south through the hundred, an area of farms, woodlands, and scattered hills known for the fertility of its clay soil. The stream took its name from the saw and gristmills beside its banks. Lumber, flour, and wheat could either be hauled overland or carried in shallops downstream. Drummond may have operated a sawmill together with his farmstead and storehouse, a common combination of rural enterprises. Like other farmers, he probably resided in a log cabin with a low roof and a wooden chimney coated in clay. In June 1731, he would sell 110 acres bordering Mill Creek to Francis Land, "yeoman." That Drummond retained one or more tracts is clear from a court judgment six years later against a neighbor whose property bordered his lands. Definitely, the family was in northern Delaware to stay, for today, long after Duncan's death in 1762, there is no shortage of landmarks bearing the Drummond name.[30]

According to the *Memoirs*, Jemmy was just one of several

servants on Drummond's farm, which also included a few slaves. Not many farmers owned more than that. In 1727 only some fifty slaves resided in the Anglican parish encompassing the town of Newcastle. One of Drummond's slaves absconded not long after Jemmy's arrival. Caught the next day and whipped, he was sold to a master in Philadelphia.[31]

Other than cutting timber, little is said of the boy's day-to-day tasks, which, depending on the season, may have included sowing, hoeing, and harvesting crops. According to a German immigrant to southeastern Pennsylvania, "Most jobs involve cutting timber, felling oak trees, and levelling, or as one says there, clearing great tracts of forest, roots and all." Not only did land need clearing, but the timber provided lumber for fencing and barrel staves, which the Delaware Valley exported in massive quantities.[32]

On occasion, a servant might have a benevolent master, but mostly conditions were miserable. Beginning at dawn, days for Jemmy were long and grueling, broken only for draughts of water and cakes of "pone" (cornbread). Meat, vegetables, and fruit were sparse. For one unaccustomed to a corn-based diet, the transition must have been difficult. A "feast" was a bowl of mush, consisting of hominy moistened with lard or bacon fat (in Pennsylvania, Moraley termed mush a "hungry food"). Newspaper advertisements usually described runaway servants clothed in leather breeches and shirts made from a coarse linen fabric known as ozenbrig—"so rough," complained Moraley, "that the shirt occasions great uneasiness to the body." A felt hat with a wide brim was customary for protection from the sun. Nights meant sleeping in a hammock made from netting or canvas. Rough-hewn quarters for servants lacked fires for warmth, even in wintertime (so cold were the winters of 1730 and 1733 that the Delaware River froze). Instances of suicide were not unknown. A former laborer from Scotland noted that "some of these poor deluded slaves, in order to put an end to their bondage, put a period to their lives." The

Newcastle servant John Fryer bore a scar beneath his chin from "having once attempted to cut his throat."[33]

Servants' bodies testified in other ways to their lives. Many, according to descriptions in runaway advertisements, exhibited facial scars from smallpox. "Pockfretten" was the usual expression. Martha Barnes, a twenty-six-year-old servant from New Jersey, had "great ring worms on her breast and arms." There were old wounds from axes, scythes, and knives. The Irish servant James Downing walked "as if he was hip shot," whereas Patrick Bourne had "a large scar on one cheek form'd like a horse-shoe." Common, too, were missing teeth, severed joints, and bent backs. A number of laborers sported tattoos, including initials inscribed with gunpowder (a technique used by courts to brand habitual troublemakers). The likeliest rogues were those said to display a "down look," a supposed sign of their duplicity.[34]

There must have been times of deep despair for Annesley. In the absence of kith and kin, sources of solace for servants were few. In vain, with the aid of a tailor, Jemmy dictated a letter to his mother addressed to the "palace" of the late Duke of Buckingham in London. Some laborers turned to drink. Despite the efforts of masters to restrict consumption, cider, rum, and beer could be had if one possessed money. Though a far cry from Philadelphia's "Hell Town," with its profusion of taverns and dram shops, northern Delaware had its share of drinking houses. Besides ordinaries, such as the Indian King in Newcastle, unlicensed houses opened their doors to servants, especially after dark when masters were hard-pressed to prevent laborers from "nightwalking." In Virginia, the planter Landon Carter condemned the proliferation of "night shops" and their popularity among poor whites and slaves. Not only did the shops dispense rum, but proprietors sold "to anybody anything whatever." Newcastle, like other communities, also hosted two yearly fairs. At least in Philadelphia, servants on such occasions attended in large numbers. There, a critic bemoaned the corruption of the city's youth, "who are at times induced to drinking and gaming in mix'd companies of vicious servants and negroes."[35]

Jemmy was said to have shunned the company of other servants, with the sole exception of an older woman. "He never partook in any of their pleasures," the *Memoirs* claimed. Seemingly his detachment, if true, stemmed from a sense of his own social superiority. During the boy's early years, there had been flashes of pride in his lineage, even as a street waif adrift in Dublin. Unlike other immigrants who sought to remake their lives in the colonies, he held fast to his identity. At the same time, he had an outward ability to adapt to different settings and new hardships. Instability had long been a way of life for him; if anything, it may have eased his adjustment to the life of a servant, however punishing the ordeal or wrenching his separation from Ireland. And the simple fact of youth may have helped to keep body and soul together. A colonial storekeeper later noted that the "younger class" of servants "become more easily habituated to the clime, [and] are able to undergo any hardships," in marked contrast to servants of "advanced years."[36]

Nor as a sustaining force should we minimize the power of retribution. A visitor to the Delaware Valley later remembered meeting Jemmy one day outside his master's house. Carrying a rifle and a dead squirrel, the boy related his remarkable tale, vowing to "come over and have satisfaction." If the *Memoirs* are correct, his uncle's betrayal became a perpetual source of torment, a "continual vulture preying on his peace." Ireland was seldom out of mind, spurring visions of a triumphant homecoming culminating in Richard's disgrace. Only after unmasking his treachery would Jemmy grant forgiveness, in a manner befitting a true lord.[37]

Or such at least, we are told, were young Annesley's thoughts on solitary days felling oak trees in the forests of Mill Creek Hundred.

4

FLIGHT

They are perpetually running away.
WILLIAM MORALEY, 1743[1]

Rarely anymore did memories of his nephew occupy Richard Annesley. In the aftermath of Jemmy's kidnapping, he could look forward to life as Baron Altham from the vantage of his brother's former home in Inchicore. Not only had the Gregorys departed, but so had the hounds, sold to a local nobleman. Pleased by his son-in-law's new rank, John Simpson belatedly blessed his daughter's union by contributing generously to the couple's support—a hefty burden in light of Richard's extravagance.[2]

At first, rumors had arisen over the boy's disappearance. In Dublin, there was no shortage of explanations, including from Richard himself. To the king at arms, responsible for certifying his title, he reported his nephew's death from smallpox (the payment of "honorary fees" for the certificate reportedly eased the herald's initial skepticism). Afterward, to a circle of intimates, Richard related "in an easy manner" that the boy "was gone." Still later, he stated to a friend that Jemmy had died in the West Indies. In an age marked by high mortality and widespread vagrancy, any of these possibilities was plausible. Had anyone attempted to investigate further, they would have found that many parish registers of burials were fragmentary. Not until the mid-nineteenth century did civil authorities in Ireland require the registration of deaths.[3]

Meanwhile, former servants of his late brother feared that Jemmy had either been murdered or transported, whereas along the quays, word of the abduction had spread swiftly, creating a "very great noise," Thomas Byrne, a childhood playmate, recalled years later. Mary Hughes, the keeper of a Dublin alehouse, recollected "that it was the common cry that" he "was put on board a ship." When the new baron passed in the streets, tradesmen could be heard muttering curses for "taking away the child's birth-right." As for Richard Tighe, the lawyer who had last been responsible for Jemmy's care, he had no doubt of the kidnapping. Long afterward, when questioned why he had not reported the abduction, Tighe asked plaintively, "Would not my Lord Altham have risen in arms against me? He would have been in a great rage, and no boy here to produce."[4]

And then there was Mr. Jones, whose alehouse in Ormond Market the new lord had twice employed in his attempts to kidnap Jemmy. An honest man by reputation, Jones only later appeared to grasp the sinister implications of the conspiracy. Owing either to guilt or to the ostracism of his neighbors, he slowly went mad. One year after the abduction, he was wont to wander the streets, repeatedly crying that "he was undone by my Lord Altham."[5]

A meatier problem for Richard was the troubled state of his finances. In Jemmy's absence, his brother's lands in New Ross had reverted to the Earl of Anglesea, as required by the 1701 will of their cousin James. Noting Richard's "unfortunate circumstances," the Irish Lords twice requested the lord lieutenant to appeal to the king "to make some fit provision for him," if only to save the House further embarrassment. As in the case of his brother, a pension of £200 was granted, but then a second blow struck. Following the death of his father-in-law in 1730, Simpson's son acquired the bulk of the family estate. Ann Annesley, now nineteen, received an annuity of just £20 and Richard a token gift of £100. So reduced were their circumstances that Richard sold the annuity. In 1732, the lord primate of Ireland, Hugh Boulter, at Richard's urging appealed to London, requesting a larger pension in light of the baron's heavy debts. "It is a pity a peer of this kingdom, and who may possibly be a peer of Great Britain, should be reduced" to "such necessities," he implored.[6]

But the Crown balked, despite an audience with the king that Richard was granted during a trip to London in 1734. Even among friends, his persistent appeals began to wear thin. Efforts to secure a plum place in the government failed miserably. "He is as poor as his elder brother, who before he died sold several reversionary estates," the Earl of Egmont sourly observed, "and his character is so bad that nobody will have [anything] to do with him."[7]

One who shared that harsh judgment was Anglesea. Despite a taste for hard whiskey, the earl, a High Churchman, possessed a stern sense of propriety, uncommon among the Annesley family. Never remarrying, the elder Tory politician remained active in the English House of Lords, where he was esteemed as one of the age's great orators. As late as 1736, he delivered an impassioned plea on behalf of his colleague Lord Arran. The earl alternated between seats in Oxfordshire and Hampshire and his residence in London. In addition to property in Dublin and the town of Drogheda, he retained extensive holdings across Ireland in nine counties. Much of the acreage was in Wexford, including the handsome estate Camolin Park, originally acquired by his great-grandfather, Sir Francis Annesley, in 1618. Construction of the mansion cost Anglesea upwards of £5,000. Known traditionally by the name of Knockangarrow, the property extended eight miles in breadth by thirteen in length. Lands let to tenants, reported a newspaper in 1737, were "set at an easy rent and long leases."[8]

To the Earl of Anglesea, the fact that Richard now stood to inherit his titles was a bitter disappointment. Whether Anglesea credited Richard's reports of Jemmy's death or, instead, the rumors of his kidnapping is not known. In part his distaste stemmed from

Richard's bigamous marriage following the desertion of his first wife after squandering her fortune. Later, in an effort to make amends, and perhaps to avert a wider scandal, the earl provided Ann Prust with an annuity of £400.[9]

All the same, there was no apparent remedy to the dilemma of Richard's place in the chain of succession; and on April 1, 1737, after decades battling the ravages of gout, Anglesea finally succumbed at his hunting lodge, Farnborough Place in northeastern Hampshire. After first lying in state, his body was interred in the parish church. "An ornament to the age in which he lived," mourned London's *Weekly Miscellany*.[10]

Remarkably, with the descent of Arthur's titles, Richard— the younger son of a younger son—became the first in the family to unite all of its many honors, totaling five separate peerages, including the barony inherited from his brother. Most important, having waited for the past decade, following his brother's death, for his elder cousin to die, Richard became sixth Earl of Anglesea. A report from Dublin unctuously saluted the new lord as a "steady patron to his country, and an enemy to oppression."[11]

On the other hand, most of the late earl's worldly goods, along with alienable lands in England, went to his cousin Francis Annesley of the Inner Temple, grandson of Francis, first Viscount Valentia (by his second marriage). The legendary Tory politician and barrister, who in 1732 married the widow of a rich jeweler, had held parliamentary seats not just in Ireland but also in England. Now seventy-four, Francis became the sole executor of Arthur's estate.[12]

That left the disposal of numerous entailed estates in England, Ireland, and Wales, the lion's share of Anglesea's wealth. By one estimate, their current worth of £10,000 per annum would quadruple after the expiration of tenants' leases in eighteen years. Ordinarily, these estates, too, would have fallen to Richard, but in a surprising twist, the second will of his late

Joseph Tudor, *A Prospect of the Parliament House, in College Green, Dublin*, 1753. The House of Lords resided in the Parliament House on the right. Today the building is home to the Bank of Ireland.

cousin James in January 1702 had inexplicably omitted Richard from the customary line of descent. The first will, executed the previous May, had included both Altham and Richard and their male offspring. Now, owing to James's infirmity or, more likely, a scribe's careless mistake, the lands were destined to fall instead to another cousin—a grandson, like Richard, of Arthur, first Earl of Anglesea—Charles Annesley of Cork, captain of the Battle-axe Guards, a military corps attached to Dublin Castle. To make matters worse, Charles was also to receive the unentailed seat of Camolin Park. "It is the clerk makes justice," declared an English saying. Arthur, who before his death chose not to contest the error, preferred to let the estates "go where the law intends them." All the same, according to Egmont, "He esteemed himself very unhappy that his title and estate should fall to such worthless persons as Lord Altham and the Annesley of Cork, the one a rogue, the other a brute." Not once in the will, in fact, did Richard's name appear despite generous bequests to others, including not only a nephew and several remote cousins but also a handful of servants.[13]

Barely had the old earl drawn his last breath before Richard decamped for Camolin Park from his Wexford residence at Monfin. There was never any question of going to court, and "possession," as the seventeenth-century adage observed, was "nine points in the law." For at least a year, Richard had had an inkling of the will's contents as well as Anglesea's desire that his tenants "attorn," for their new landlord, to Charles Annesley, whose agents managed to seize most of the remaining lands on both sides of the Irish Sea.[14]

Not only did the will's wording favor Charles, but he was better prepared for a protracted legal battle in view of the high cost of litigating a suit at the Court of Chancery. Despite Richard's occupation of Camolin Park, his cousin's resources promised to be far greater. Still, the new earl retained the family's titles, and few persons with knowledge of the dispute could blindly dismiss the merits of his cause.

Desperate for hard cash, Richard began to seize tenants' goods for unpaid rents due on May 1. He also cleared a portion of the estate's thick woodlands, threatening all the while to fell every last tree. Since the early seventeenth century, landed gentlemen had laid waste to the countryside for its most valuable natural resource. Timber fetched high prices, with the consequence that rotting stumps marred much of the terrain. In contrast to the forestlands of rural England, enormous portions of the Irish landscape, except for the country's more rugged reaches, were strangely barren. What landowners did not sell, the poor pilfered for firewood. In 1726, the lord chief justice concluded that in the "southern parts" of the island there was "scarce a tree or hedge to be seen for twenty miles."[15]

According to one estimate, the oak woods at Camolin Park were worth at least £6,000. The prospect of such an immense loss drove Charles to obtain a temporary court order forbidding their destruction; and, upon the arrival of both parties from Ireland, negotiations quickly followed at Francis Annesley's London house in Lincoln's Inn Fields. Already, in an act of kindness, Francis had bestowed on Richard the elegant furnishings at Farnborough Place along with Anglesea's robes and the signet of his arms. Implacable, the new earl insisted upon all of the entailed estates in England and two-thirds of those in Ireland. He had little taste for compromise. It was surprising, nonetheless, that on June 16, after repeated meetings, the two cousins reached an accord that appeared to satisfy Richard's demands. He would also retain Camolin Park, the jewel among the family's Irish properties, to which he finally returned with a large retinue in late August. As many as five hundred tenants were said to welcome the sixth Earl of Anglesea at the Wexford border as the county's lord lieutenant and *custos rotulorum* (keeper of the rolls), historically the county's principal justice of the peace.[16]

As things turned out, neither Richard nor his lawyers had reviewed deeds and other documents in Francis's possession. Later, upon closer inspection, there appeared reason, in fact, to conclude that the flawed will of December 1701 had been revoked and that Camolin Park, as an entailed estate, should have devolved directly to Richard. Moreover, Francis Annesley had interests of his own to advance, which became clear soon enough. In 1738, he filed a bill at the Court of Chancery in London for a large portion of Richard's Irish lands, arguing that none had been entailed. Incensed, Anglesea refused to honor the previous agreement, drafting instead an alternate proposal that Charles swiftly rejected. Richard also dispatched to London an attorney to lobby members of both houses of Parliament to oppose a bill designed to exemplify the late earl's will (i.e., render the document official with a royal seal). The bill was successfully defeated once word spread that cousin Francis, the executor, had been expelled decades earlier from the Irish

House of Commons for Tory sympathies. By this time, Richard's agents had taken control of all Anglesea estates in Ireland, including the collection of tenants' rents. Even the heirs of Catherine Phipps, the daughter of James, third Earl of Anglesea, notably her son, Constantine, now insisted on a say in the rancorous proceedings. Meanwhile, quickening land values in Ireland, after years of famine and depression, raised the stakes even higher.[17]

So there it was. As with other aristocratic houses that fell prey to rifts over inheritance, Anglesea's death in 1737 had exposed the family's fault lines. Former fissures arising from envy and mistrust had dramatically expanded. In just months, a barrage of court suits was threatening to sunder the house of Annesley—a conflict that never would have arisen had Jemmy been allowed to succeed his father. As tempers flared, allegations of duplicity and deceit flowed freely between cousins. Tormented on all fronts, Richard began to voice the unthinkable—retrieving his nephew, if still alive, from the wilds of America. Charles, he swore to friends, "should never have a foot of the estate, for if the worst came of it, he knew how to produce a man who should inherit all."[18] Almost certainly this was a bluff, but we can never know for sure; for within a short while, Richard's bluster had been overtaken by events, originating not in Dublin or London but across the Atlantic.

Just like colonial slaves, scores of white servants in America routinely absconded from their masters. They remained at large for days, even weeks, if not, finally, escaping altogether. Far more Irish than German servants ran away, a probable consequence of their harsher treatment. Favorite destinations included the western backcountry and crowded cities like Philadelphia and New York, which offered both anonymity and the chance of employment. Some fugitives, disillusioned with prospects in the colonies, sought to board ships bound for home. Convict servants, who had not opted to enlist for America to begin with, became particularly notorious for embarking before the expiration of their terms. "Great numbers have been come back before half their time was expired," Bernard de Mandeville noted in 1725.[19]

From 1720 to 1760, Philadelphia newspapers printed advertisements for nearly 2,400 white runaways from the Delaware Valley. So prevalent were they that Benjamin Franklin, during his famed journey in 1723 to Philadelphia, aroused suspicion in southern New Jersey. "I cut so miserable a figure," he recounted in his autobiography, that "I was suspected to be some runaway servant, and in danger of being taken up." Ordinarily, fugitives' chances were poor. With bounties in the offing, reports circulated rapidly by word of mouth, even in the absence of newspaper advertisements. If caught and questioned, theirs was the burden of proof; they had to produce either a valid pass or an expired indenture. For servants as well as slaves, freedom of movement, at least during daylight, was closely monitored. "Notwithstanding these difficulties," noted William Moraley, "they are perpetually running away."[20]

Philadelphia papers during the 1730s carried ads for thirty runaways from Newcastle County. All but three were male, with most in their twenties. In view of the cost and inconvenience of newspaper advertising, there seems little doubt that the actual number of fugitives was far greater.[21]

No advertisement ever appeared for Jemmy, though he fled at least twice. The first attempt took place during his fifth year of servitude. Grueling labor, periodic whippings, and thoughts of Ireland all drove him to abscond, traveling east, so he thought, along a "rout the runaway slaves usually take." Armed with a hedge bill, a hooked blade with a long wooden handle for cutting brush, he hoped to board a departing vessel on the Delaware as a sailor. But after days of making his way through thick forests, he came instead to the Susquehanna River in Pennsylvania, some fifty miles due west of Mill Creek Hundred. Following three days of backtracking, he joined a party of fugitives from Pennsylvania

THREE POUNDS REWARD.

RUN AWAY from the Sub-
scriber, living at Warwick fur-
nace, Minehole, on the 23d inft. an
Irifh fervant man, named DENNIS
M'CALLIN, about five feet eight
inches high, nineteen years of age,
has a freckled face, light coloured
curly hair. Had on when he went
away, an old felt hat, white and yel-
low ftriped jacket, a new blue cloth coat, and buckfkin
breeches ; alfo, he took with him a bundle of fhirts and
ftockings, and a pocket piftol ; likewife, a box containing gold rings, &c. Whoever takes up faid fervant and fe-
cures him in any goal, fo as his mafter may get him again,
fhall have the above reward and reafonable charges
paid by   JAMES TODD.

N. B. All mafters of veffels, and others, are forbid
from harbouring or carrying him off, at their peril.

Advertisement for a Runaway Servant, *The Pennsylvania Packet; and the General Advertiser* (Philadelphia), January 27, 1772. Toward the close of the colonial era, illustrations occasionally accompanied runaway advertisements in Philadelphia newspapers.

bound for a ship on the Appoquinimink River in southern New-castle County where it entered Delaware Bay. Though they traveled by night, all in turn were captured by men on horseback with lanterns, and Jemmy found himself confined for five weeks in a jail in Chester, Pennsylvania, southwest of Philadelphia. On his return to Newcastle, not only did Drummond whip him "without mercy," but a court added two years to his original contract, extending the remainder of his term to four years. Unlike most colonies, which attached a fixed period of time to a runaway's indenture depending on the length of absence, Delaware left the severity of the penalty to the discretion of county courts.[22]

Magistrates also performed the task of hearing complaints of abuse from servants. In view of petitions submitted to the court of quarter sessions for Chester County in Pennsylvania, grievances

ranged from "barbarous usage" to the nonpayment of "freedom
dues" (e.g. clothing and tools) granted servants on the expiration
of their terms. Ann Doughterry, having "thro' necessity" been
forced to leave Ireland, complained that her three children, indentured as servants like herself, had been sold illegally to a trader in
Virginia. No such petitions have survived for Newcastle County,
though, according to the *Memoirs*, Jemmy protested Drummond's
mistreatment to Newcastle magistrates shortly after his return.
Apparently the evidence was strong enough to prompt his sale
to a new master, though conditions remained harsh during the
succeeding three years. Then, with just twelve months remaining, Annesley, now twenty-one, boarded a ship, ostensibly bound
for Europe, at the encouragement of several sailors—only to be
apprehended and punished with four additional years of servitude.
Thirteen years for an indentured servant was extremely onerous,
alone rivaled, among white laborers, by the fourteen years reserved
for the most notorious transported convicts.[23]

Several dramatic incidents described in the *Memoirs* are at
best implausible, and in this respect the account resembles other
eighteenth-century narratives set in foreign lands that blended
fact with fiction. Jemmy, at one point, reportedly became the
romantic object of not one but two maidens: Maria, the daughter
of his second master, and an Indian girl named Turquois. The
colony did contain a negligible population of natives, some of
whom Jemmy probably encountered over the course of his servitude. A former Newcastle minister wrote in 1709, "They strag-
gle up and down among the English plantations and villages" on
"leaving their winter quarters" in order "to meet with a chapman
for their burden of skins, or with a meal of victuals." Annesley's
encounters, however, were likely less titillating than the *Memoirs*
suggest. Supposedly, the rivals met one day in a meadow beside
the Delaware, despite Jemmy's efforts to discourage both suitors.
Turquois, seizing Maria "by the throat, gripped her neck so fast

between her hands that she was very near strangled." But Maria escaped, and the Indian maiden, "mad with despair and frustrated revenge," ran "directly to the river, and plunged headlong in, putting an end at once to her unhappy love and life." On a later occasion, according to the *Memoirs*, Annesley found himself attacked by two Iroquois braves. Slashed in the hip by a knife, he escaped after a furious struggle when several men appeared in search of a runaway slave.[24]

Yet more heroic was Jemmy's supposed foiling of a plot by his master's wife and the servant Stephano. Together, the pair planned to kill her husband until Jemmy chanced upon the conspiracy. Barely, we are told, did he himself escape being poisoned by his vengeful mistress. A cat by mistake consumed his basin of soup, only to begin "foaming at the mouth"; displaying "all the signs of the most terrible agony," it "fell down dead." These events, never themselves reported in a newspaper, almost certainly were inspired by a sensational murder in Newcastle County not long after Annesley's arrival. According to Benjamin Franklin's *Pennsylvania Gazette*, in 1731 Catherine Bevan and her lover, a "young servant man," plotted to kill her elderly husband. In contrast to the fictional account, however, Henry Bevan suffered an agonizing death—first poisoned with roman vitriol (cupric sulfate) and then beaten, he was at last strangled with a handkerchief. At the funeral, a county magistrate, on finding the coffin nailed shut, ordered the lid opened, and discovered a badly bruised corpse. Following a coroner's inquest and trial, the servant was hanged and Mrs. Bevan burnt alive in the capital.[25]

Not until 1740, having just turned twenty-five, did James Annesley regain his freedom (it had been years since anyone called him Jemmy). Never, apparently, did he contemplate remaining in the colonies. Instead, he struck out for Philadelphia to seek transport to Ireland. The *Memoirs* suggest that he had completed his servitude, but the timing is premature in light of the six

additional years imposed for running away. Almost certainly, he
was a fugitive, finally escaping on his third attempt, as a London
newspaper subsequently reported.[26]

Lying between the Delaware and Schuylkill Rivers, Philadelphia was the second largest city in the colonies, after Boston, with
a population in 1740 nearing twelve thousand. Lined with elegant
Georgian homes of stone and brick, the broad avenues contained a
number of handsome churches, including Christ Church, among
the grandest in North America, with an organ imported from London. "It takes almost a whole day to walk around the city," a German immigrant reported at mid-century. Warehouses, wharves,
and piers dominated the bustling waterfront, as vessels departed
for all corners of the North Atlantic and the Caribbean. The servant William Moraley, during a visit to the harbor, counted at
least forty ships.[27]

The port drew large numbers of runaway servants from the Delaware Valley and northern Maryland. Temporary lodging was found
at taverns and boardinghouses, which were notorious for conceal-
ing servants and apprentices on the lam. Philadelphia newspapers
alerted readers that fugitives might seek to board outbound ships,

G. Wood, *The Prospect of Philadelphia from Wickacove*, 1735.

and captains were admonished not to admit disreputable persons as either sailors or passengers. A notice in the *Pennsylvania Gazette* warned of "suspicious fellows, lurking on board the ships or hanging frequently, on evenings, about them at the wharfs."[28]

James found passage on a merchant vessel bound first for Jamaica, then for London, just as war with Spain had broken out in the Caribbean. As a runaway, he probably had no other choice. In early August, following an uneventful voyage, he disembarked at Port Royal on the island's southeastern coast. Located at the tip of a crooked spit of land, Port Royal had suffered the reputation, a half-century earlier, of being the most wicked town in the west— a "dunghill" populated by pirates, prostitutes, and rogues of all stripes. In 1692, more than a few persons discerned a measure of divine justice in the horrific earthquake that, late one June morning, plunged half of the town into the sea, resulting in the loss of hundreds of lives.[29]

By the time of Annesley's arrival, the remains of Port Royal had been converted into Britain's principal naval base in the Caribbean. Eight years earlier, Spanish coastguards off Cuba had boarded the brig of an English captain, Robert Jenkins, who was beaten severely and half-strangled. After severing his ear, the Spanish commander bid him "to carry it to his master King George." Years later, Jenkins purportedly displayed the pickled remains to enraged members of the House of Commons, igniting long-festering tensions between Britain and Spain over trade.[30]

The War of Jenkins' Ear erupted in October 1739, and the base at Port Royal quickly began to draw men and ships. Assembling in the waters off Jamaica was the most powerful armada in English history, nearly two hundred warships, transports, and support vessels, with most destined to attack the key Spanish fortress of Cartagena in the spring of 1741. Commander of the fleet was Vice Admiral Edward Vernon, fresh from a victorious assault on the Panamanian stronghold of Porto Bello with just six ships. Arriving in an expeditionary force from Virginia, Lawrence Washington, George's half-brother, later named Mount Vernon in his honor. Among sailors, the admiral was less fondly known as "Old Grog" for diluting their daily rum ration with water, along with lemon juice to prevent scurvy.[31]

On August 11, 1740, according to a surviving muster book, Annesley enlisted as a seaman aboard His Majesty's fifty-gun ship, the *Falmouth*. A ship of the line with a burden of 760 tons and a crew of three hundred, the *Falmouth* had returned to Port Royal in early July after helping to capture a Dutch vessel carrying Spanish goods. As an able seaman, "pulling and hauling" likely consumed James's hours in port—mending sails, hoisting cables, and repairing rigging. For relief, seamen flocked at night to punch-houses, to Vernon's dismay. Despite the demanding regimen, it was less arduous than life aboard a merchantman, which might explain why Annesley enlisted in the navy, notwithstanding the longer service.[32]

Or, just maybe, he expected to find a more receptive audience aboard a naval vessel, for it was there that he decided to declare his true identity. Word spread in short order across the massive fleet at Port Royal, now approaching the size of a large provincial town, brimming with soldiers as well as seamen eager for the latest gossip. Annesley found himself confronted by two crewmen of the fireship *Eleanor*: James Simpson, a master's mate, and seaman John Bowen. Simpson, oddly enough, was the cousin of Richard Annesley's second wife, Ann; skeptical at first, he was soon convinced. Bowen, who had attended school with James in Dublin, had no such hesitation. "This is the man," he loudly declared, clapping James on the shoulder among a crowd of sailors. Then still others who had known the boy came forward, including Robert Collier, a former coachman to Lord Blessington, once a close friend of Baron Altham. A marine private stationed in nearby Kingston, Collier, after speaking with James, swore an affidavit before a justice of the peace affirming his identity.[33]

Such was the "great noise" that Admiral Vernon himself shortly met with Annesley, only to be persuaded by his remarkable saga. Besides advancing the young man money, he instructed Captain Douglas, commander of the *Falmouth*, to treat him as a gentleman for the duration of his tour. In addition, he was promoted to midshipman in the navy's highly stratified chain of command, a rating normally occupied by young gentlemen training to become sea officers.[34]

It might at first seem strange that after so many years Annesley should encounter a handful of distant acquaintances in a remote corner of the Caribbean. But in the early 1740s, Port Royal was fast becoming the military epicenter of the western hemisphere. And, too, the breadth of the Atlantic had by then effectively shrunk, becoming smaller, more intimate, and far less mysterious. Voyages required fewer weeks, greater numbers of people circulated more freely, and information traveled more swiftly. On February 12, 1741, the *Daily Post* in London published a dispatch from Jamaica reporting that a seaman recently entered aboard the *Falmouth* had been identified by a mate as "the only son of the late Lord Altham, who was heir to the title and estate of the earl of Anglesea." Two additional gentlemen, the correspondent noted, had corroborated the claim, whereas Admiral Vernon had ordered that he should "walk the quarterdeck as a midshipman," pending his voyage home. Before the month was out, the letter also appeared in the popular London periodical, the *Gentleman's Magazine*.[35]

Suddenly Annesley's prospects had dramatically improved, with word of his gripping ordeal spreading rapidly. What had once seemed a distant dream—returning to Ireland—had now become a distinct likelihood. Not even the *Falmouth*'s participation in the disastrous land and sea assault on Cartagena commencing in mid-March would interfere. Ordered to block provisions to the besieged Spanish fortress, the ship patrolled El Dique, the channel separating the island of Grand Baru from the mainland of present-day Colombia. In late April, Vernon decided to abandon the assault, leaving the *Falmouth* and other vessels to make their way back to Jamaica. Left behind were more than ten thousand dead out of fourteen thousand British and American soldiers committed to the battle. The number of seamen who perished is not known, but probably some ships had barely enough hands to man the rigging. Malaria, dysentery, and yellow fever ("black vomit") exacted a heavier toll on British and American forces than did fire from the enemy, which was heroically led by the one-eyed admiral Don Blas de Leso.[36]

With Annesley aboard, the *Falmouth* left the Caribbean in early July, destined for London after first escorting a ship to Virginia bearing the governor, William Gooch. Two months later, it reached the Thames naval yard at Woolwich, established in 1512 by Henry VIII for his flagship, the *Henri Grace a Dieu* (*Great Harry*), where it was slated for numerous repairs, including fresh planks of wood on the underside of its hull to replace what little sheathing remained from shipworms and decay. Quarters in the yard were cramped. Forced to wait for one of just two dry docks, the *Falmouth* finally entered on September 30, two days after the departure of a battered warship named the *Anglesea*, later to be scuttled off the Kent coast.[37]

5

DELIVERANCE

*Great as the misfortunes of my life have been, I shall always
consider this unfortunate accident as the greatest of them all.*
JAMES ANNESLEY, 1742[1]

J ames Annesley found himself in a sprawling metropolis of
675,000 people. By the mid-eighteenth century, London
was the biggest city in western Europe. At no other time would
it so dominate the English nation—politically, economically, and
culturally. Containing 10 percent of the country's population, the
city occupied both banks of the Thames, stretching from Tothill
Fields, home of Bridewell, England's first debtors' prison, as far
east as Blackwall, site of one of the foremost private shipyards
in the world. Daniel Defoe calculated that London's perimeter
totaled thirty-six miles. Within this vast expanse lay a patch-
work of parishes, precincts, and wards, with streets, large and
small, bustling with life, pedestrians and carriages all in perpetual
motion. "The variety that we met with as we went along is amaz-
ing," remarked James Boswell during a stroll from fashionable
Hyde Park in the West End to Whitechapel Turnpike beyond
London Bridge. "One end of London is like a different country
from the other in look and manners."[2]

On October 14, 1741, pursuant to orders from the Admiralty,
Annesley was discharged from the Royal Navy. More than thirteen
years had elapsed since he had fended for himself in the streets of

Dublin, a city altogether different from London in size and appearance. Lacking friends or family, he came armed with the names of prospective allies supplied by well-wishers in Jamaica. Given his aristocratic pretensions, employment was out of the question. Instead, while the *Falmouth* still lay anchored in the Thames, James had written a letter to Sir Maurice Thompson, second Baron Haversham, who four years earlier had married his paternal aunt, Elizabeth—also, unfortunately, the sister of his Uncle Richard, with whom her interests had long lain. Following Haversham's rejection of his appeal, James applied in person to Francis Annesley, yet embroiled with Richard over the lands of their deceased cousin Arthur. Caught by surprise at his home, Francis was gracious but noncommittal, suggesting over a meal that James carry his cause to Ireland. James also received a trifling sum of money as a token of the barrister's goodwill. An appeal to the widow of the Duke of Buckingham, his step-grandmother, fared no better. The duchess, he was told, was traveling in France.[3]

Unable to find a patron among London's upper crust, Annesley turned to a man of more humble repute. For years, the Quaker William Henderson had acted as an agent for both Lord Altham and Arthur, Earl of Anglesea, collecting rents in England as well as Ireland. Until a recent falling-out, he had been in Richard's employ. Henderson's past was checkered. Prior to the protections scandal in the Irish Lords, he had been the beneficiary, while imprisoned for debt, of the certificate forged by Altham. Still, Henderson, who now resided in London, had intimate knowledge of the family, including memories of the boy Jemmy. Not only did Annesley receive food and lodging, but, more important, Henderson put him in touch with a tireless Scottish merchant by the name of Daniel Mackercher.[4]

It is no small irony that Mackercher, a man of modest origins, should have been enlisted to help defend James's birthright.

Having read of Annesley's ordeal in the press, the Scot welcomed the chance, through Henderson's offices, to meet the young claimant. That James had been forced as a child to live by his wits may have sparked Mackercher's interest.

The orphaned son of a Presbyterian minister, Daniel had left the care of an uncle at age thirteen to join the British army during the Jacobite rising of 1715. Only after repeated attempts to enlist near Stirling was he finally successful despite his youth. After serving in the Scottish Greys for three years, he studied divinity at Edinburgh before embarking for the Continent. During years of travel, Mackercher acquired a valuable network of influential friends and a handsome fortune from a variety of commercial enterprises. It was an era of expanding trade and growing opportunities for energetic entrepreneurs. Fluent in French, he was even on hand in 1734 to observe the siege of Phillipsburg during the War of the Polish Succession, all the while cultivating the friendship of high-ranking French officers.[5]

Less successful was a visit to Virginia in 1737 during which a scheme to purchase tobacco for the French Farmers-General collapsed in disarray, owing largely to the machinations of his partner, a Swiss *abbé* named Jean James Huber. The Scot bore partial responsibility for inflated trade projections meant to entice tobacco planters, many of whom in the end grew skeptical about his assurances.[6]

At a time when rank normally derived from birth, Mackercher was the quintessential self-made man—hardworking, shrewd, and upwardly mobile. There is no denying that he was an adventurer given to investing in high-stakes enterprises. To some degree, his itinerant life exemplified the adage, "A man's country is where he does well." But he was no charlatan. Nor, contrary to the popular stereotype of merchants, was he lacking in sophistication and gentility. Like many successful men of commerce, he aspired to upper-class respectability. Upon the outbreak of war with Spain in 1739, he reportedly "called in" his numerous investments "with a view," finally, toward "sitting down for the rest of his life."[7]

A portrait of Mackercher by Justin Pope-Stevens in 1744 depicts a compact, muscular man in his early forties with a full face, snub nose, and penetrating eyes, with one hand on his left hip. His right hand appears to clutch a legal document. From his periwig and sword to his embroidered waistcoat, he radiates prosperity, though any suggestion of self-satisfaction is belied by an expression of indignation. Beneath the portrait is an inscription from the Roman playwright Terence: *Nihil a me alienum Puto* (Nothing that is human is alien to me).

Mackercher and Annesley forged a close relationship over the weeks after they met, as Mackercher assumed the roles of mentor and master tactician. In James, he found a candidate unusually deserving of his time and resources despite the risks of failure. Whatever compensation, if any at all, he hoped to receive remains a mystery.

For a time, James lodged at Mackercher's house in the affluent environs of Westminster, furnishing details of his peripatetic childhood in Ireland. In return, he received instruction in the speech and deportment befitting a gentleman—an effort to make up for the genteel education he had lacked ever since being shunned by his father.[8]

To be sure, prospects for success were uncertain. For James to reclaim his family's estates and honors, he would first need to prove his identity as Baron Altham's son, a daunting task for a young man not heard from for more than a decade—hence Mackercher's efforts to plumb the depths of his memory. James had borne no distinguishing scars or blemishes as a child, and even his exposure to smallpox at twelve years of age had left no lasting marks. There were no fingerprint or dental records to consult, no modern DNA tests or photographs; blood analysis to determine parentage would not be devised until the early twentieth century. Samples

John Brooks after J. Pope-Stevens, *Daniel
MacKercher*, 1744.

of his handwriting? Even had his penmanship not changed during
the intervening years, anything that he might have scribbled as a
child was long gone. Then, also, if Annesley's identity could be
verified, there remained the issue of his legitimacy; it had to be
proved that Lady Altham, rather than one of Altham's "whores,"
was his mother. The late baron's notorious reputation as a philan-
derer threatened to undercut the presumption of legitimacy that
ordinarily favored married couples.

To judge from literary works dating to Shakespeare's romance
Cymbeline (1610), the introduction of commoners into noble families, including counterfeit claimants, had long been a source of
upper-class anxiety. The most sensational controversy during the
preceding century had occurred after the death in 1632 of the Earl
of Banbury, a royal courtier who, it seems, left no male heir. Not

only did his widow wed her longtime lover, Lord Vaux, five weeks later, but she attempted to pass off an infant as the late earl's son. Upon the youth's untimely death, the countess tried the gambit a second time by bringing forward another male child. Although known as the Earl of Banbury, he was never allowed to sit in the House of Lords.[9]

An absence of written records magnified the problem of confirming Annesley's bloodline. Any documents or correspondence belonging to his late father, if not destroyed, remained in Richard's hands. And though some parishes might maintain registers of such vital statistics as births, marriages, and deaths, not only was recordkeeping erratic, but in Dunmain's Tintern parish, the picture was at best confusing. Notwithstanding contemporary reports that no register existed at the time of James's birth, Mackercher later claimed to have briefly seen both a register and a small pocketbook of baptisms kept by the former curate, Reverend Lloyd. What's more, the original leaves for the spring and summer of 1715, the period covering Annesley's birth, had been torn from both books.[10]

In the absence of written documentation, much had to be done. Witnesses would need to be located, interviewed, and ultimately conveyed to court—those, that is, who remained alive. Not only were James's parents deceased, but also dead were the midwife who had attended his birth, all three godparents, and the minister who had presided at his christening.[11] Others with an intimate knowledge of the family's affairs—the Annesleys' former servants—might find their veracity challenged owing to their low social station. And, too, among the living, there was always the danger that long memories would prove shallow. It would be a hard slog, steeply uphill, with daunting legal bills. By contrast, James's powerful adversary was a nobleman with five titles and seemingly unlimited resources. The possibility of defeat was very real.

All the same, it would be difficult to exaggerate Richard's alarm following his nephew's return, a homecoming that he had dreaded since first reading of the young sailor's appearance in Jamaica. Told by a former servant of James's arrival in London, the earl fumed, "You fool, he is dead," insinuating that Annesley was an impostor. Only after consulting with attorneys did Richard's temper show signs of cooling. To Donat Leary, a friend from County Tipperary, he first heaped scorn on James as the "son of a whore" who "had dishonored" the bed of his late brother. Still, Leary expressed misgivings. If born in wedlock, he fretted, James could be "troublesome." "There is no such son now in being," Richard shot back, "and if there is, he is in such a part [that] he will never be heard of here!" More calmly, he remarked that "there was a care taken that" the young man "would never be seen or appear in this part of the world."[12]

But that was before Mackercher's meddling, and by January 1742, on arriving in London, Richard's mood had again soured. No sooner had James taken up his new quarters than Richard's attorneys accosted Mackercher, urging that he abandon a pointless enterprise with little chance of success. Soon afterward, Mackercher met with the earl himself and three associates just to the east of Buckingham Palace in St. James's Park, long a favored retreat of the royal family (when asked by Queen Caroline the cost of closing it and other royal parks to the public, Sir Robert Walpole answered tersely, "Only three Crowns").[13]

At first, Richard seemed subdued, explaining in a measured tone that "the pretender" was the bastard son of his late brother. But finding the Scot skeptical, he unleashed a torrent of abuse, only to be chided by Mackercher for failing to protect James as a child, whether or not his birth had been legitimate. That he had been shipped to America, Mackercher bluntly added, demonstrated the depths of the earl's duplicity.[14]

Far from producing a settlement, the meeting proved

disastrous. For the first time, Mackercher now began to fear for James's physical safety. Not long afterward, two armed men were seen lurking near Mackercher's home (they were later identified as Thomas Stanley and Michael Morgan, both newly arrived from Dublin). Obviously his young protégé would have to be moved. While Mackercher continued to lay the groundwork for a lawsuit, he dispatched James to an estate belonging to a friend, Sir John Dolben, near the hamlet of Staines. There, in western Middlesex, at the manor of Yeoveney, James would be out from under his Uncle Dick's nose and still just a morning's ride from London.[15]

His nephew's return only complicated the earl's escalating legal squabbles with other branches of the Annesley family. After negotiations in 1738 had broken down, Charles had filed a bill in the Court of Chancery in Dublin about the time of Francis's own Chancery suit in London. The Dublin court ruled first. In early 1740, Charles obtained a decree reinstating the original settlement agreed to by Richard in June 1737. In addition, Charles was to be reimbursed one-third of all Irish rents, plus interest, collected in the intervening years. Meanwhile, Francis, awaiting a decision in London, continued to claim lands in the counties of Kildare, Kerry, Clare, and Armagh and the town of Drogheda. Not only did these quarrels severely drain Richard's purse, but he would ultimately need the goodwill of both men in staving off his nephew.[16]

Precisely for that reason, Richard did not reveal his recent marriage to either Charles or Francis. Following his desertion of Ann Prust, his first wife, he had remained married for thirteen years to Ann Simpson. Although he was not above giving her a "drubbing," he had enough affection for her to furnish a generous inheritance. As late as 1740, during a serious illness, he had executed a deed granting the countess an annuity of £2,000 and their three daughters bequests totaling £25,000 in the event of his death. There was no son.[17]

Upon his recovery later that year, however, both the deed and his marriage fell by the wayside. Richard had grown infatuated with Juliana Donovan, the seventeen-year-old daughter of a deceased Wexford merchant "not worth a shilling," whose widow was one of Anglesea's tenants. By the fall harvest, the earl was spending most evenings at the Camolin alehouse kept by her brother and returning home in the small hours of the morning. In January, Ann brought suit for cruelty and adultery in the Ecclesiastical Court in Dublin, which awarded her legal costs and alimony at the rate of four pounds per week. Richard's headstrong refusal to pay either sum resulted in his excommunication from the established Church of Ireland for life, as well as Ann's steady descent into poverty (by late 1747, the unpaid alimony exceeded £1,300).[18]

In a private ceremony on September 15, 1741, the earl and Juliana wed in the great parlor at Camolin Park. In attendance were his steward, Charles Kavanagh, the bride's brother, Nixon Donovan, and the Reverend Lawrence Neil, an English clergyman. Just four weeks earlier, Ann Prust had died at her Devon home. Having requested alimony from Richard shortly after his accession to the earldom, she had been paid £3,500 for disavowing their marriage.[19] By waiting until her death to remarry, Richard displayed uncommon caution. Then again, possessing two wives was one thing, three would be pushing the odds; and those were not currently running in his favor. Now at least he could make the case, if necessary, that his first marriage had invalidated his second, and that with Prust's death he was free to take a new wife.

Why, then, keep this, his third marriage, a secret? Absent a male heir, Richard's titles and estates would devolve to Charles Annesley. Next in line, absent a son born to Charles, were Francis and his sons. It took no great stretch of the imagination to foresee his cousins' reaction on learning of the marriage to Juliana. Both almost certainly would have thrown their legal and material support to James in the hope of reaching a private settlement. As

Thomas Fitzgerald, one of the earl's attorneys, later reflected, "If the marriage had been avowed, and any male children born, the whole family would have rose against his Lordship."[20]

So by early 1742 Richard was still under siege. Everywhere he turned, he was the target of lawsuits, past and pending, while his nephew James, his most dangerous adversary, was nowhere to be found. In March, with the earl's return to London, matters only worsened upon his appeal of the Chancery ruling in favor of Charles. The English House of Lords denied the petition, and Anglesea was ordered to pay more than £10,000 in unremitted rents. Owing to his past recalcitrance, all future income from tenants' rents was ordered sequestered, allowing Charles, as a lawyer observed, to "pay himself the rents and profits of his one third from 1737, and the costs of the suits." Anglesea, for his very subsistence, was "entirely in the power" of his cousin until the arrears were repaid.[21]

His spirit broken, Richard sent for his solicitor of the past sixteen years, John Giffard. A close friend who had done his share of the earl's dirty work, beginning in 1725 to avert his conviction for highway robbery, Giffard had seen Anglesea's mood darken in recent months. There, at his Bury Street home near St. James's Park, Richard grimly announced that in exchange for £2,000 to £3,000 a year, he would "surrender up" his titles and estates to James. His intention, he informed Giffard, was to live in France, for "if Jemmy had the estate on those terms, he [Richard] should live much happier and easier in France than he was here, as he was tormented by law." Further, he said that "it was his [Jemmy's] right, and he would surrender it to him (for he did not value the title[s]) rather than [to] Frank and Charles Annesley, and those that were striving to take it from him." Already, out of desperation, Anglesea had hired a valet to tutor him in French— Charlotte Charke, a struggling actress infamous for dressing in men's clothes on and off the stage. Ridiculed by friends, Richard discharged Charke five weeks later. Giving her a "small pittance," he retained an Irishman in her stead, Captain Stephen Hay, the son of a tenant and a former officer in the French army.[22]

In the early afternoon of May 1, James, as was his habit, accompanied Joseph Redding the younger, the Yeoveney gamekeeper, on his daily round of the estate. This Saturday, James carried a fowling piece with which to shoot sparrows, a common pest for farmers. Spying a crow, he raised the gun but stopped short of firing. Too far off, young Redding advised. Before long, they came to a meadow, Hare Mead, where they discovered two poachers beside the Staines River, a shallow tributary of the Thames. Clumps of willows lined the bank. Later identified as Thomas Egglestone, a carpenter, and John, his seventeen-year-old son, they were fishermen, not hunters. The pair's only weapon was a casting net, which the father quickly tossed into the water as the men advanced. Vaulting a small hedgerow, Redding at once grabbed the elder Egglestone by the jacket. Suddenly, without warning, a gun discharged. "I am a dead man," declared the father as he fell face down amid the thick smoke. Some of the lead shot, penetrating the upper left hip, had torn into his belly, and within minutes he was dead.[23]

"Lord, sir, what have you done!" shouted Redding to Annesley. Stunned in disbelief, James only grasped the enormity of the calamity after finding the gaping wound beneath the flap of Egglestone's jacket. "What shall I do!" he cried out, before collapsing on the ground. Years of abuse had not hardened his emotions. Beating himself repeatedly with his fists, he exclaimed, "What have I done!"[24]

Riddled with fear, he and Redding both ran off in the direction of a small farmhouse, as the son rushed to Staines to fetch a surgeon and a constable. A short while later, the constable, with a small band of villagers, found James on the estate in the attic of a washhouse. On giving himself up, he was taken in a cart to the

Staines "round house," or gaol, where he expressed a wish "to be killed out of the way" for the death of an innocent man. The next day, in the village of Laleham, he was examined before Sir Thomas Reynolds, a justice of the peace, as were witnesses to the shooting. Redding, who initially eluded capture, surrendered several days later.[25] Finally, it seemed, James's luck had run out.

In the English legal system, only the crime of treason exceeded the gravity of murder, defined as the killing of another human being with malicious intent. Not included was manslaughter, which by definition was unpremeditated, or the killing of someone either by accident or in self-defense. In contrast to modern criminal procedure, whereby charges are brought beforehand on the basis of police work, juries determined the severity of a crime in their deliberations, should the defendant, in fact, be thought guilty. Unlike manslaughter, for which offenders were normally "burnt in the hand" (branded), the punishment for murder was hanging—"till the body be dead! dead! dead! dead!"—which, for those tried in London, ordinarily took place at the King's Gallows in Tyburn, a village overlooking Hyde Park. Even so, if Annesley was convicted of murder, he could still receive a lesser penalty— especially as a first-time offender—either at the hands of the jury or the judges, who recommended royal pardons. Were mercy shown, chances are that James would be banished as a convict to America, either for fourteen years or for the remainder of his life.[26]

Word of the shooting reached Richard the next day in London. In an instant, he was revitalized. Jolted out of his despair, he summoned John Giffard to the White Horse Inn in Piccadilly. Jubilation reigned. The solicitor was ordered straight away to Staines, first to make certain that James could not escape and then to undertake his prosecution. At Giffard's urging, Anglesea himself would remain in the background. Further instructions would be relayed through intermediaries, principally John Jans, a surgeon by trade, later described as Richard's "companion" and "manager."

No expense was to be spared, the earl declaring to Giffard that "he did not care if it cost him £10,000 if he could get" Annesley "hang'd, for then he should be easy in his titles and estates."[27]

Although conducted in the name of the crown, criminal prosecutions in the 1700s lay largely in private hands. Not for another century would the government assume the burden of gathering evidence, interviewing witnesses, and proceeding to trial. Instead, it was left to the victims to manage prosecutions, chiefly because of political opposition to appending a prosecutorial arm to the state. Only in recent years had victims begun to retain lawyers to take the initiative in court. The system's shortcomings were numerous, not least the inability of many individuals, given the costs involved, to bring offenders to justice.[28]

In Staines, Giffard's offer of assistance was happily received. After attending the coroner's inquest on May 4, leading to grand jury indictments against Annesley and Redding for murder, he spent the ensuing weeks examining witnesses, issuing subpoenas, and conferring with four counselors retained to try the case. There were frequent trips back and forth between Staines and London, along with meetings with John Jans and others at the White Horse, long favored by the earl for stabling his coach and six. Jans also disbursed funds to cover Giffard's preliminary expenses, which by the end of the month exceeded thirty pounds.[29]

James, almost immediately, had been transferred to New Prison in Clerkenwell, a neighborhood in north London. Constructed in the early 1600s, the prison was used to detain prisoners awaiting trial. In most cases of felony, bail was out of the question. For inmates able to afford the cost, a room and a "good bed" could be had for one shilling for the first night and three pence for each subsequent evening. Others were forced to languish in a common room offering only the barest amenities. Of the prison, Middlesex justices complained in 1720 that "many persons . . . wanting money, being destitute of friends, or falling sick, are in danger of perishing."[30]

And yet Clerkenwell was markedly superior to the city's
best-known prison, Newgate, lying just northwest of St. Paul's
Cathedral. Overcrowding, abysmal sanitation, and the prevalence
of smallpox and "gaol fever" (a variety of typhus spread by lice)
made the place a death trap. "A tomb for the living," one person
remarked. Doctors refused to enter its gates; nor was it uncommon for 10 per cent of the inmates to die in a single year. Giffard
attempted to arrange Annesley's transfer there from Clerkenwell,
imploring a Staines magistrate to sign the necessary order. Fortu-
nately for James, Mackercher had learned of the shooting shortly
afterward at his London home. Without question, if his interests
were purely mercenary, now would have been the time for the Scot
to cut and run. Instead, he had increasingly assumed the role in
preceding months of an elder brother, if not, in fact, of a surrogate
father. On receiving the alarming news, he dispatched an able
London solicitor, John Paterson, to Staines, who made certain that
James stayed put.[31]

Annesley's arraignment was set for Friday, June 4, barely five
weeks after the shooting. The trial itself would follow immediately afterward. Eighteenth-century justice, if not always fair, was
nonetheless swift, especially in London. As the chief criminal court
for the city and the surrounding county of Middlesex, the Old
Bailey sat eight times a year, in contrast to quarter sessions courts
in England that met four times annually and assize (provincial)
courts, which convened just twice. The threat of disease helped
to discourage backlogs in the capital. Nor was there widespread
concern over the brevity of trials. The overwhelming number of
defendants, after all, belonged to London's lower orders. As Alexander Pope wrote in 1714, "The hungry judges soon the sentence
sign, / And wretches hang that jury-men may dine." One's day in
court seldom exceeded half an hour.[32]

Constructed after the Great Fire in 1666, the Old Bailey lay
across a small yard from Newgate. Hidden from the street, it

could only be approached through an alley. The courtroom occupied most of the first floor, with a dining room and offices on the top two stories. Built of brick at a cost of over £6,000, it was "a fair and stately building," noted an admirer of the Italianate design. Because of concerns about pestilence and inadequate ventilation, the back of the courtroom opened onto a courtyard, not unlike a partially enclosed amphitheater. Surrounding the yard, where attorneys and prisoners gathered, was a forbidding brick wall topped by spikes. Sessions could be raucous as defendants waited their turn. In 1714, one of them shot a turnkey while in line for his trial. Two years later, a convicted highwayman vaulted over the wall. In 1736, however, the courtroom was enclosed, presumably to afford protection from the weather and perhaps to lend a greater measure of dignity to the colorful deliberations.[33]

On the morning of June 4, the keeper of New Prison escorted

Anonymous, *The Old Sessions House in the Old Bailey in 1750*, n.d. The original of this copy had to have been completed before 1736, the year the courtroom was enclosed.

Annesley into the courtroom. His posture erect, James's pluck in the intervening weeks had returned. Joining him, as an accessory to the crime, was Joseph Redding, who had remained free on bail. The room, despite its spacious dimensions, was even more crowded than usual. The judges presided from an elevated bench, their backs to a wall with towering windows at either end. Beneath them sat attorneys, scribes, and clerks. At the bar, a wood railing facing the bench, witnesses delivered their testimony, as the jury sat in rows to their right. Just above the bar hung a mirror designed to reflect natural light onto a witness's face—all the better to evaluate his truthfulness. The accused occupied a separate box, while spectators watched from galleries on either side of the room.[34]

"Silence," proclaimed a bailiff.

"James Annesley," instructed the clerk, "hold up your hand." James, and then Redding, in turn, complied.

Most of the language read aloud in the formal indictment was familiar enough, though that did little to make the words less bracing:

> You stand indicted in the county of Middlesex, by the names of James Annesley, late of Staines, in the county of Middlesex, labourer, and Joseph Redding, late of the same, labourer; for that you, not having God before your eyes, but being moved and seduced by the instigation of the Devil, on the 1st day of May, in the 16th year of his present majesty's reign, with force and arms, at the parish aforesaid, in the county aforesaid, in and upon one Thomas Egglestone, in the peace of God, and our said lord the king, then and there being, feloniously, willfully, and of your malice aforethought, did make an assault . . .

"How say you, James Annesley, are you Guilty of this felony and murder whereof you stand indicted, or Not Guilty?"[35]

Due to Annesley's purported "quality," he had received the courtesy of sitting in front of the bar despite being labeled a "labourer" in the indictment.

"My Lord," James replied. "I observe that I am indicted by the name of James Annesley, labourer, the lowest addition my enemies could possibly make use of; but though I claim to be earl of Anglesea, and a peer of this realm, I submit to plead Not Guilty to this indictment, and put myself immediately upon my country, conscious of my own innocence, and impatient to be acquitted even of the imputation of a crime so unbecoming the dignity I claim."[36]

Further counts followed, including being charged with violating the notorious Waltham Black Act of 1723 for the malicious discharge of a firearm — a perverse application of a law whose principal purpose was to punish poachers.

"Culprit, how will you be tried?" demanded the clerk.

"By God and my country," repeated James.

"God send you good deliverance."

After the arraignment, the court deemed the day too far advanced "to proceed to a trial of such expectation." Rather than reconvene in the morning, however, the prosecution requested a continuance, inexplicably citing its inability to attend. A critic later alleged that the delay was another ruse to remand Annesley next door, to Newgate, until the succeeding session in July. If so, the ploy failed. The delay was granted, but remarkably both defendants were freed on bond in the amounts of £200 for Redding and £1,000 for Annesley.[37]

On the morning of Thursday, July 15, the trial finally got under way, despite yet another prosecution petition for a continuance—"not alleging any sufficient reason for the delay," the court noted testily in denying the request. The defendants were again arraigned, and a jury of twelve men impaneled. Attracting, among others, persons "of the first rank," this would be anything but an ordinary trial. From beginning to end, the courtroom remained packed, as a total of twenty-one witnesses were called to testify, not including the two defendants. The judges, some half-dozen in number, included George Heathcote, the lord mayor of London, and Sir John Strange, the solicitor-general and recorder of London. The defense, funded by Mackercher, assembled five lawyers to counter the prosecution's four counselors. Only recently had defense counselors been allowed in criminal trials, and usually only in cases of treason. That slowly started to change in the 1730s, when courts granted them the right to examine witnesses in order to balance the presence of prosecuting attorneys.[38]

Two counselors gave opening remarks for the prosecution, declaring both defendants guilty of murder. Their prime witness, John Egglestone, son of the deceased, was sworn in. Clearly nervous, he was instructed by his examiner, Serjeant Abraham Gapper, to speak slowly and deliberately.

Several minutes into his testimony, Egglestone leveled his most explosive charge. Just before the shooting, James Annesley had angrily threatened his father, swearing, "God damn your blood, deliver your net, or you are a dead man!" The gun, Egglestone related, had been held chest high and aimed straight at his father (in contrast, he had testified at the coroner's inquest that the barrel had been pointed downward). Annesley's knees had been slightly bent. What's more, after the shooting, the defendant had raised the butt of his gun, declaring to John, "You rogue, I will knock out your brains too!" In answer to a question from the jury foreman, the witness assured listeners that his father, before the shooting, had not spoken an "ill word" in provocation.

Nearly as damning, a friend of Annesley had approached young Egglestone the following day in Laleham, offering him £100 a year not to testify. Worse, Annesley himself had been present and, pleading poverty, reduced the offer, according to Egglestone, to £50. Although assaults were known to be resolved out of court by means of monetary settlements, in cases involving a death there was a thin line at best between obstructing justice and compensating the family for the inadvertent loss of a loved one.

"What is the reason you did not comply with this offer?" inquired Gapper.

"I told them that I would not sell my father's blood at any rate!"

And on that dramatic note, the prosecution's examination of the witness ended.

Commencing the cross-examination, the defense counsel asked Egglestone to describe the scene of the shooting.

"You say you stood by and saw Mr. Annesley point the gun at your father. Did you see him cock the gun?"

"I did not see him cock it. The gun was cocked when he came up to my father."

"Do you know one Giffard?" the counsel abruptly inquired, followed moments later by asking whether he also knew a man named Williams. To both questions, Egglestone answered yes.

Quickly, it became apparent that after meeting in Staines with John Giffard, Egglestone had been brought to London late one night by John Williams, keeper of the White Horse. There, Egglestone had resided, free of any expense, during the weeks before the trial.

When asked whether he had seen the Earl of Anglesea at the inn, the court interjected, calling the question improper. Egglestone did, however, admit to meeting with a man named Paul Keating, newly arrived from Ireland, and to seeing a mysterious note that Keating had drafted at the White Horse. As to the contents, he denied any knowledge. What followed was just as mystifying.

"Were you ever at New-prison to see Mr. Annesley?"

"Yes."

"What did you go for?"

"I cannot tell."

"I ask you what you went for?"

"I went for my own fancy."

"Did you not send up word to him, you were sure he would be glad to see you?"

"I believe I might."

"What was the reason for which you thought Mr. Annesley would be glad to see you?"

"I cannot tell; I was willing to see him."

After a last set of inconclusive questions, Egglestone returned to his seat. Just three additional witnesses testified for the prosecution, including John Bettesworth and John Fisher, who had witnessed the shooting from the opposite bank of the river. Neither, from that distance, had heard an exchange of words beforehand.[39]

Nor in other respects did their testimony benefit the prosecution. Fisher, in fact, during his cross-examination, related a surprising conversation with Egglestone prior to their examinations before Justice Reynolds on May 2. "He said he believed it was not done willfully," reported Fisher, and mentioned Annesley's offer of £50 a year. "What did you say to him?" asked the defense counsel. "I said your father is dead, and the money will do you good. Do not swear any thing against him, if you think it was done accidentally."[40]

Once the prosecution rested, the court invited Annesley's personal testimony. Resentment, verging on self-pity, colored his opening remarks. "My lord, I am very unable to make a proper defence, having by the cruelty of those whose duty it was to protect me, been deprived of the advantages of an education I was entitled to by my birth."

But then he turned to the shooting—in his words, a "melancholy accident." Once the net had been thrown into the river, testified James, he had stooped to grab a rope trailing behind. At that moment, the gun, "hanging by my side," fired "to my great grief as well as surprise." As for fleeing, he continued, "My behaviour, immediately after the accident, was, I hope, inconsistent with a temper that could murder a man I had never seen before, without one word of provocation." "Whatever may be the determination of your lordship and the jury," he concluded, "great as the misfortunes of my life have been, I shall always consider this unfortunate accident as the greatest of them all."[41]

Redding's account echoed that of Annesley, whereupon one of the defense counselors, Hume Campbell, pointed to the defendants' legal right to prevent the Egglestones from poaching. Because the shooting was the "accidental consequence of that act," Annesley, he insisted, was innocent as charged, and the deceased a victim only of "chance medley."

A string of defense witnesses testified to Redding's duties as gamekeeper. Of greater interest were the next three witnesses, two of whom had spoken with John Egglestone in the wake of his father's death. One testified that Egglestone had shown him with a stick the manner in which Annesley had held his gun by the middle of the barrel next to his hip—a direct contradiction of Egglestone's earlier testimony. Another acquaintance, his former master, reported being told that the shooting was accidental, whereas the third witness had overheard him make the same statement to Annesley himself as the two men shook hands.[42]

If this testimony was not damaging enough, the court next heard from a surgeon who had examined the body of the deceased. Only recently had medical testimony played any role in courts, and for that reason, the Annesley trial has traditionally been thought a landmark case.

In light of their novelty, expert witnesses still invited skepticism. As the surgeon James Bethune neared the bar, Serjeant Gapper protested to the bench. "My lord, this is another person that is brought to contradict the evidence of Egglestone, in what he said with respect to the position of the gun." As for a more cogent objection, Gapper was at a loss.

"Egglestone said the gun was pointed downward," countered the defense, preferring to cite his original testimony during the coroner's inquest. "Now we will show you, from the nature of the wound, that it was morally impossible it should be so."

In clinical detail, Bethune described the trajectory of the lead shot, having previously inserted a probe into the wound. With the instrument pointing downward, he had failed to discern a passage. Inserted upward or from a level direction, the probe had entered the stomach cavity effortlessly.

Questioned whether the shot, on hitting Egglestone's hip bone, might not have been "thrown upwards," Bethune demurred, citing the upward penetration of the bone itself, thereby demonstrating that the gun could not have been fired at chest height. "This is not a matter of judgment," he asserted, "but I have given you a demonstration of it." On the heels of this testimony, yet a second surgeon testified to having reached the same conclusion during his own examination.[43]

The coroner responsible for the original autopsy was sworn in, though not to discuss his colleagues' testimony. Instead, he recited the initial attempt by John Giffard to have Annesley confined to Newgate. "There was a lord mentioned," he added, "but I cannot remember that he was named."

The final defense witness, Paul Keating, left no doubt as to the nobleman's identity. Having often spoken with Egglestone at the White Horse, Keating disclosed to the court Lord Anglesea's close involvement in managing his nephew's prosecution. "Says he [Egglestone], I am here at the expense of the Earl of Anglesea."

"This is reflecting upon a noble person's character," objected the bench.

But the damage was done. And there was more. Undaunted, Keating told of Anglesea's frequent visits to the inn. In addition, Keating had composed a note for his friend to sign obligating the earl to pay Egglestone's elder brother several hundred pounds, allegedly for carpentry previously performed by their father. In return for such largesse, Egglestone had agreed to testify for the prosecution.[44]

On resting, the defense, followed by the prosecution, each delivered closing statements. Whereas defense counselors argued at length for a verdict of "chance medley," prosecutors, chastened by the damaged credibility of their star witness, suddenly seemed amenable to a finding of manslaughter. Their case in disarray, a small troupe of rebuttal witnesses unexpectedly appeared in the closing minutes to commend John Egglestone's character. None did so enthusiastically, though most denied that he would commit perjury.

"Do you," asked a prosecutor of the final witness, "think he would forswear himself?"

"I do not think he would forswear himself."

"Upon your oath, do you not think he is much addicted to lying?"

"Why, that is not taking a false oath?"[45]

After the court's oral summation of the evidence, the jury began its deliberations. Ordinarily, the members might have been sequestered without "meat, drink, fire, or candle" in order to expedite a verdict; instead, they conferred in their seats. The jury did not take long.

"Chance medley," on all counts, the foreman announced.

"And so say you all?" asked the clerk, all but drowned out amid shouts of joy.[46]

And thus concluded one of the longest trials at the Old Bailey in recent memory. Consuming seven hours, it produced a transcript of more than twenty-two thousand words. Due to its length, the case was published, "with all convenient speed," apart from other trials held during the court's four-day session in July—more than forty cases in all, including three other murders and two rapes. The *Proceedings of the Old Bailey*, as compilations were called, normally sold well on London's streets, but the appeal of the Annesley case, as the publisher noted, was unique, having "engaged the attention of several persons of distinction, and raised a general expectation in the world."[47]

Any hope for a conviction had ended with the abrupt arrival, in the midst of the trial, of the Earl of Anglesea, resplendent in a suit of scarlet and silver *point d'Espagne*. Not unlike a pacing lion, he alternated between a seat in the rear and another on the bench, as was his prerogative as a peer. In a single stroke, his appearance all but confirmed the defense allegations of prosecutorial abuse; it was a brazen attempt, James's friends later claimed, to cow the jury.[48] Perhaps. More likely, he had felt powerless to stay away.

6

HOME

For God's sake, go off, for you will all be murdered!
ANONYMOUS, 1743[1]

The trial cast a long shadow. More than ever, Annesley and his uncle remained bitterly at odds. Publicly humiliated, in London no less, Richard was not likely now to back down. Even less inclined to negotiate was James, his confidence bolstered by the acquittal. Then, too, by the summer of 1742, he had added reason to press ahead. Following his months in Staines, he had taken a wife, Miss Lane, the stepdaughter of a villager named Richard Chester—what may have been an impulsive choice by one starved of affection during much of his youth. Daniel Mackercher appears to have thought ill of the union, viewing it as a distraction or, worse, an impediment, owing to the bride's humble origins.[2] For James, by contrast, marriage and the prospect of a male heir no doubt underscored the importance of his quest.

Annesley's heightened confidence may be gleaned from a petition dated September 14 seeking the assistance of Sarah Churchill, Duchess of Marlborough. In addition to her wealth, coupled with a reputation for aiding people in distress, she possessed a strong streak of independence, to her occasional detriment at court. Despite her declining health at eighty-two years of age, the dowager was not an unlikely patron. Although Mackercher or the Quaker William Henderson, who delivered the petition (to no avail), may have participated in crafting it, there is no reason to gainsay the authenticity of Annesley's sentiments. The principal portion offers a litany of his tribulations, from his abduction and years as a "slave" to his arrival in London after serving in the Caribbean. It is his "paternal right" for which he solicits the duchess's assistance, to which end he requests the opportunity "to wait upon your Grace in person."[3]

For all of the trial's anguish, a happy consequence was the renewed attention Annesley's saga received in London newspapers, even before the proceedings had begun; by the 1740s the city claimed at least a dozen papers. Several childhood acquaintances, since resettled in London, paid visits during his imprisonment at Clerkenwell. The London linen draper James Cavanagh, a long-time friend of Lord Altham in County Wexford, immediately recognized "Jemmy" at the trial. From these encounters, the names of additional witnesses were acquired—old playmates, servants, and neighbors. With talk of litigation quickening, Mackercher now had reason to hope that a trip to Ireland would greatly improve their prospects at court, as well as lay to rest any lingering doubts of his own. Already, with William Henderson's aid, a few former servants at Dunmain had been brought to London for interviews.[4] All the same, innumerable other witnesses remained in Ireland. It was time for the prodigal to return home.

In the fall, James set out for Dublin, accompanied by Mackercher, two friends, and three servants. They likely traveled overland by coach, a quicker route than by sea from London. Even so, it was an arduous journey to the Welsh coast—260 miles—which normally required more than a week. The first half, across the English Midlands to the Shropshire town of Shrewsbury, mostly followed the ancient highway Watling Street, constructed by the Romans. From there, the road narrowed as it snaked through the craggy terrain of north Wales. Eventually, travelers were forced to proceed on horseback. At Bangor, Annesley's party would have crossed the dangerous Menai Straits by ferry to the Isle of Anglesey, less than a mile offshore—the historic site of the family's earldom. The island was traditionally known as *Môn mam Cymru* (Anglesey, mother of Wales) for the bounty of its rich farmland. Just off its western coast lay Holy Island and the port of Holyhead. "A scurvy, unprovided, comfortless place," Swift found in 1727. "Muddy ale and mouldy bread." Once the winds and sea permitted, passengers boarded a packet-boat for the voyage to Dublin, a distance of sixty miles, which usually took fewer than twelve hours. (Today, halfway across the Irish Sea, the slightest glimmer from lighthouses on opposite shores can be spied at night).[5]

It had been fourteen years since Annesley had last seen Dublin Bay or walked the city's streets. Although the sounds and scents of Dublin remained the same, there had been a number of changes during his absence, from the construction, commencing in 1729, of a new Parliament House to a steady surge in population, probably spurred in recent years by the flight of rural families during the harrowing famine of 1740–41 arising from the failure of potato crops. The increase in newcomers was especially noticeable in the rapidly expanding neighborhoods northeast of the Liffey. It was there that James and his companions took up residence at the sign of the Bear on Jervis Street, just blocks from Essex Bridge, where he had been thrust into a carriage during his abduction.[6]

Over the coming weeks, potential witnesses in Dublin were invited to Jervis Street, whereas others, on hearing of Annesley's arrival, traveled from the country of their own accord. Several more wrote letters detailing their recollections. Twenty years earlier, Patrick Plunkett, the son of a brewer, had lived next door to Lord Altham and his son on Phrapper Lane. Reaching the Bear just at candle-lighting, he was shown to a parlor where James and others stood inside. "You are welcome to Ireland," declared Plunkett, warmly extending a hand in greeting and kissing his cheek. Another former friend, Thomas Byrne, brought by coach to Jervis

Joseph Tudor, *A Prospect of the Custom House and Essex Bridge, Dublin,* 1753.

Street, was asked upon entering a room of men, "Tom, do you know any of these Gentlemen's faces?" Immediately he recognized "Mr. Annesley's face as perfectly as any face in the world"—a common reaction among those who had known him as a child.[7]

Heartened by the growing number of prospective witnesses, Annesley and Mackercher in November pushed on to New Ross. Hopes ran high, though no one could predict the reception they would receive there or elsewhere in Wexford. Much of the town, along with portions of the countryside, lay in Richard's hands, and Irish tenants were renowned for their servility. The Irish people, complained Samuel Madden in 1738, "[are] the most addicted to follow their great lords and gentlemen of distinction of any in the Christian world."[8]

For centuries, the hierarchical relationship between landlord and tenant defined rural life, marked by unswerving bonds of loyalty. With the Protestant Ascendancy the casts gradually changed, but the roles remained the same. Local magnates, with few exceptions, exercised absolute authority over their domains. "A landlord in Ireland," noted Arthur Young during his tour, "can scarcely invent an order which a servant labourer or cottar dares to refuse to execute." In return for subservience, tenants gained their patron's protection—hence the customary saying, "Defend me and spend me." In hard times, rents might even be deferred or leases loosened. Should tenants run afoul of the law, prosecutions could be quashed or charges reduced. Disrespect toward one's superiors, on the other hand, was punished harshly, typically with a caning or horsewhipping. "Knocking down is spoken of in the country in a manner that makes an Englishman stare," remarked Young.[9]

Not that all of Wexford lay under Anglesea's thumb. As in other parts of Ireland, the county contained different factions of landowners, including cliques led by Nicholas Loftus, a longtime member of the House of Commons (and a future baron), and Caesar Colclough, whose cousin Anthony had been a godfather to James. Known as the Great Caesar, Coclough, a convert to Protestantism, had represented the town of Enniscorthy in Parliament since 1727.[10]

Further, despite the prominence of Anglesea's titles, he wielded less influence than might be expected of a landed aristocrat. His local ties were short-lived, including among his tenants. On first inheriting the earldom, he had assumed the traditional mantle of a country grandee. Besides organizing hunting parties for the gentry, he donated cash purses for the winners of horse races. But as an interloper, Richard lacked any longstanding identification with either the land or its people—a problem aggravated by his prolonged absences in London. A critic later alleged that to attach the people of New Ross "to his interest" following his nephew's return to London, he began to treat them "with more complaisance" than his tenants elsewhere, even paying for the church's fresh coat of paint.[11]

As James and Mackercher neared the town on horseback, with the Blackstairs Mountains looming to the north, a large crowd appeared on the dirt road. News of the trip had preceded the two men, drawing numbers of people outdoors. All at once, amid cries of welcome, Annesley was engulfed by the throng, some kissing his hands, others voicing prayers for his success. As he started to dismount, a town official steadied his stirrup in a time-honored gesture of respect.[12]

Their stay appears to have been brief—several days spent meeting with former neighbors able to affirm James's identity. Probably sentiment, as much as anything, took him to Dunmain. His father's lease had long since reverted to Aaron Lambert, the original tenant. Having left at the age of three, Annesley was unlikely to remember the estate, and Altham's staff of servants had quitted the grounds within two years of his own departure.

During the remainder of his pilgrimage, James revisited every spot where he and his father had once resided, including Kinnea and Carrickduff, drawing former acquaintances at each stop. By the time Annesley and Mackercher returned to Dublin after a month's absence, they had culled more than one hundred potential witnesses from James's past. Plainly, the trip allayed Mackercher's fears. That so many persons—most of them tradesmen, tenants, and servants—were prepared publicly to embrace Annesley's cause testified both to its merit and to its likelihood of success. A few, like Richard Geraldine of New Ross, who knew little of the matter, doubtless had scores to settle. Owing to a financial loss for which he blamed the earl, Geraldine vowed to testify against the "old rogue," whom he branded a "very bad man." But for most folk, a larger issue was at stake. Ultimately, one's fealty, as they saw it, belonged not to the current lord but to the house of Annesley and the rightful heir of Baron Altham.[13]

That same fall, upon returning by sea from England, the Earl of Anglesea disembarked at Ballyhack, a small port on Wexford's southern coast barely ten miles from New Ross. There he found a crowd assembled for his arrival. Among the first to welcome him home was an elderly woman named Anstace O'Connor. Decades earlier she had peddled oysters at Dunmain. "How do you do, are you alive still, Anstace?" Richard joked, motioning for the widow to sit beside him on a bench. He asked if "Nurse Landy"—James's former wet-nurse—was living and where she dwelled. New Ross, he was told. Then he inquired what had become of the bastard she'd borne.

"He died of smallpox," answered Anstace.

"No, no," corrected Richard, "he is not dead, he went over sea."

"No, my Lord, it was Lady Altham's child went over the sea, and the people are moaning because a great many here say you transported him."

Startled, Anglesea snapped, "No, you fool, it was Joan Landy's child went over sea! Hold your tongue!"

After regaining his composure, the earl offered £40 if she'd swear to that, which Anstace adamantly refused, adding that she would not "take such an oath for all the world." And there the conversation ended. Rising to leave, Richard reached into his pocket and handed her an English sixpence.[14]

Most members of the Irish aristocracy kept silent during the Annesleys' escalating confrontation, warily letting matters play out in court before allying themselves with one side or the other. Privately, at least, many grandees sided with James, to judge from a letter written in early 1743 by Dr. Edward Barry of Dublin to the Earl of Orrery. "No unprejudiced person doubts of the justice of this cause; but such a complicated scene of wickedness and such hair-breadth escapes from imminent danger could only be unravell'd and directed by providence; 'tis beyond the reach of human power. The Lord is universally unpity'd, abject in his misfortunes; the young man modest and humble in his success."[15]

Though Barry's claims were overstated, Richard had few friends willing to lend public support. Much like his late brother, he was seen as a rapacious upstart, even by the Ascendancy's lax standards. With his estates besieged by his cousins, Charles and Francis, only his titles conferred any respect among other peers—titles that might in fact be ruled counterfeit if his nephew had his way at court.

Still to be settled was the field of battle. There were several alternatives for bringing suit against the earl, all complicated by the fact that his lands and titles lay both in Ireland and England. Modeled after the English judicial system, Irish courts were wholly independent except for the final stage of the appeals process. During a constitutional crisis in 1719, the English House of Lords had managed to extend its appellate jurisdiction to Irish lawsuits. The following year, to underscore the point, Parliament in London enacted the Declaratory Act confirming the supremacy of the House of Lords and affirming, more broadly, Parliament's right to legislate for Ireland (thereby providing a blueprint for the Declaratory Act of 1766 targeted against the American colonies).[16]

To reclaim his English titles, James Annesley might have submitted his case directly to the English Lords, who were empowered to resolve peerage conflicts. A similar appeal would also have been necessary to the Irish House, which still retained jurisdiction over its membership. All the same, even if Annesley prevailed in recovering his titles, further litigation would be required to regain his estates.[17]

A stumbling block was Anglesea's right to "privilege" as a member of the House of Lords in both kingdoms. Initially, beginning in the late Middle Ages, peers had enjoyed protection from civil lawsuits and other legal actions not including criminal prosecutions. What at first had been a broad grant of immunity was narrowed during the first half of the 1700s to include periods when Parliament was either in session or in recess for less than two weeks. Otherwise, by virtue of a law passed as recently as 1738, peers, the distinguished jurist William Blackstone later noted, "may be sued like an ordinary subject."[18]

Annesley acted swiftly in the spring of 1743 while both parliaments stood adjourned. Before departing for London, he leased 1,800 acres of land in County Meath to a country squire named Campbell Craig for a period of twenty-one years, a standard technique employed by claimants for bringing disputed titles to court. Although a tiny portion of Annesley's prospective inheritance, it was no mean estate, representing part of the acreage awarded his father by the third Earl of Anglesea, James's namesake. Worth upwards of £300 per annum, the property contained 110 homesteads, fifty gardens, and two mills spread over 800 acres of arable land, 600 acres of pasture, and 300 acres of meadow. The remainder consisted of bogs and wasteland. Craig took possession on May 2, but his tenure was brief. As expected, he was forcibly ejected, the next day no less, by Richard's agents. The earl himself, by then, had returned to London.[19]

Of the major courts in Dublin, the Court of Exchequer would seem an unlikely arena in which to seek justice. Established in England during the reign of Henry I, it was the oldest of England's common-law courts. Its principal purpose was to enforce the collection of royal revenues, with the king its only plaintiff. The accounting of sums due the Crown reportedly occurred on a table covered by a checkered cloth resembling a large chessboard—hence the court's name. By the eighteenth century, however, the Courts of Exchequer in London and Dublin were adjudicating growing numbers of private suits normally reserved for the Court of Common Pleas, the common-law court traditionally employed for civil actions. By filing a writ of quo minus, the plaintiff in an Exchequer suit could insist that the injury in question impeded his ability to honor his debts to the Crown, whether taxes, duties, or excises. By means of this expansive legal fiction—a "matter of form and mere words," noted Blackstone—virtually all subjects enjoyed access to the Courts of Exchequer, which offered litigants the possibility of a reasonably quick and inexpensive resolution of their claims.[20]

Money remained a mounting concern due to the drain on Mackercher's reserves. In late January, he had written a Lancashire acquaintance, Richard Standish, in the hope of reclaiming a debt of £120—in all likelihood just one of a number of outstanding obligations that the Scot now attempted to recoup. "I should not urge this," he explained, "if I was not much pressed in affairs of the utmost consequence (not only to me but to the great cause I am embarked in)."[21]

On June 3, the Dublin court heard Campbell Craig's bill of complaint during its Trinity term. Claiming damages in the amount of £100 caused by his ejection, Craig was "less able," according to his lawyer, "to pay the debts he now owes" to the king. Rather than proceed directly to trial, however, the court honored the request of Anglesea's lawyers to put off proceedings until the Michaelmas term in November—at worst a minor setback, since Richard was required to relinquish his right to privilege despite his strenuous protests.[22] Should Craig in the end prevail, besides the enormous symbolic importance of such a victory, Annesley's claim as landowner would be affirmed, affording a source of income with which to finance future suits.

At roughly the same time, lawyers in London launched a second offensive by filing a suit on James's behalf at the Court of Chancery in Westminster Hall, an ancient court of equity in which parties petitioned for relief in civil matters without being bound by the rigidity of common-law procedures. That, at least, was the tribunal's role in the medieval era, though by the 1700s it was fast becoming known for its costly and protracted hearings—long before Charles Dickens's scathing depiction in *Bleak House* (1852–53). Nonetheless, with investigative powers unrivalled by other courts, Chancery remained a favored venue for complicated suits encompassing multiple estates. Unlike common-law courts, whereby witnesses attended a trial to testify before a jury, Chancery witnesses were deposed out of court by examiners, a signal advantage in cases involving long distances. In view of the properties left in 1737 by Arthur, fifth Earl of Anglesea, in England, Wales, and Ireland—some entailed, others not—resorting to Chancery seemed, at the time, a sensible course.[23]

On July 15, James and his attorney submitted his bill of complaint. The document was written in tightly packed script, totaling nearly three thousand words, on a massive piece of parchment. It began by tracing Annesley's lineage and his right to the titles and estates of both his father and the late earl. The kidnapping was recounted, as were his years as a "common slave" in Delaware—all of which was laid to Richard Annesley, "called earl of Anglesea," who in James's absence had "taken upon himself" the titles, manor lands, tenements, and heritaments that were his nephew's rightful inheritance. On a practical level, the bill concluded by seeking an injunction forbidding Richard to collect rents and cut timber on the disputed estates, coupled with a request for the liberty to conduct formal examinations of witnesses in England, Ireland, America, and "other parts beyond the seas."[24]

By early September, both James and Richard had returned to Ireland in advance of the trial at the Court of Exchequer. Annesley and a small party of companions, including Mackercher, disembarked in Dublin, while the earl landed just to the south at Dunleary. From there, he traveled the short distance to his coastal estate at Bray.[25]

Richard, at last, had fresh reason to feel encouraged about the approaching contest. As recently as January, such was his need of cash that in London he had auctioned the elegant furnishings received years earlier from Farnborough House, including Japanese cabinets, tapestries, and velvet settees. He had also ordered his agents in Wexford to fell selected forestland. But after a six-year struggle with Charles and Francis over the estate of their cousin Arthur, an accord had been reached among the family's major branches. In the aftermath of the settlement with Charles imposed by the English House of Lords, he and Richard had come to terms with Francis in March. By agreeing to forgo a small number of estates in England, Francis acquired all the lands he had been demanding in Ireland. For Richard especially, the price was steep, but he had at least solidified the support of two vital allies. Already, of course, they had reason to take Anglesea's side, convinced as they were that they and any male heirs stood next in the line of succession to the earl. Now, even more importantly, portions of their own lands were potentially at stake.[26]

Especially critical was Charles's backing—not only for his wealth but also for his influence in Dublin. Years later, an attorney recalled, "The late earl [Richard] had . . . the misfortune of being generally disliked, so that in case of an attack against his property and honours, he must in a great measure depend on the assistance of his relations. Charles Annesley stood not in the same light; his connections and influence gave him weight." Family sentiment played little role. Richard's "scheme," as the attorney called it, "was to attach Charles Annesley by motives of interest." "Affection," he noted, "there was very little between them." In the meantime, Anglesea, his enemies afterward alleged, took steps to suborn additional members of the family who might aid James as material witnesses. Foremost among these was Francis Annesley of Ballysax in County Kildare, who had known James as a boy at Kinnea. The earl's distant cousin, Francis reportedly received an estate worth £500 a year.[27]

Every September, for as long as anyone could remember, members of the rich and mighty traveled to County Kildare for the races at the Curragh. Less than thirty miles southwest of Dublin lay a gently rolling plain comprising nearly 5,000 acres of common land, where flocks of sheep grazed from nearby farms. Twice each year, in September and either March or April, the vast Curragh heath became the kingdom's premier racecourse, drawing thousands of spectators of all ranks and religions, including most of Dublin's Anglo-Irish establishment. "Horse racing is become a great diversion in the country," reported the *Dublin Intelligencer* in 1731.[28]

Not just the Curragh's terrain, but the soft quality of the turf itself, which lay atop a layer of fine dry loam, made the plain peculiarly well suited for flat racing. "It is a fine sod for that diversion not to be equalled in the universe," noted an English traveler. The very name derived from *Cuirreach*, the Gaelic word for racecourse. Organized contests dated to the 1670s, though informal races had gone on for decades if not centuries; as early as 1634, a horse owned by the Earl of Ormond bested another belonging to Lord Digby in a four-mile heat. Prizes at the Curragh were extravagant, some totaling hundred of pounds for sprints of different lengths, usually held over a period of several days. To judge from the 1730s painting *Race on the Curragh*, some spectators, either on horseback or in carriages, rode abreast of the course rather than stationing themselves on the sidelines. Heavy wagers between lords with rival mounts only added to the excitement, as did the occasional threat of violence among the bystanders.[29]

Friends of James later stated that he and his party attended the races for a "diversion" while awaiting November's trial. The weather by mid-September had turned inviting, sunny and warm following an early cold snap. The Curragh also served as an opportunity to rub elbows with Ireland's finest, including, perhaps, potential jurists and jurors. At the very least, it afforded the young claimant a stage to display the manners and deportment of a nobleman. The trip, however, was not without risks. Already there had been trouble in Dublin. Within days of their arrival from Wales, someone had attempted to shoot a blunderbuss into a coach carrying James and Mackercher as it clattered down Dame Street at night. The gun misfired, and there was no second shot.[30]

Anonymous, *Race on the Curragh*, 1730s. The famed round tower of the town of Kildare may be seen in the background of this early depiction of flat racing.

On the morning of September 14, a Wednesday, they departed Dublin with servants and two close friends, Hugh Kennedy and William Goostry. Nearly everyone carried pistols, or, as Mackercher recalled, they traveled "in furniture." After taking their lodgings at the New Inn in Newbridge, the men rode to the course to view the day's final race, the King's Plate for £100 in prize money. Later, as they made their way back through the crowd, they passed Richard, standing in a circle of gentlemen next to a tent. "That Mackercher, though he appears here like a gentleman, is an arrant scoundrel," he shouted, pointing toward the Scot. "And the coat you see upon his back, I saw not above a month ago in Monmouth Street" (a London lane known for shops peddling secondhand clothing). If he was stung by the gibe, Mackercher betrayed no sign of it. Keeping his head, he instructed his companions to ignore the provocation, and they left the field without interference. On Thursday, no races were scheduled, so he and James visited at the homes of local squires who remembered Altham and his boy during their residence in Kildare.[31]

As Friday, the final day, unfolded, James's party reached the Curragh on horseback at the end of the first race. Signs of trouble arose as they began to cross the field toward a small hill on the opposite side. All of a sudden, a coach drawn by six horses at full gallop approached the riders. As they rushed out of the way, the coachman turned sharply about for a second pass. Only a railing protected the four men and their servants. "There he is, there's the shoe-boy," taunted the driver as he motioned toward Annesley with his whip. Worse, as if issuing a call to arms, he cried to onlookers, "Black your ball!" By the third run, someone had identified the coachman as Joseph Lawson, one of Anglesea's men.[32]

Incensed, Mackercher rode off in search of Richard, whom he found amid a crowd at the winning post. Retainers and footmen were thick on the ground, some wearing the earl's blue livery faced with red. Mackercher dismounted and strode forward, with James, Kennedy, and Goostry following behind on horseback. Attired in a brown coat and a lace hat, Anglesea sat astride a bay mare.

"My Lord, I beg to speak with your lordship aside," Mackercher said in a low voice, trying to restrain his anger. Startled, Richard mistook the request for a challenge. According to a witness, his face appeared to change color. "This is no time nor place, you see I have no pistols before me," he answered.

"For what I have to say to your lordship, every time and place is proper. I come only with a complaint against one of your servants, who has insulted a gentleman. And I should be glad to know, my Lord, whether it be by your orders or approbation he behaveth so." Then Mackercher added, "As the affront was very public, it is proper the satisfaction should also be. So, therefore, it is expected that you should strip your servant [of his livery], and turn him off in the field."

"Who was the gentleman that was insulted?"

"That is the gentleman, my Lord," Mackercher responded, indicating James just beyond the crowd.

"He is a gentleman? A shoe-boy, by God, a blackguard and a thief. No, by God, I won't, and you are a villain, a scoundrel, and a thief!" screamed Anglesea.

"You lie!" exclaimed Mackercher. "Mr. Annesley is no bastard. He is the lawful son of Lord Altham. Before two months are about, it will appear to the world to be so!"[33]

Instantly, Francis Annesley of Ballysax, who had accompanied Anglesea to the races, rode forward and struck Mackercher on the forehead with the butt end of a whip. A trickle of blood flowed down his face, as he countered with his own lash. Goostry, in turn, hit Mackercher's assailant with a riding crop. At this point, Richard rose in his stirrups to rouse the milling crowd, calling James a bastard and a shoeblack. Frightened for their safety, Mackercher shouted to the others to leave quickly or they would be murdered.

"There is one of the villains," exclaimed Richard as he delivered a hard blow to Kennedy's head with the butt of his whip. More blows rained down from Anglesea's men, causing Kennedy to fall from his horse, his head bleeding badly. Managing somehow to remount the horse, he received repeated lashes from Anglesea, who only desisted when others in the crowd began to cry "Shame!"

Meanwhile, as Goostry tried to maneuver his own horse, Richard yelled, "There's Goostry, another of the rogues, as great a rogue as any in Ireland, knock him down!" Struck to the skull by Francis Annesley, he too would have fallen had sympathetic spectators not reached up to support him.

James, the intended target of the melee, had been forced aside by Mackercher, just as two strangers implored them to flee. "For God's sake, go off," said one, "for you will all be murdered!"[34]

Both spurred their horses, only to hear Anglesea cry out,

"Follow the son of a whore, and knock his brains out." Forty to fifty men on horse and foot set off in pursuit, armed with staves, pistols, and swords. On overtaking Mackercher, they pursued James instead, proceeding as far as the Newbridge Road, about a quarter of a mile from the racecourse, where he abruptly turned his horse to face the oncoming mob. Maybe James expected to confront his uncle, pistols drawn, or perhaps he halted to avoid the ignominy of being shot from behind without first attempting to defend himself. According to one account, several bystanders shouted a warning just before he pulled up. Whatever the reason, in turning, his horse's hind feet slid into a ditch, causing the full weight of the animal to fall momentarily atop its rider. Knocked senseless, Annesley was immediately approached by a dozen men. One on horseback, John Archbold, boldly advanced to the front. Having heard the initial ruckus from his tent, he had followed the others, hoping to prevent further bloodshed. "I believe he is dead already," Archbold announced. "There is no need to kill him again." With that, the crowd slowly dispersed, some shouting, "The pretender is killed." Meanwhile, a surgeon, William Hackett, unsuccessfully tried to bleed James's arm. Moments later, Mackercher arrived, with Kennedy and Goostry close behind. Mackercher at first thought young Annesley lay dead.

Had it not been for the fall, they would have ridden right away to Dublin, despite the gathering darkness—or at least as far as the safety of Naas, the county seat, along the way. Accompanied by the surgeon, they laid James in a chaise and retreated to the inn. By then, he had regained consciousness, badly bruised but with no broken limbs or other serious injuries. The day's fray had left the entire party bloodied and battered, with no shortage of wounds to be washed and dressed. That done, they retired in order to leave as early as possible Saturday morning. Several other lodgers at the inn, fearing the worst, fled that night.[35]

Shortly before daylight, the innkeeper rapped frantically on the door, rousing the company from bed. The building, he reported, was surrounded by a hundred armed men. However exaggerated the claim, Mackercher knew that their pistols were no match for carbines and blunderbusses. Barricading themselves in their second-story room, they waited until an hour after daybreak. Goostry ventured downstairs only to learn that a warrant, on the complaint of the Earl of Anglesea, had been issued by a justice of the peace for the arrest of himself, Mackercher, and Kennedy. The charge was assault. Seconds later, the earl's steward, Michael Lacy, arrived with a constable in tow. Lacy insisted that the three men return to the justice in order to give bail. "No," responded Goostry, "we do not care for that, we have got enough of this country. I am all over blood. I don't like it so well to go into it again." During the heated exchange, the constable whispered to James and the others, "Naas is the county gaol, gentlemen, and if you say you will go in that gaol [to give bail], I must carry you there." With Naas lying seven miles to the northeast, Mackercher agreed, sending word ahead to solicit aid from friends in the town.[36]

They quitted the inn without incident. The entourage consisted of Mackercher, Kennedy, and a Mr. Carrick, who volunteered his services, all riding in a coach, with the constable and Lacy trailing behind on horseback. In front, almost three abreast, were Annesley, Goostry, and the surgeon Hackett, followed by several servants. Annesley had refused to ride in the coach. He was also one of the few permitted to carry a pistol, for the three under arrest were denied weapons.

A few miles beyond Newbridge, an armed man in a green coat passed the coach from behind. As Goostry dropped back, the rider slowed his horse to a trot and started to approach Annesley on the left. Hearing the cock of a gun, Goostry spied the muzzle of a rifle, aimed directly at James, lying across the pommel of the man's saddle. "Mr. Annesley, you'll be shot," shouted Goostry, rushing him at once into the coach with Hackett's help. The mysterious rider, later identified as Angus Byrne, quickly fell to the rear toward Lacy and the constable. Minutes later, in response to Mackercher's appeal, fifteen armed men on horseback appeared from Naas to escort the party for the remainder of the journey.[37]

Inexplicably, Byrne continued to follow the coach, even riding as far as the home of a Naas magistrate named Bonner. Once inside, Mackercher demanded that Byrne be questioned.

"Whose gun is that?" Bonner asked.

"It is my Lord Anglesea's," Byrne answered.

"What were you to do with this gun?"

"I was desired to pursue Mr. Lacy's directions."

"What directions had Mr. Lacy?"

"In case there had been a rescue," he replied tersely.

"In case of a rescue, what were you to do with this gun, loaded as it is with eight bullets?"

At that juncture, Lacy himself burst into the room. "Sir, answer no more questions. You are not obliged to answer." And the examination was over.

Once Lacy proclaimed himself Anglesea's steward, the magistrate hesitated to proceed further, referring the entire company to a justice of the peace. With bail supplied to the justice by Mackercher, Goostry, and Kennedy, James and the men at last returned to Dublin.[38]

That Byrne was meant to murder Annesley is clear. Later, under oath, Angus was more forthcoming. As Richard's huntsman, he had indeed been told that morning to take directions from Michael Lacy. A quarter mile beyond the Kilcullen Bridge on the road to Naas, Lacy had handed him a screw-barreled gun of the type popular with gamekeepers. "Angus, your bread is baked. You shall be provided for while you live. You are to use this thing. Fire at the pretender, [and] be sure not to miss him. We have horses to carry us off, and never fear, if we are taken, we'll make a rescue of it. We have people enough here to prove it for us."

But at the critical moment, Byrne had flinched, later telling Lacy that he would "have no hand in any man's blood." Even after Annesley had dismounted and entered the coach, Lacy still implored Byrne to act. "You might be done for as well as any man in the world," he promised.

"By whom, pray?" Byrne asked.

"By my Lord Anglesea," came the reply.[39]

7

REDEMPTION

All the streets seem'd to be in a blaze.
Westminster Journal,
December 10, 1743[1]

Barely fifty feet from the Dublin crypt containing the corrupted remains of James Annesley's father, Lord Altham, stood a nondescript stone building known as the Four Courts. Ever since 1608, the central law courts of Ireland had been housed in the former two-story home of the dean of Christ Church. Located beside the cathedral, the building had last been renovated at the end of the seventeenth century. Simplicity itself, the main floor of the edifice was neither elegant nor functional. A French visitor pronounced the building and its denizens equally gloomy. The compact courtrooms faced a common hallway without doors or curtains. There was minimal ornamentation—arched doorways and windows, pilastered frames, and a dome in the center of the ceiling. On one side were the courts of Exchequer and Chancery; directly across the vestibule lay King's Bench and Common Pleas—all "fill'd in term-time," quipped Swift, "with those who defend their own estate or endeavour to get another's." The clamor must have been overwhelming. Adding to the noise, both the cellar and the upper floor of the building were leased to spinners and shopkeepers, a source of "great annoyance" to the lawyers and judges sandwiched in between.[2]

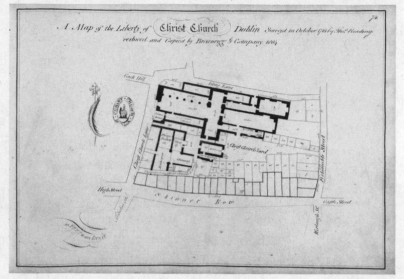

Thomas Reading, *Map of the Liberty of Christ Church Dublin Survey'd in October 1761 . . . ,* 1761. The drawing offers a detailed layout of the Four Courts as well as of Christ Church. The alley known as "Hell" appears as the "Passage from Christ Church Lane."

An alleyway ran from Christ Church Lane (on the western edge of the cathedral) to the Courts' rear. As dark as it was narrow, the passage, like a trench, lay partly below ground. Along the path, a door opened onto the central hall inside, just to the left of the Court of Exchequer. Owing either to the passage's appearance or to its terminus, it was famously dubbed "Hell." An advertisement for nearby lodgings announced the availability of "furnished apartments in *Hell*." "They are well suited to a lawyer," the ad declared.[3]

Crumbling plaster, decaying joists, and loose floorboards were among the problems besetting the Four Courts. In 1739, the courtroom belonging to Exchequer was found to be in "ruinous" condition. Beams had to be placed as "props" to forestall the ceiling's collapse. Equally problematic were the building's cramped quarters. On a June afternoon in 1721, the sight of billowing smoke from a clogged chimney sent persons from all four court-rooms spilling into the hallway, where one of the few doors was locked to prevent the escape of prisoners. More than one hundred men and women were injured, with between twenty and thirty either suffocated by the smoke or trampled to death in the crowd's frenzy.[4]

The first week of November was windy and wet, followed by frosty temperatures and gusts from the north and northwest. A spell of "dark mizzling weather" then set in for most of the month—cold and drizzly. All the same, neither the weather nor, for that matter, the Courts' physical deterioration could detract attention from the singular case Exchequer was set to hear. Since his arrival from the Caribbean, the saga of James Annesley had become a sensation throughout the British Isles—"the common conversation of the coffee-houses," observed a London resident. Now, with another dramatic trial looming, public interest had only intensified. As early as January, Dr. Barry had written to the Earl of Orrery, "We all expect the trial with impatience." Recent events at the Curragh, awaiting a separate hearing, fed the anticipation. "We hear from Ireland," the *Westminster Journal* reported, "that the life of the Hon. James Annesley, Esq. has been twice attempted there."[5]

Certainly, there were no illusions about the contest's significance. Ostensibly a dispute over competing leases, the case's larger import—as the first step toward Annesley's vindication—was apparent to all. Never, potentially, did any jury have five peerages and such an immense estate at its disposal, now worth by one account at least £50,000 a year. No less momentous in the public mind were the lurid allegations of aristocratic wrongdoing, which, for James's following, had robbed a peer of the realm of his birthright and broken the chain of succession within the house of Annesley.

Richard's circle, by contrast, bewailed the prospect of elevating a false claimant to the family's hereditary honors, not unlike Jacobite efforts to place a Stuart heir on the throne. Opponents commonly derided James as a "pretender," the slur attached to successive generations of Jacobite claimants. With the outbreak of the War of the Austrian Succession and renewed Protestant fears in 1743 of a Franco-Jacobite invasion of Ireland, the label "pretender" had widespread resonance.[6]

Plainly no previous peerage controversy, except for struggles over the throne itself, so captivated the popular imagination. The current contest, wrote Viscount Perceval to his father, the Earl of Egmont, was "perhaps of greater importance than any tryall ever known in this or any other kingdom."[7]

The court convened at eight o'clock on the morning of Friday, November 11, despite an attempt by Anglesea's lawyers to obtain an injunction halting the trial. The first day occasioned, in the words of one correspondent, "the greatest concourse of people, hurry, and confusion in a court of justice that has been known in the memory of man." Nearly everything about the proceedings suggested their enormity. Fearing violence, the lord lieutenant, William Cavendish, third Duke of Devonshire, stationed a military guard just across the street at the Tholsel. Parliament met sporadically at best for the duration of the trial, with many of its members among the throng that each day packed the courtroom.[8]

At least two of the three judges, attired in silk robes trimmed with miniver, were figures of weight and reputation. The chief baron of the Court of Exchequer was John Bowes, who besides serving as solicitor-general and then attorney-general had represented the borough of Taghmon in County Wexford in the Irish House of Commons, where he had been a staunch advocate for English interests. As a lawyer, he was praised for "the music of his voice, and the gracefulness of his elocution."[9]

Anonymous, *John Bowes*, Chief Baron of the
Exchequer, mezzotint by John Brooks, ca. 1741.

The second baron, Richard Mountney, was a fellow of King's
College, Cambridge, and a classical scholar before being called to
the bar in 1732. Arthur Dawson, the court's third baron and only
native of Ireland, had served as member of Parliament for County
Londonderry from 1729 to 1742. He was less well known for his
legal expertise than for his authorship of a bacchanalian ditty that
proclaimed, "Ye lawyers so just, / Be the cause what it will, who
so learnedly plead, / How worthy of trust! / You know black from
white, / Yet prefer wrong to right."[10]

Each side in the contest employed an imposing legion of lawyers. As barristers, all came from the upper ranks of the country's
legal establishment, in contrast to attorneys and solicitors, who
were not allowed to plead in higher courts. Opponents of the earl
later alleged that he had monopolized the city's most eminent

barristers; and, in fact, his fifteen counselors included the top four lawyers in the kingdom, not only the attorney-general and his deputy, the solicitor-general, but also the prime serjeant and the recorder of Dublin, all of whom had the right to accept private clients so long as the king was not a party. To represent Campbell Craig and Annesley, as the "lessor of the plaintiff," Mackercher retained the second and third serjeants to lead a panel of thirteen lawyers. With some two hundred barristers in Dublin, nearly one in seven participated on one side or the other during the trial.[11]

Equally remarkable were the jurors brought from County Meath, site of the disputed estate. From a pool of twenty-four men of independent wealth, as required by law, twelve were selected, their names written on tickets picked out of a box. Included were many of the county's biggest landowners, possessing estates collectively worth more than £70,000 per annum. Although several jurors reportedly stood to lose lucrative leases to pieces of the disputed property should Craig and Annesley prevail, they were not disqualified. Fully ten were members of the House of Commons. "Nor ever was there a jury composed of gentlemen of such property, dignity, and character," reported a letter from Dublin.[12]

Once the jurors had been sworn in, Craig's formal complaint, describing his ejectment "with force and arms," was read in court. The events of May 3 were not contested by Anglesea's lawyers. Instead, two other issues came to dominate the proceedings. Most important was whether James Annesley was the son and rightful heir of Arthur, Baron Altham; and second, whether, after a prolonged absence abroad, the lessor of land to Campbell Craig was in fact Annesley and not an impostor.[13]

Serjeant Robert Marshall gave the opening remarks for the plaintiff. Forty-six years old, he was a native of County Tipperary, which he had aggressively represented in Parliament since 1727. A practicing lawyer for twenty years, he spent close to an hour tracing the chronology of the case, beginning with the union of Annesley's parents and concluding with his recent trial at the Old Bailey. As for his kidnapping, Marshall was deliberately coy, promising to reveal the villain's identity in the course of the trial. "It will much more properly come out of the mouths of the witnesses," he stated. Not scheduled to testify was Annesley himself—nor, for that matter, his uncle, the earl. In contrast to accepted practice in criminal trials, interested parties in civil proceedings would not be permitted to give testimony until the mid-nineteenth century.[14]

Over the remainder of the day and into the night, fourteen witnesses took an oath not to forswear themselves. Following the clerk's admonition to "tell the truth, the whole truth, and nothing but the truth," each was required to kiss the Bible. Consisting, in the main, of former servants, neighbors, and family friends, most gave detailed descriptions of Lady Altham's pregnancy and Jemmy's birth. With the courtroom aglow in candlelight, two women, Mary Doyle and Ellen Murphy, claimed to have been in the room during the delivery. The absence of a parish register made such testimony critical. Memorable events, such as the festive celebrations following Jemmy's birth and christening, stood out in the statements. The most compelling witness was Major Richard Fitzgerald of Prospect Hall in Waterford, on leave from serving in the Queen of Hungary's troops in the Rhineland. On the day after the boy's birth, he had visited Dunmain. Having been pressed to stay for dinner, he recalled kissing the baby and giving his nurse a half-guinea. Lord Altham, he testified, was "in high spirits with the thoughts of having a son and heir." In contrast, however, to other witnesses, Fitzgerald recalled that the birth had occurred not in the spring but in the fall.[15]

In the late evening, the jurors also heard from the widow, Deborah Annesley, who twenty-five years earlier had refused to board Baron Altham at her Kildare estate. At sixty years of age, she was the aunt of Francis Annesley of Ballysax as well as Anglesea's cousin. More important, she remained a figure of strict propriety and in the weeks approaching the trial had rejected her nephew's urgent pleas not to testify as doing so, he claimed, would cause the family's ruin.

Called to the bar, Deborah stood her ground. Volunteering that she had never seen the baron's boy—preferring, as she did, not to visit Kinnea—she nonetheless insisted that he was always thought to be Altham's heir. Members of her household were known to drink Jemmy's health. Her late brother, Deborah Annesley testified, "was a sober, grave man" who "would not have toasted the health of the child if he had been a bastard." What's more, on Altham's death in 1727, they had "enquired what was become of that boy, but never could learn."

Not until 11 p.m. did the court finally adjourn. Rarely, particularly in the short days of fall and winter, did courts sit so late. It was only the second time in memory that such a trial had extended beyond a single day, and there was no end in sight.[16]

All day Saturday and well into the next week, Sunday excepted, the court heard from a steady stream of witnesses for the plaintiff. Any notion that this would be a routine trial had long been abandoned. Sessions continued to run late, convening at 8 or 9 a.m. and not adjourning until long past dark, with only brief intervals for "refreshment."

Among those to appear on Saturday was Joan Laffan, Jemmy's former dry-nurse. In recounting the fracas preceding the baroness's expulsion from Dunmain, she told of the cut inflicted upon Tom Palliser's ear. Immediately afterward, she related, Jemmy had pointed to drops of blood on the floor. On cross-examination, Anglesea's counsel questioned whether she had ever resided at Dunmain. Besides challenging her knowledge of other servants, he expressed surprise at her ignorance of one of Altham's neighbors.

"Did not you know that he was reckoned a gentleman of estate and a justice of the peace?" demanded the defense.

"Well," replied Laffan, without hesitation, "there are a great many indifferent men [who are] justices of the peace in our country."[17]

In this instance and others, cross-examinations, initially perfunctory in tone, grew sharper. Nor did opposing counsel shrink from impugning a witness's social credentials. James Dempsey testified to his employment at Carrickduff as tutor to Jemmy for six months in 1721. Recently, he had been reintroduced to his former student, whom he had immediately recognized.

"Do you go to mass or to church," asked the defense lawyer during cross-examination, playing upon anti-Catholic animus among the jury.

"I go to mass, but I did not know much of religion when I tutored Mr. Annesley, for during the six months that I staid in the house I neither went to church or mass, but I have a better notion of religion now," he said, adding, "thank God."[18]

By contrast, Nicholas Duff, a tavernkeeper who had known Altham and his son during their residence on Cross-Lane, was ridiculed for his genteel pretensions. "Have you ever carried a chair?" questioned the defense.

"What of that? I am a gentleman now."

"Are you a porter to Mr. Mackercher?"

"No, I don't go of errands."

"Do you open Mr. Mackercher's door to people?"

"Sometime, I open it," Duff confessed, "but I have no wages. I tend to oblige Mr. Annesley and Mr. Mackercher."

If that was not humiliation enough, the counsel asked if he had ever swept the walk before Mackercher's door.

"No!" came the angry reply.

"How long have you had the coat now on your back?" goaded the defense.

"Ever since I bought it last spring. Why don't you ask me where I bought this wig?"

Finally, questioned at whose direction he stood at Mackercher's door, Duff responded, "By my own directions, to divert me, for my own pleasure, for unless I did it I should go into an ale-house to drink."

Of the exchange, a witness in the gallery reported that Duff's posturing "made the court very merry."[19]

Moments of levity, however mean-spirited, were few. Lighter in tone was the testimony of Bartholomew Furlong, whose wife, he stated, had been interviewed years earlier by Lady Altham as a potential wet-nurse. Determined to cast doubt upon his testimony, the defense counsel pressed for accurate descriptions of Altham and his wife. The baron, Furlong replied, was a "very small faced, thin, little man, and spoke very loud." Asked whether his wife was a "lean or a fat woman," he replied, "She was not a fat woman."

Pointing to a man in the audience, the counsel then inquired whether she was "as fair as that gentleman?"

"She was not so fair," answered Furlong.

"Of what complexion is your wife?"

"She is a brown woman. Lady Altham was not of the same colour, [and] that they ought not (in one day) to be compared together," adding, "to be sure, Lady Altham was fifty times beyond my wife, though my wife is more pleasing to me."[20]

By Monday afternoon, the court had heard thirty-nine witnesses for the plaintiff, evoking vivid memories of Jemmy Annesley at varying stages of his youth. Now, the focus of the testimony shifted abruptly to the period preceding his kidnapping. Still a butcher, brawny John Purcell approached the bar. What followed was a riveting tale of the months Jemmy had spent with Purcell and his family on Phoenix Street—and of the earl's attempt to abduct the boy while under the butcher's care.

Asked by the plaintiff's lawyer whether he could identify James in court, Purcell pointed to Annesley and replied, "That is the gentleman there. I know him as well as I know the hand now on my heart." During the cross-examination, the counsel directly challenged Purcell's veracity. Why, he wondered, had the butcher not reported the attempted kidnapping in Ormond Market to the authorities? "If a man had come to take away your own child by force, would not you have gone to a justice of the peace to have given examinations against him?"

"I believe not," replied Purcell, "for I thought myself capable of vindicating that cause " (i.e., redeem or rescue, according to the biblical meaning). Left unsaid was the deep distrust that tradesmen, especially Catholics like Purcell, felt toward constables and magistrates. In a letter to Lord Orrery, a friend reported that the four-hour testimony of the "brave, bold butcher" had caused most persons in the courtroom to weep.[21]

Still more unsettling was the account given early Tuesday morning by two men, Mark Byrn and James Reilly, who had participated in Jemmy's abduction. With remarkable candor, they related not only their role in the day's events but also Anglesea's— the first evidence to link the earl directly to the kidnapping. Nothing was held back, not the boy's wrenching capture nor his plaintive cries for help. Reilly, a former servant, testified to Richard's frustration soon after his brother's death. "I have heard the present Lord Anglesea very often say, when people used to affront him for destroying the boy's birthright, that he would . . . [get] even with him." Subsequent testimony by a customs officer as well as that of a former clerk to the merchant James Stephenson left no doubt that Annesley had departed Dublin aboard the *James* on April 30, 1728.[22]

It was not until the afternoon that the court called John Giffard, one of the final witnesses for the plaintiff. Anglesea could not have contemplated without alarm the testimony of his former attorney. For twenty years, Giffard had represented the earl, in and out of court, most recently as the manager of James Annesley's prosecution for murder.

Costs stemming from the prosecution had totaled £800, well short of the £10,000 pledged by the earl during his initial euphoria. But, livid over his nephew's acquittal, he had doggedly refused to pay Giffard a final sum of £330, filing instead a suit at the Court of Exchequer in London contesting Giffard's claim, daring him to "set forth particularly all the business that he hath done." It was a colossal blunder. Not only did Giffard respond by documenting his grievance with a detailed schedule of costs, listing names, places, and dates, but he also answered a series of interrogatories put by the court—all of which Daniel Mackercher, ever on the alert, caught wind of. Although Anglesea's involvement in the prosecution had been alleged at the Old Bailey, few people at the time realized the extent of his participation. Stunned by Giffard's incriminating evidence, Mackercher presented the solicitor with two choices: either come to Dublin to testify or face being subpoenaed—or such, at least, was Giffard's subsequent explanation for his startling appearance Tuesday afternoon.[23]

Certainly he gave no sign of being a reluctant witness. Barely seconds into his testimony, John Fitzgibbon (nicknamed Wily John) enquired about the shooting at Staines. The defense objected, and Fitzgibbon countered by telling the court that Anglesea had funded the prosecution of his nephew, despite the possibility of his innocence—an allegation, responded the defense, wholly irrelevant to the case at hand. At that juncture Serjeant Marshall rose to speak. Anglesea's role, he declared, revealed a deliberate design to prevent his nephew "from any possibility of asserting his birthright." "What we now propose to lay before your lordship and the jury," he emphasized, "is the very extraordinary part that the Earl of Anglesea took in that trial."[24]

Taken aback, the barons promised to give their opinions in the morning on whether or not to admit Giffard's testimony about the Staines shooting. "The immense consequence" of "the present cause," noted Baron Mountney, "will incline me to hesitate upon such points, as I should otherwise be most extremely clear in." Reported a Dublin newspaper the next day, "The great tryal between the Right Hon. the Earl of Anglesea and James Annesley, Esq. which begun last Friday in his Majesty's Court of Exchequer, still continues; and we hear, they have not yet examined all the witnesses for the plaintiff."[25]

When court convened at ten o'clock, William Harward for the plaintiff immediately revived the controversy over the admissibility of Giffard's testimony, provoking, once again, the defense's opposition. Before ruling, the court appeared anxious to hear further arguments. The defense counsel Francis Blake put forth a new line of reasoning by claiming attorney–client privilege: "An attorney or solicitor might not, nor is he compellable to disclose the secrets of his client." It is a privilege, he argued, "not merely and solely" inherent in the office of the counsel "but is, in law and reason, the right and privilege of the client."[26]

In fact, the concept of attorney–client privilege was neither broadly defined nor deeply ingrained in the common law by the eighteenth century. First invoked in Elizabethan courts, the privilege only gained wider recognition during the second half of the seventeenth century. Even then, judges did not routinely uphold the principle, nor was it ordinarily thought applicable to solicitors and attorneys, like Giffard.[27]

If both sides in the trial acknowledged the principle's legitimacy, both also accepted the need for restrictions. Beyond that, there was little consensus, particularly in relation to permitting Giffard's testimony. Counselors spent the rest of the morning in vigorous debate, introducing early precedents but also expanding the boundaries of current law in new directions.

For the plaintiff, privilege in the present instance was objectionable for three reasons. First, Anglesea's conversations with Giffard bore only an indirect connection to the pending litigation, occurring, as they had, well before the filing of Campbell Craig's suit.

Second, the bulk of their discourse regarding the earl's nephew had occurred under the guise of friendship. No cause, not even Annesley's prosecution, was then underway. Finally, privilege, counsel argued, could not be invoked to shield illegal behavior, *malum in se*, on the part of an attorney and his client, including the planning of a malicious prosecution. "Surely there never was a stronger instance of iniquity," admonished Harward, "than the present; a design of the blackest dye against the life of an innocent person."

Defense lawyers hotly disputed the validity of such burdensome criteria. Instead of rebutting specific arguments, they argued for a broader application of privilege. After all, declared John Smith, the earl's status as Giffard's client had commenced from the time of his initial retention until that of his dismissal. "Whatever my lord said to him during that space of time, touching his affairs, was plainly said to him under confidence as his attorney."[28]

By mid-afternoon, the court was ready to render its verdict. In a landmark decision that would influence rulings on the issue for another half-century, the barons unanimously found in favor of the plaintiff, all but gutting the principle of privilege. Giffard would be allowed to testify. For the chief baron, no comprehensive rule as to privilege existed. Each case needed to be examined on its own merits. In the matter at hand, the principle only protected discussions relating to pending litigation and even then could not be employed to conceal a criminal act. "As this was in part a wicked secret," he stated, "it ought not to have been concealed; though, if earlier disclosed, it might have been more for the credit of the witness." On these points his colleagues strongly concurred, with Lord Mountney taking the opportunity to chastise the defense for misconstruing existing case law on the subject.[29]

Giffard's testimony lived up to its billing: direct and devastating. Richard quit the courtroom just as his former attorney approached the bar. Testifying to Anglesea's legal battles with

other members of the family, Giffard related the earl's decision
to abandon his titles and estates in favor of removing to France.
Worse, Anglesea had conceded his nephew's right to both.

"And, pray," asked the plaintiff's counsel, "what altered his
resolution then?"

"Why, on the 1st of May, Mr. Annesley had shot a man at
Staines." And thus began the sordid story whereby Richard had
ordered Giffard to initiate a prosecution, irrespective of either the
cost or Annesley's guilt or innocence.

The cross-examination of Giffard was combative. Turning to
his role in the prosecution, the defense only succeeded in fixing
blame for countenancing Anglesea's malfeasance.

"When my lord Anglesea said that he would not care if it cost
him £10,000 so he could get the plaintiff hanged," inquired counsel, "did you apprehend from thence, that he would be willing to
go to that expense in the prosecution?"

"I did."

"Did you suppose from thence that he would dispose of that
£10,000 in any shape to bring about the death of the plaintiff?"

"I did."

"Did you not apprehend that to be a most wicked crime?"

"I did."

"If so, how could you, who set yourself out as a man of business,
engage in that project, without making any objection to it?"

"I may as well ask you, how you came to be engaged for the
defendant in this suit," Giffard sharply retorted.

Moments later, counsel returned to the subject of Giffard's
culpability.

"Did not you apprehend it to be a bad purpose to lay out money
to compass the death of another man?"

"I do not know but I did. I do believe it, Sir. But I was not to
undertake that bad purpose. If there was any dirty work, I was not
concerned in it."

"If you did believe this, I ask you, how came you to engage in this prosecution without objection?"

"I make a distinction," he parried, "between carrying on a prosecution, and compassing the death of a man."

In short, not unlike Anglesea's current counselors, Giffard, in his role as attorney, was merely following his client's wishes, not conspiring to abet a crime—an argument at odds with that made by plaintiff's counsel for waiving attorney–client privilege.

No matter. Linking Giffard to Anglesea's misconduct did nothing to diminish the force of his earlier testimony. Nor did defense suggestions that he would profit by a finding for the plaintiff. "I desire to know," demanded the defense, "if Mr. Annesley gets this suit, whether you will be paid your bill of costs [owed by the earl]?" "No, Sir," Giffard replied, "I shall lose every shilling of it." Asked why he had agreed to testify about a former client, he replied, "This bill of costs of mine [for managing Annesley's prosecution] would never have come to light, had I not been obligated to sue for my right."[30]

Late Wednesday afternoon, St. George Caulfeild, the attorney-general of Ireland, rose in a black silk gown to deliver opening remarks for the defense. The son of an Irish judge, he had been educated at the Middle Temple and later served in the Irish Commons. No portion of the plaintiff's case went unscathed. At the center of Caulfeild's attack was the issue of Annesley's birth, which he attributed to an adulterous relationship between Lord Altham and the kitchen-maid Juggy Landy, the servant whom opposing counsel had already identified as Jemmy's wet-nurse. Landy, Caulfeild pointedly noted, had not been summoned as a witness for the plaintiff (in truth, the defense had no plans to call her either, having had only limited success trying to suborn her testimony). But hadn't the boy been kidnapped and shipped to America? Nonsense, Caulfeild insisted. He had traveled abroad voluntarily "without the least interposition on the part of the earl." Maliciously prosecuted for homicide? A web of deceit spun by a disreputable witness. By contrast, the counselor promised to produce testimony over the coming days from "persons of the best conditions in the neighbourhood of Dunmain."[31]

After nearly two hours, the first witnesses were called, including Colonel Thomas Palliser, Sr. A former sheriff, he evidently harbored no ill feelings, at least toward Anglesea, for Lord Altham's thrashing, years earlier, of his son Tom. Just the opposite. The baron's only offspring, Palliser testified, was Landy's bastard. What's more, not long after the birth, she had been dismissed from Dunmain for "whoring"—an "infamous woman" whom the colonel "would not trust for the value of a potato." Cross-examined for three hours, Palliser proved vague in many of his recollections, a consequence, intimated the defense, of his advanced age. During the testimony, he was permitted to deliver his remarks from a chair before the court finally adjourned at ten o'clock in the evening.[32]

Much of Thursday's evidence continued to revolve around Juggy Landy's illegitimate son. That she had borne a boy, counsel for the plaintiff had never disputed. But a sailor, they'd insisted, had fathered the child. Moreover, the infant was slightly older than James, and he had died at three years of age from smallpox. In fact, contended the defense, Juggy's bastard—Jemmy Annesley— had been born in the Landys' ramshackle cottage. Only after Lady Altham's departure was the boy given a home at Dunmain and his father's name. According to William Elmes, a neighbor, the baron forbade any intercourse between Landy and her son lest "the child should know his mother." Once, on discovering her near the great house, Altham had threatened to set his hounds on her.

So different was this from the testimony of Joan Laffan that the court ordered her to return. Resworn after curtsying to the bench, she recalled only briefly encountering Elmes at Dunmain, though she judged him an honest man. For his part, Elmes, a former high constable, testified that Laffan had previously been charged with theft. He also described her as a laundry-maid, which she strongly denied, having been the boy's dry-nurse. As for Jemmy, he was attired, she testified, as a nobleman's son, usually in a silk or velvet coat, which Elmes claimed never to have observed.

He also disputed the condition of the Landys' dwelling. "I saw no furniture at all. There was a wall made up with sods and stones."

"Oh fie! Mr. Elmes," exclaimed Laffan, clapping her hands. "I wonder you'll say so. By the Holy Evangelists there was never a sod in the house!"

As with most of the defense's witnesses, Elmes was questioned by counsel for the plaintiff by right of *voir dire* ("to see to speak"). This entitled counsel to probe whether the witness had an interest in the trial's outcome. In Elmes's case, he denied leasing land from Anglesea. Others responded along similar lines, disputing, as well, any expectation of compensation for their testimony. "I am no way concern'd to the value of a farthing," responded one indignant witness.[33]

With evening coming on, Anne Giffard, the next person called, introduced a fresh line of defense. Lady Altham could not have given birth in the spring of 1715, for she, Giffard, and other ladies had traveled to the town of Wexford for a week to attend the assize trial of two men indicted for Jacobitism. Giffard even recollected that they had sat next to the young squire Caesar Colclough.

At eight o'clock, the court adjourned, though not before the chief baron forcefully urged opposing counsel to expedite their examination of witnesses. The case, he noted, was "of so extraordinary a nature that the business of the whole nation was postponed on account of it." So ended the first week of a contest that was barely half over. "If Mr. A[nnesle]y carries it," reported an observer, "it will be with the good will of all people here."

Nevertheless, he added, "What will be the event of it is impossible to determine."[34]

Over the next three days of testimony, a total of twenty-eight defense witnesses paraded before the court, most called to dispute either the birth of a son to Lord and Lady Altham or the quality of James's upbringing. As a group, the witnesses were every bit as diverse as the plaintiff's supporters, including not only a Dublin alderman but also servants and tradesmen, most of whom resided in County Wexford. Again and again, they affirmed the absence of a legitimate heir. Unlike Landy's bastard, no such child had ever been seen or spoken of. Notably absent from the witness pool were any members of the Annesley family, including the earl's cousins Charles and Francis, who may have chafed at the prospect of perjuring themselves.

The defense waited until Friday to call its prime witness. For thirteen years, Mary Heath had been the personal servant to Lady Altham, from the time of her arrival in Ireland until her death. Heath's portrait of the Althams' marriage, which consumed most of the afternoon, suggested little affection, much less love.

"Was there ever a child," queried defense counsel, "either christened or living at that home while you were at Dunmain?"

"No, never."

"Did my lady ever talk to you any thing of her being with child, or having had a child during that time?"

"No, never a word."

Nearly as protracted was Heath's cross-examination, though it was of little value to the plaintiff. A formidable witness, she had, by the end of the day, proved equal to the task, confirming not only the absence of an heir but also, for good measure, Lady Altham's trip to Wexford in the spring of 1715.[35]

With the defense resting on Monday, plaintiff's counsel exercised their right to call rebuttal witnesses. Right from the start, they attacked Heath's testimony. According to Caesar Colclough, neither the baroness nor Mrs. Giffard had attended the Wexford assizes. If they had, he would have remembered them. "In a country town of that sort, if a lady of distinction comes, everybody hears it." In his view, it was rare for women of privilege to attend such trials. As for the veracity of Mrs. Giffard, Colclough observed, "The family is reduced and very poor; their circumstances are altered, and so may their honesty."[36]

Worse, a London acquaintance of Heath, John Hussey, was also called to challenge her testimony. A reluctant witness, he had been subpoenaed late one night at his home in County Kildare. (As soon as the messenger pretended to bring news from Hussey's sister, he had grudgingly opened his outer gate.) To the court, he testified to a conversation that he had with Heath over tea at her Holborn home in late 1741. Of Annesley's arrival from the Caribbean, she had remarked, "Nobody knows that young man's affairs better than I, because I long lived with his mother, the lady Altham." In fact, Heath had "expressed a great deal of concern for him." And, too, that during their final meeting in London, she had reported plans to travel to Ireland to testify, inexplicably, on behalf of the Earl of Anglesea.

The cross-examination was withering, but Hussey was adamant. A prolonged inquiry ensued into the nature of his trade, in which he denied ever having been a tailor but professed instead to deal in fabrics. He had also served as a steward aboard one of the royal yachts, Hussey proudly volunteered, thereby handing the defense an unexpected opening.

"You mentioned, that you had an employment under the Crown," countered the counselor. "Pray, what is your profession in point of religion?"

"My Lord, I desire to know if that is material," Hussey protested, "and I appeal to the court whether I must answer the question or not."

"It is criminal," interjected Serjeant Marshall for the plaintiff, "if a man accepts of an office under the Crown, and is not a Protestant," adding, however, that Hussey was not required to incriminate himself. After further debate over the nature of his royal commission, Hussey at last attested to being a Catholic.

Minutes later, Heath was resworn to answer his allegations. Acknowledging their acquaintance, she related an altogether different set of conversations. "I have several times talked about it [Annesley's reappearance], and said what a vile thing it was to take away the earl's right, and that my lady never was with child; and I cannot say no more if you rack me to death."

Turning to Hussey, she declared, "I never thought that you were such a man; I've heard people say that you were a gamester, and lived in an odd way, but I would never believe it till now. But I always took your part, and said you behaved like a gentleman."

"I am a gentleman," he insisted. "I can bring several people to justify me to be a gentleman, and a man of family; indeed I have heard you say it [i.e. that Annesley's rightful inheritance had been usurped], and speak it with all the regret and concern imaginable."[37]

For the remainder of the day and all of Tuesday, more witnesses followed, rebutting as best they could pieces of the defense's case. Thomas Higginson, a former surveyor for Baron Altham, swore to having seen Lady Altham, "big belly'd," at Dunmain in the spring of 1715. A few charged the defense with soliciting perjured testimony, the most sensational instance involving an elderly Catholic priest by the name of Michael Downes, the member of an old Wexford family. According to the priest of a neighboring parish, Downes had accepted a bribe of £200 for swearing falsely to Annesley's illegitimate birth—a grave sin for which he reportedly intended to seek absolution. (Of his accuser, Downes responded in court, "He is a vile, drunken, whore-master dog.") Finally, at 6 p.m., both parties rested, with the court announcing that they would reconvene on Thursday the 24th, after a day's respite.[38]

The trial's penultimate stage commenced at eight o'clock with closing arguments by three counselors for either side. For eight hours, defense lawyers, led by the prime serjeant, Anthony Malone, recounted the testimony of the previous ten days. A prominent member of Parliament for County Westmeath, Malone was a polished orator. Along with other members of the defense, he expressed persistent surprise that the birth of a lawful heir had not attracted greater attention among neighbors and other members of the Annesley family. "It is impossible it should be a secret to all the world," contended Malone, "except [for] two or three of the meanest servants." Indeed, he asserted, not one person in the vicinity of New Ross worth more than £10 a year had testified to the boy's birth. No more credible was Altham's constant neglect of the child in Dublin. Such cruelty toward a legitimate son was inconceivable, as was the failure of John Purcell and Richard Tighe, among others, to bring the baron to account for his negligence. After all, "no man [was] more odious to the people generally [and] to people of power universally," stated the solicitor-general, Warden Flood (if such harsh words about his late brother gave Richard pause, there is no report).

Vainly, however, did the defense rebut the two most glaring weaknesses in their case: Jemmy's kidnapping and his subsequent prosecution for murder—"the only colours for this suit," Malone claimed. "Were they out of the question," he insisted, "I dare venture to say that this cause would be hooted out of court." Flood likened the incidents to "a romantic cobweb." All three counselors emphasized the enormity of the jury's decision—"a cause, perhaps, of the greatest moment that ever was tried in a court of justice in this kingdom, and a stake of the greatest value that ever was in the disposal of any jury before." Not only was the estate the largest ever contested in court, but numerous lives stood to be injured by a finding for the plaintiff, including those of countless tenants. Even more alarming was the potential danger to the social order. Personal property and the country's system of inheritance, sanctioned by custom and the common law, stood imperiled should the plaintiff prevail, setting a precedent whereby every illegitimate son might be tempted to contest a lawful bequest. All the more reason, then, for the plaintiff's evidence "to be proved beyond all contradiction." Otherwise, asked Malone, "What family can be safe?" Echoed Flood, "Is not putting a suspicious man into a family, not only an injustice to posterity, but to the first founder of the family?"[39]

After a half-hour's refreshment for the jury, Serjeant Marshall rose to speak for the plaintiff. Straightaway he declared his belief that "there has scarce been an instance in any age of such a scene of iniquity, cruelty, and inhumanity as this." Apart from reviewing the evidence on both sides, Marshall contrasted Annesley's disadvantages in going to trial with the wealth and influence of his uncle. The passage of time had only compounded the difficulty of the task. After so many years, the serjeant wryly noted, "it is impossible for any man to keep his witnesses alive." More surprising was the earl's failure to produce a single member of his family to dispute the boy's lawful birth. As for those witnesses whom the defense did call, "the most favourable construction," argued Serjeant Philip Tisdall in his remarks, "is that they are ignorant of a fact so notorious to the rest of the country."

Most important of all, testimony regarding Annesley's kidnapping, a deed that "speaks stronger than words," had gone uncontroverted, as had allegations respecting his prosecution. The uncle, "being of a proud avaricious disposition, tempered with cruelty," proclaimed Marshall, "could not bear that a boy in those low circumstances should succeed to Altham's estate and title, or be presumptive heir to the Earl of Anglesea." It was an extraordinarily blunt indictment of a nobleman. At 10 p.m., the defense rested.[40]

Until their summations on Friday morning, the court's barons had remained silent during much of the proceedings, except for ruling on the admissibility of John Giffard's testimony. The chief baron, on occasion, had expressed dismay over the contradictory nature of the testimony and once admonished a defense witness for suggesting that the earl himself was James's father. "This dirt will do the defendant's cause no service," scolded Bowes.

Judicial summations, while not critical in legal proceedings, frequently helped to guide a jury's deliberations. The bench was obligated to identify the trial's salient issues and to evaluate the relevant evidence, all the while clarifying basic points of law.

Bowes spoke first and at great length, followed by extended comments from Mountney. Although Dawson, the last to talk, took less than an hour, the three summations consumed most of the day. All noted the gross inconsistencies in testimony. Seldom, in all likelihood, had so many persons in a court of law lied so brazenly and with such apparent conviction. A witness for the defense, at the outset of her testimony, was seen to kiss her thumb rather than the Bible, only to have the oath administered a second time. "One or the other must speak false," observed Bowes of the two camps; "which of them have done so, God only knows." And, as a consequence, all three justices attached great weight to the known circumstances of the case—particulars that had emerged from the legal crossfire largely intact.

According to the common law, circumstantial evidence, in the absence of "positive proof," was both a proper and necessary substitute as long as it led to a "violent" (extremely strong) "presumption" as to the act in question. "Light, or rash, presumptions," William Blackstone later wrote, "have no weight or validity at all."

One of the circumstances, in Bowes's view, favoring the defense was the seeming ignorance of James's birth among the distant relations of Lord and Lady Altham. On the other hand, Bowes laid great stress upon the youth's kidnapping, adding, however, that

Anglesea may have acted merely to avoid the "trouble he might have from this lad," notwithstanding his illegitimate birth. For Mountney, however, both the prosecution and the kidnapping created a *violenta presumptio* that Annesley was his father's lawful heir. Addressing the jury directly, the baron declared, "Witnesses, gentlemen, may either be mistaken themselves, or wickedly intend to deceive others. God knows, we have seen too much of this in the present case on both sides! But circumstances, gentlemen, and presumptions, naturally and necessarily arising out of a given fact, cannot lie." In sharp contrast, Dawson stressed the implausibility of Annesley's legitimacy, owing to witnesses able to contradict his birth at Dunmain. "You will consider," the baron told the jury, "how far the transportation [to America] will make you give credit to a fact you should otherwise think improbable."[41]

The trial was the longest ever known in the British Isles. For twelve days, the jury had listened to testimony and diligently taken notes. They had been sequestered from family and friends, with the injunction to ignore anything that might be heard outside the courtroom. At long last, with the summations completed, the case was the jurors' to decide as they withdrew to a nearby chamber late that afternoon.

As if on cue, Dublin's weather had dramatically improved by the final week of November, reverting to the welcome warmth of summer, with a gentle breeze from the south and southwest. At 5 p.m., in less than thirty minutes, the jury had its verdict.

"Hear ye, hear ye," proclaimed the clerk. "Gentlemen, which do you find, for the plaintiff or the defendant?"

"We find for the plaintiff," announced the foreman.

That evening, as the Earl of Anglesea prepared to leave Dublin in disgrace, church bells pealed and bonfires lit up the streets. So quickly had word of the verdict spread, a newspaper reported, "all the streets seem'd to be in a blaze."[42]

8

EQUITY

He that goes to law holds a wolf by the ears.
English proverb, 1600s[1]

News of the stunning verdict traveled in all directions. For two weeks, newspapers on both sides of the Irish Sea had struggled to keep readers abreast of the trial's progress. Word reached London by express rider in just five days. At long last, a paper announced, the "great cause" had been decided in favor of the "Hon. Mr. Annesley." In Westminster, a genteel delegation congratulated James's wife at her house on Millbank Road. Outside, a crowd gathered in the street around barrels of beer as the bells of St. Margaret's rang in celebration. Meanwhile, publishers in London and Dublin awaited transcripts of the proceedings to print for an eager public.[2]

In the afterglow of the trial, all of Dublin seemed to delight in the outcome. "Never was there so universal joy," wrote a resident. "A verdict," reported Viscount Perceval, "much to the satisfaction of almost everybody who is not affected by it." More bluntspoken was the Dublin lawyer Richard Tighe, who reported to Lord Orrery that the jury had "smelt the rat," not believing that Anglesea would have taken such "pains about a bastard." When the Dublin Music Society honored James at an evening gathering, six hundred people attended to catch a glimpse.[3]

The verdict could only have brought Annesley a deep sense of vindication. Suddenly, the end of his ordeal, so long in coming, appeared at hand. According to a newspaper report, he gave Mackercher a deed of gift for £2,000 per annum, but the Scot declined the present. It was around the same time that Annesley sat for an oil portrait, which was reproduced by the prominent engraver John Brooks, whose past subjects included Chief Baron Bowes and William Aldrich, the lord mayor of Dublin. Bearing the caption *Veritas Praevalebit* (Truth Will Prevail), the mezzotint engraving depicts a mature young man clad in genteel attire, looking none the worse for his tribulations. The face exhibits a mood of confidence and resolution. Crowned by a broad forehead and a periwig, the eyes frame a sharp nose, with a fashionable cravat wrapped about the neck. The portrait bears a passing resemblance to an early likeness of James's paternal great-grandfather, the first Earl of Anglesea.[4]

Predictions circulated that Annesley would soon be seated in the House of Lords, in Dublin if not at first in Westminster. The *Daily Post* of London reported on December 17 that a writ of summons to the Irish Lords had been newly approved. Lending credence to such rumors, Annesley had by then met at Dublin Castle with Devonshire, Ireland's lord lieutenant, to discuss petitioning the king for the Irish titles of Viscount Valentia, Baron Mountnorris, and Baron Altham. About the same time, Bowes requested a visit, later finding James "a very sensible young man" in spite of his "low education." Even Charles Annesley, who had footed a portion of his cousin's legal expenses, briefly considered negotiating a separate peace with the claimant. Of the verdict, Anglesea's sister, Lady Haversham, feared, "It must necessarily have a very great influence on all future questions at law."[5]

Considering Annesley's compelling saga, the magnitude of his popular support in Ireland and England is not surprising. As the *London Evening Post* later observed, "The case of Mr. Annesley does, indeed, contain every thing that can excite the curiosity, as well as compassion of the public." For ordinary folk in Ireland, especially Catholics able to empathize with James's persecution, his uncle's disgrace may have given vent to pent-up animosity toward the established order. More remarkable was Annesley's embrace by much of the upper class, notwithstanding the threat that his lawsuit posed to property holders. As defense counselors had warned, the trial might encourage like-minded litigants to file lawsuits, whether or not their claims, or their births, were legitimate.[6]

But the Earl of Anglesea had a scandalous reputation, which the trial's dramatic disclosures exacerbated. In the eyes of Lord Mount Alexander, the earl was "the greatest rogue in Europe." According to Devonshire, "There is scarce any one here (at least amongst those I see or hear of) but thinks the jury have gained great reputation by their behaviour." It was said that other peers, after the trial, turned their backs when Richard entered the small, ornate chamber of the House of Lords, graced by a tapestry of the Battle of the Boyne. "If it was for his vices," he reportedly exclaimed, "they were too late. If for his misfortunes, they were too early."[7]

Not long before, Annesley's cause would have stood little chance of success, owing to a court system in which influence-peddling, judicial favoritism, and jury-packing were endemic. Indeed, the verdict appears to have taken English officials aback. Lord Duncannon, Devonshire's private secretary, reported from London, "The verdict being given for the plaintiff has occasioned great surprise in this place." In 1726, Archbishop King had complained of "corruption" that "spread from the High Court of Chancery to the petty guilds." In part, its decline resulted from a drive by the Irish government in the 1730s to reduce the influence of "persons of great rank" in judicial proceedings. By the following decade, the campaign even enjoyed the growing support of many landed magnates.[8]

For no less important was the changing character of the Protestant Ascendancy itself. During the middle decades of the eighteenth century, the manners of the Irish elite underwent a profound reformation. Along with grander homes, civic improvements, and intellectual circles like the Dublin Society emerged new standards of behavior among men anxious to buttress their cultural and political legitimacy, in England no less than in Ireland. Then, too, a greater sense of civic responsibility may have arisen from the horrific death toll in 1740 and 1741 resulting from the "Great Frost" followed by famine and the "Year of the Slaughter" (*Bliadhan an Áir*). In a typical display of magnanimity, jurors at the conclusion of Annesley's trial donated their daily stipends to a local infirmary for the poor.[9]

Sharp practices and hard usage were more apt to face condemnation, and despite the persistence of dueling, there was less tolerance of violence. Lord Santry, on being tried in 1739 for the murder of a commoner, was convicted by a jury of Irish peers. Although the beneficiary of a royal pardon, he was ostracized by close friends. Lord Orrery, once a harsh critic of the Irish, informed an English acquaintance in 1747, "I have known this kingdom fifteen years. More improvements than I have visibly observed of all kinds could not have been effected in that space of time," adding that "politeness is making some progress" and that "literature is close behind her."[10]

Richard's misconduct, in this changing climate, served as an embarrassing reminder of a recent time when aristocratic crimes occasionally escaped punishment by higher courts. That he was personally disliked only made it easier for the upper class to reaffirm its devotion to the rule of law by championing his nephew's cause.

Still, there were limits to the spirit of reform. Moved to action by accounts of Annesley's kidnapping, the Irish House of Commons drafted a legislative proposal in December 1743 "for better securing the liberty of the subject, and for the prevention of imprisonment beyond the seas." Following the addition of several amendments, the draft, extending the right of *habeas corpus*, was passed and ordered sent to the lord lieutenant and the Irish Privy Council for review before transmission to Westminster. (By virtue of Poynings's Law, established in 1494 at the behest of the lord deputy of Ireland, legislation could advance through Parliament only after preliminary approval by the English Privy Council.) But the proposed bill never left Dublin, as it was rejected by the administration and with it any chance that the government might crack down on kidnapping that session. In addition to having a longstanding antipathy to legislation that broadened the bounds of *habeas corpus*, Dublin authorities feared that the bill could potentially protect persons charged with treason in Ireland from facing trial in England. More successful, by contrast, was a bill the same session to expedite the transportation of felons and vagabonds to America. On learning that shipmasters had occasionally unloaded their cargoes elsewhere in Ireland or in Europe, Parliament, with the king's consent, made that offense punishable by death.[11]

Seven weeks after the trial, James and his uncle each traveled to New Ross in an attempt to consolidate popular support in advance of further litigation. Richard arrived first, in mid-January. According to a partisan letter in the *Dublin Journal*, "one hundred and fifty gentlemen and inhabitants of the town" received him, as ships in the Barrow saluted his arrival with cannonfire. On Sunday, he attended church before dining with a large body of wellwishers, who escorted him from town the next day on his return to Camolin Park. In contrast, a subsequent letter, published in London, disputed the generosity of the town's reception. "There is not one word of truth [in the first report] from beginning to end, notwithstanding the great pains taken with the populace of that place by an all-powerful faction in that county to have him well received."[12]

In all likelihood, both accounts were exaggerated. Whatever the exact truth, it would be surprising if Anglesea no longer enjoyed the backing of a portion of the population, if not out of loyalty than out of self-interest, especially among his tenants.

Less mixed were reports of Annesley's own trip, a victory lap that commenced in Dublin. On January 12, having passed through villages aglow with bonfires, he and a retinue of more than fifty gentlemen and servants arrived in Naas, where they found the streets thronged with supporters. In New Ross—two days after the earl's departure—another large crowd met James two miles from town with garlands and streamers. Amid the pageantry, guns were dragged from ships in the river to heights overlooking the town and reportedly fired in celebration (it seems a fair surmise that some townspeople, hedging their bets, attended both homecomings).[13]

Following his meeting with the lord lieutenant, Annesley had already sent separate petitions to His Majesty King George II requesting his Irish and English titles. Both appeals, after tracing his lineage, recounted his uncle's treachery and the recent verdict at court. On the advice of the lord high chancellor of England, the petitions would be referred to the attorneys-general of Ireland and England for review. Only on receipt of their reports would the king transmit the petitions to the House of Lords of each kingdom for formal consideration. "This will in all probability be a very tedious affair," forecast Lord Duncannon.[14]

In Dublin, matters at first moved quickly. By December 21, Devonshire had received the king's blessing to transmit Annesley's petition to the attorney-general, which he did the next day, also sending it to the solicitor-general and the prime serjeant. All three, of course, had represented the earl at the Court of Exchequer, for which reason, perhaps, they declined to give an opinion other than urge a thorough investigation by the House of Lords.[15]

The officers' joint report, in spite of its brevity, did not reach Devonshire's hands for three weeks. By the time the King had received the document and then returned it to Dublin Castle a second time, the House was about to adjourn, with Devonshire set to leave for England. The officers' dilatory counsel dealt a mortal blow to Annesley's hopes for a quick resolution of his Irish titles. Not for another eighteen months, until the lord lieutenant's return to Ireland, were the Lords due to reconvene. From Devonshire's perspective, the postponement was welcome. Not only could he return home as scheduled—no small thing for a lord lieutenant from England—but the delay would permit the House of Lords in London to rule on Annesley's English titles first— a "more prudent" course, Duncannon had advised Devonshire in late December.[16]

Just as worrisome for James, on the heels of the Exchequer verdict in November, Richard's lawyers had requested a writ of error requiring the court to reconsider the jury's verdict. Until its judgment, the verdict was stayed and James was prevented from claiming his lands or rents in County Meath.[17]

Stymied suddenly in Ireland, Annesley and Mackercher returned in March to London. There, in a remarkable twist of fate, James, a former indentured servant and a runaway at that, received an audience with King George, whose curiosity had doubtless been piqued by the trial's notoriety (as to what, if anything, was said, there is no existing account). Still expected was a report from the attorney-general, Sir Dudley Ryder, who, as a rule, preferred to "keep out of all scrapes, all enmities," as he wrote in his diary. A fresh petition filed by Francis Annesley, urging a new trial in County Wexford to determine the merits of James's claim, may have been all that was necessary to convince Ryder, whom Anglesea had formerly retained as a lawyer in the suit against his cousin Charles, to delay his review.[18]

And then there was the matter of the letters. In still another blow, Francis that spring produced a small bundle of receipts, legal documents, and correspondence, supposedly unearthed among the papers of the late Duke of Buckingham. Included in the cache were four letters sent to the duke between July 11, 1715, and December 2, 1718. The first three, written by Lord Altham, dealt with his growing indebtedness, while the last, from his wife, described her own financial plight following their separation. Not one of the letters, ranging in length from a few lines to a single page of writing, contained any mention of a son, as Anglesea's partisans were quick to point out. In London, William Murray, the future Earl of Mansfield, weighed in as solicitor-general. Like Ryder, his close confidant, Murray had previously represented the earl against his cousin. The letters, he pronounced, "plainly proved the claimant to be an impostor." Backers of James countered that the single letter from Mary, if authentic, represented a tiny fraction of her regular correspondence with her father and stepmother, which otherwise seems to have disappeared (not even the four "original" letters exist today, just copies). As for Altham's correspondence with Buckingham, it contained few domestic details of any sort.[19]

None of these setbacks, however frustrating, affected Annesley's suit in London at the Court of Chancery, which was designed to recover all of his rightful estates in Ireland, England, and Wales—a full-bore attack whose outcome, he and his supporters hoped, would benefit from the earlier victory at the Court of Exchequer. In answer to James's original complaint of July 1743, lawyers for the earl had responded that fall, denying there was any "legal issue" of the late Baron Altham. Nor, according to their response, had James been spirited to America against his will but had instead voluntarily indentured himself as a servant.[20]

Despite Chancery's origins as a pragmatic alternative to common law courts, equity proceedings were typically protracted. The volume of litigation by the eighteenth century was staggering. During the yearly term in 1734–35, for example, 3,240 new suits were filed, adding to an existing logjam of 4,840. Charged with shepherding cases through the judicial maze was a small army of clerks. In the end, however, suits could only be heard by the lord chancellor or, in his absence, the master of the rolls, neither of whom were full-time judges. The court's yearly calendar was restricted to four terms and to certain days of the week. In 1706, the legal reformer John Sparke bitterly complained that many suits "have been depending, some ten, others twenty, and others almost thirty years."[21]

Quickly it became clear that Anglesea's goal at Chancery was to stall the proceedings, long enough at least to exhaust his nephew's modest funds. Virtually every action required the payment of steadily rising fees—in addition, of course, to the increasingly burdensome expense of legal counsel. From the late 1600s to the mid-eighteenth century, the cost of going to court in London doubled. Woe to litigants with limited resources. With the support of his cousins, Richard could afford to exploit arcane technicalities in the law by blanketing the court with repeated motions. "Injunctions upon injunctions," a critic later groused. The lone consolation was that the court denied Anglesea as well as James rents from the disputed estates in Meath.[22]

Annesley had two tenuous sources of income to defray costs: Mackercher's dwindling fortune and donations from supporters, stirred by the cause's spreading fame. Such notoriety would have been inconceivable at the start of the century when news circulated less freely, confined, for the most part, to a narrow national elite. The ensuing years witnessed not only the rapid expansion of newspapers and periodicals but also a growing number of meeting places for discussions of public affairs. London by 1739 contained more than five hundred coffeehouses and nearly as many taverns. "All Englishmen are great newsmongers," observed a Swiss visitor.[23]

Annesley's struggle received increased attention from a variety of sympathetic publications, including numerous editions in London and Dublin of *Memoirs of an Unfortunate Young Nobleman* . . . , which concluded its colorful account of his life just short of the Exchequer trial. Costing three shillings, the book had first appeared on Fleet Street in February 1743, shortly before the *Gentleman's Magazine* began to serialize an abridged edition. Curiously, Annesley and Mackercher took out a notice in a London newspaper alleging that the book's misrepresentations were designed to harm James's legal prospects, presumably by undermining the credibility of its factual contents, of which, wittingly or not, he had been the source. Annesley also likely resented losing the opportunity to first tell the story of his ordeal in his own words, an exercise that might have proven both cathartic and remunerative.[24]

Equally partisan, and cast in religious verse, was *The Book of the Chronicle of James* . . . (1743), which appeared in London shortly after the Exchequer verdict. *A Letter to a Nobleman in the Country* . . . (1744) offered a more straightforward account of James's tribulations. Of his uncle, the author of *Altamira's Ghost* . . . (1744) railed, "Then foul Impostor, howl, despair, / The mock of friends below; / When plung'd in never-ending pain, / and ever'living woe." In sum, whether by design or chance, no print medium was neglected, including broadsides intended for mass consumption. Not a single publication, by contrast, appeared in Anglesea's support.

Widely available, too, in Dublin, London, and Reading were competing trial transcripts that went through multiple reprintings. An abridged transcript appeared in Newcastle-upon-Tyne, while newspapers as far away as Bristol, Salisbury, and Sherborne serialized the proceedings, as did London papers and the *Gentleman's Magazine*.[25]

Annesley's spreading fame also brought forth new witnesses. Already in September 1743, even before the trial, commissioners appointed by the Court of Chancery had begun to depose his supporters in Dublin. In a brash maneuver to delay the hearings, another year passed before Anglesea permitted the examination of

*The Hon^th^ James Annesley Esqr*

George Bickman the Younger, *James Annesley*, ca. 1744. It is not known whether Annesley posed for this portrait, which appeared in one of the published Exchequer trial transcripts. Note the ship to the left, with an infant held aloft in a stern window, and to the right an American scene replete with a palm tree, a half-naked youth with a horn, a pack of hounds, and a pair of beavers.

his own witnesses. Later, the earl's opponents also alleged a darker purpose. In advance of the trial, Richard's agents, complained a critic, "had an opportunity of knowing the whole of Mr. Annesley's plea before the evidence of their own witnesses was fixed by any previous examination."[26]

Over the course of two years, commissioners in Ireland took upward of four hundred statements. Many added new details, while others dovetailed with testimony at the Court of Exchequer. A clear majority of the affidavits favored the young claimant. Outside the capital, numerous interviews occurred in County Wexford, not only in New Ross and Wexford but in smaller communities like Taghmon, Ryland, and Tintern. An extensive list

Chancery Deposition of Ellen Murphy, March
10, 1744. A laundry-maid at Dunmain,
Murphy, both in the above deposition
and during the trial in 1743 at the Court
of Exchequer, was one of two people who
testified to having witnessed Annesley's birth
in 1715.

of questions steered the inquiries, the answers to which clerks
recorded on sheets of parchment for the court.[27]

What by outward appearances was an orderly process belied
a ferocious campaign to influence deponents. With partisans
on both sides eager for an advantage, allegations of influence-
peddling should not surprise us. "Bribery can split a stone,"

declared an Irish proverb. Mackercher, for one, was accused of suborning the deponent Rutherford Green, who for some time had been in "very wretched and necessitous circumstances." The allegation, however, appeared less credible coming, as it did, from Green's brother, himself an inmate of the Marshalsea Debtors' prison in Dublin.[28]

Only Richard commanded the wealth or power to systematically court—or coerce—witnesses, especially in Wexford. Although law enforcement in the provinces had long fallen prey to aristocratic influence, Anglesea's followers went to uncommon lengths. Warnings were blunt: one's home might be pulled down or, worse, a family ejected from its farm. In the town of Wexford, the county seat and an Anglesea stronghold, the earl brought an ejectment suit against Thomas Cole, whose wife had testified in Dublin for his nephew. The widow Anne Moore, whose father had attended the christening of James Annesley, was told by the earl's partisans that "they would sweep the kennel" with her.[29]

Not surprisingly, deponents in County Wexford chose locations at which to give their statements with care. Witnesses favorable to young Annesley testified in places beyond his uncle's control, including Dunmain, where Chancery commissioners examined twenty-seven persons, from elderly widows to gentleman farmers. A handful were tradesmen, including a carpenter, a blacksmith, and a staymaker. By contrast, twenty-five of Anglesea's backers testified next door in New Ross, where seventeen resided, probably as the earl's tenants. They, too, represented a mix of occupations, though most appear to have been better off. At the end of their statements, all but one of the New Ross deponents were able to sign their names, whereas just over half of the deponents at Dunmain signed with a mark.[30]

In the midst of what had become a daunting and protracted struggle on all fronts, the assize court in County Kildare prepared to try

Anglesea in August 1744 for the attack at the Curragh the previous September. James and Daniel Mackercher returned to Dublin in July, to be welcomed by bonfires and pealing bells. With little good news in recent months, the trial offered a possible change in fortune. Also charged were five of Anglesea's companions, including Francis Annesley of Ballysax, Michael Lacy, and Angus Byrne. Drawn by the county grand jury, the indictments were wide-ranging, encompassing incidents both on and off the racecourse. Thrown out, on the other hand, were the charges originally preferred by the earl against members of James's party.[31]

All six defendants were indicted for assault, a misdemeanor involving the threat or infliction of personal injury. Given the violence of the age, courts frequently treated physical altercations as civil disputes between private parties.[32] That Anglesea and his retainers were tried at all, much less by an assize court—normally restricted to hearing provincial felonies and serious misdemeanors—testified to the earl's notoriety as well as to the site of the ruckus. Noblemen, after all, were not expected to behave like commoners, at least not in public.

The assize court normally alternated between the rival towns of Athy, in the south of County Kildare, and Naas in the north. The more centrally situated town of Kildare was said to lack accommodations for the large numbers that attended sessions, if not for the trials than for the heavy press of administrative business dispensed by justices, from setting local taxes to awarding contracts for public improvements. Sessions also gave rise to markets and fairs, significant attractions in their own right.[33]

The county was but one location on the Leinster circuit. Comprising seven counties in all, the circuit was traveled twice each year, during Lent and summer, by judges from Dublin and senior barristers acting as deputies, accompanied by an entourage of servants and clerks. In a festive ceremony, full of pomp and tradition, local notables typically greeted judges upon their arrival, and entertained them to a lavish dinner. Both of the justices assigned to Anglesea's trial were veterans of the Exchequer contest, Lord Mountney and St. George Caulfeild, the attorney-general.[34]

Commencing at eleven o'clock on the morning of July 3, the trial lasted more than twelve hours. For the prosecution, Mackercher related the chain of events in painstaking detail, followed by corroborating testimony from Hugh Kennedy, William Goostry, and others in the party that traveled to Naas on the last day. In a surprising turn, the final prosecution witness was Angus Byrne, who had already pleaded guilty to four counts of assault. The faint-hearted assassin described Anglesea's conspiracy at length. Lacy, who had accompanied Byrne on the Naas Road, failed to appear despite a warrant for his arrest.[35]

Just one of the defendants, Francis Annesley of Ballysax, testified for the defense, which called three other witnesses, none of whom undermined the prosecution's case. Neile O'Neile, a surgeon from Naas, was contradicted by Richard's own lawyer. Worse, after he blamed the row on Mackercher's provocative behavior, O'Neile was abruptly challenged by the jury foreman, John Digby.

"Did you meet me coming home on the road that day?" asked Digby.

"Yes, Sir, I believe I did. I cannot recollect."

"Did you say anything to me?"

"I cannot say I did."

"Did not you express concern to me at the treatment Mr. Mackercher and Mr. Annesley had received?"

"I do not remember that I did."

At the conclusion of the trial, O'Neile would be charged with perjury, and was later convicted and pilloried for the crime.

Little better was the testimony of the dancing master Patrick Cavenagh. After alleging that Mackercher had made a threatening gesture toward Anglesea with the butt of a whip, he could not recall the type of whip or its length. The final witness,

Dennis Tynan, was thought so compromised by his participation in Annesley's prior prosecution at the Old Bailey that the defense retracted his testimony.[36]

In the end, the court found the defendants guilty of assault, for which each was fined, with the largest sum, in excess of £30, imposed upon the earl. "My Lord," reprimanded Baron Mountney, "your quality . . . greatly aggravates the offence," adding that "a number of people there by your lordship's example, might . . . [have been] led to take part on the one side or the other; and if they had done so, it is to be feared that there might have been more fatal consequences."[37]

The fines, though modest, far exceeded those normally imposed for assault. More important, the trial afforded additional evidence of Richard's visceral hatred of his nephew, all amply documented in transcripts published later that year in London and Dublin. When the court asked Mackercher whether he intended to sue for damages, he replied no. "We prosecute," he explained, "for public justice, for the safety of our own and Mr. Annesley's life."[38]

There was scant time to savor the moment. In the first flush of joy, Annesley and Mackercher already looked forward to another contest, their prosecution of Mary Heath for perjured testimony at the Court of Exchequer. Not that others had not forsworn themselves; but Heath, as the defense's prime witness, offered an inviting target, not least for her betrayal of James and his late mother. Perjury, under the common law, was a grievous offense, often punishable, as a felony, by either transportation or incarceration. At issue was her emphatic denial that Lady Altham had been pregnant, much less borne a child. With little progress yet in London or Dublin, a conviction would lend added credence to Annesley's legitimacy. So strong did the prosecution evidence appear that the odds in coffeehouses reportedly ran twenty to one in favor of an adverse verdict. Anglesea himself might even be indicted for suborning Heath, or so his opponents hoped.[39]

First, Annesley and Mackercher returned briefly to County Wexford for a third visit, hoping to rally supporters in advance of the imminent arrival of Chancery commissioners. Met by a large troop of horseman six miles north of New Ross, Annesley's party was engulfed by a surging crowd as they prepared to enter the town. Amid bonfires, garlands, and music, they were entertained on the road to Dunmain by one hundred couples, performing in two lines facing one another the long dance, or *rinnce fada*. That evening, in surrounding villages, fires blazed in celebration.[40]

Mary Heath's trial was scheduled for October in County Dublin, but in a surprising maneuver it was moved by a writ of certiorari to the Court of King's Bench with the approval of the chief justice, Thomas Marlay. Although originally designed to transfer egregious cases to the court, the writ was increasingly abused by the early 1700s as a ploy to postpone proceedings and pile up prosecution costs.[41]

Lying just across the hall from the Court of Exchequer, King's Bench was Ireland's superior criminal court. With the trial reset for November, Heath, at the last minute, received a continuance until February, stranding numerous witnesses from England at great expense to the prosecution.[42]

Critics later alleged that Marlay's financial ties to Anglesea rendered King's Bench an improper venue. By one account, he stood to lose six to seven thousand pounds should Annesley, in the end, acquire the earl's estates. Moreover, Marlay's son, Anthony, had served among Richard's lawyers during the Exchequer trial and now represented Heath as a senior counselor. An Irish native who had sat in the Commons for County Longford, the judge was no stranger to political infighting on or off the bench, having been chief baron of the Exchequer before his selection in 1741 as chief justice. More often than not, judicial appointments, as in his case, were made on the basis of political service rather than legal expertise; and despite Dublin's changing legal culture, judicial abuses involving conflicts of interest still occurred. At best, the chief justice blithely skirted the common law rule barring any man from "acting as a judge in his own case." Marlay, at sixty-seven years of age, was joined by two associate judges, Michael Ward, a native of County Down, and Arthur Blennerhassett from County Kerry.[43]

Even before the trial got underway, tempers flared as the court assembled on an icy morning early in February. A key witness named Sarah Weedon, the prosecution alleged, had been abducted by the defense; and with Daniel Mackercher and still other witnesses delayed on the Welsh coast by contrary winds, there were ample grounds for a continuance until spring. Citing the inconvenience to the defense, Marlay not only denied the request, but seized on the occasion to condemn the conduct of Annesley's lawyers fifteen months earlier at the Court of Exchequer. "Jugglers cannot play so well the same trick twice," he warned. Just as alarming, the original panel of jurors contained the names of men long dead and others too infirm to attend court, leaving only a small pool from which to select a total of twelve. At least several were known partisans of the earl. The court also forbade any mention of Anglesea's past malice toward his nephew, leaving the jury, in assessing Heath's veracity, to choose between the testimony of witnesses with dramatically different recollections of Annesley's childhood.[44]

Those testifying for the prosecution provoked a chorus of objections from both the defense and members of the bench, who grew increasingly annoyed. "I never heard that there was safety in a multitude of witnesses," snapped Marlay, who found their quality equally objectionable, declaring, "If you have any person of undoubted credit, in the name of God produce him." The jury also appeared anxious to expedite the proceedings, declining, when asked, to pause for refreshment.[45]

In all, the court heard twenty-five witnesses for the prosecution, including Dr. Samuel Jemmat, who only recently had stepped forward on learning of Annesley's cause. A former president of the Royal College of Physicians in Dublin, he had examined Lady Altham during her pregnancy toward the end of 1714, as had a midwife, Hellena Moncrieffe. "Upon the word of a Christian," Moncrieffe swore, "both by the judgment that I have had since and before, my lady Altham was as much with child as ever I was, and I have had 21 children."[46]

The defense, in turn, produced fifteen witnesses, equally emphatic in support of Heath's veracity, followed soon afterward by the judges' summations. These sounded a common refrain. In any trial for perjury, insisted the bench, the evidence must be conclusive. "The testimony to convict any person of so great and infamous an offence ought to be so full, clear and consistent, that there can be no room to doubt the truth of what is offered to prove," prodded Marlay. Lest there be any indecision, Blenner-hassett volunteered that juries often "incline to mercy" when faced with contrary evidence of equal weight. At half past four in the morning, after conferring for twenty minutes, the jury returned its verdict: "Not guilty." The defense had carried the day.

"Heath is acquitted," declared a wag, "and Lord Chief Justice Marlay is found guilty." Reported London's *Daily Post*, "Notwithstanding the facts she was charged with were fully and clearly proved, by witnesses of undoubted credit, she was acquitted."[47]

With each new disappointment, public interest in Annesley's ordeal ebbed. No longer by the fall of 1745 were his tribulations the talk of coffeehouses and drawing rooms, either in Dublin or London. The spotlight, by then, had shifted to more momentous events. In addition to the outbreak of war with France in 1744, Scottish Jacobites had risen in rebellion a year later to claim the British monarchy for the "Young Pretender," Charles Stuart, grandson of James II. By October, his army had invaded England, eventually marching as far south as Derby before mounting a hasty retreat, only to be routed the following April at the battle of Culloden. The failed uprising, followed by trials of the rebel leaders, easily eclipsed lingering interest in Annesley's protracted legal woes, apart, perhaps, from creating an invidious association in the public mind between a pair of "pretenders."[48]

With Mackercher's wealth all but drained and public contributions reduced to a trickle, James found himself starved for money. One by one, each of his lawsuits slowed to a standstill owing to the costly and obstructive tactics of Richard's lawyers. At Chancery, despite the accumulation of several hundred examinations by the spring of 1745, the expense of proceeding to trial had become prohibitive. Contrary to fears expressed during the Exchequer trial that a verdict for Annesley would open the floodgates to a torrent of counterfeit claimants, these setbacks offered a cautionary lesson in the perils of litigation. "He that goes to law," averred an English proverb, "holds a wolf by the ears."[49]

Between Ryder's foot-dragging and Anglesea's intransigence, the outlook was not encouraging. With no report forthcoming from the attorney-general, the House of Lords could not take up the case, inhibiting, in turn, the Irish Lords from proceeding. In 1745, after first imposing a deadline of April 16 for Anglesea to respond to his nephew's petition, Ryder extended the date to May 23. By late June, the response remained overdue, nor did Richard's lawyers agree to the suggestion from opposing counsel that Ryder begin examining Annesley's evidence in order to save time. In the face of such flagrant defiance, Ryder continued to dither, and the delays continued. The earl knew his man.[50]

To compound their misfortunes, a post chaise containing Annesley and Mackercher overturned that September near Hungerford on the way from Bath to London. Though there appeared to be no evidence of foul play and neither was seriously injured, their friend, William Livingstone, was suspicious enough to notify the under-secretary of state, Andrew Stone, before setting out to inspect the mishap.[51]

It was not long afterward that one of Annesley's oldest supporters hatched a plan to betray him. Little is known of the plot, though Tobias Smollett later included some of the details in his novel *The Adventures of Peregrine Pickle* (1751). In Smollett's rendering, the traitor was William Goostry, who, despite his savage beating at the Curragh, evidently recognized a losing cause. On meeting with an agent for the earl, he volunteered to trick Annesley into signing a deed designed to forfeit any claim to Richard's titles and estates. In return, Goostry demanded of Anglesea a bond for £6,000 and an annuity of £700.[52]

Whether or not Smollett's version of the story was true to the details, clearly something was up, to judge from a curious letter sent to the earl in August 1746 by one of his retainers, Stephen Hay, who had been his tutor in French years earlier. Anglesea had recently returned to his Bray estate from England, and Hay had himself just arrived in Ireland from London. From Dublin, he reported, "I have brought over from them ["Mackercher's party"] a person who could be of the greatest use to them, . . . and the man is actually here and, if he informs me right, can be of very great service to your Lordship if there should be any occasion for him."[53]

But that was not all. The scheme's success, according to Smollett, ultimately depended upon poisoning James's friendship with Mackercher, his stalwart champion. Somehow, Goostry succeeded in convincing Annesley that the Scot, seeking to recoup his lost fortune, intended to file a lawsuit that would ensure James's incarceration in a debtor's prison for the remainder of his life. Mackercher, for his perfidy, was to be generously rewarded by Anglesea himself.[54]

Persuaded that he might soon be arrested, Annesley in November of 1747 brought suit in London at the Court of Chancery against his friend, alleging an illicit "combination" between Mackercher and "other persons at present unknown." "All which actings and doings of the said Daniel Mackercher and his confederates," asserted the complaint, "are contrary to right, equity, and good conscience."[55]

Mackercher learned of Goostry's intrigue just in time to bring James to his senses and foil his uncle's plot.[56] But the betrayal had to have been deeply demoralizing to Annesley's thinning ranks, all the more because Goostry had courageously come to his aid when he had been threatened on the Naas Road. Not since his kidnapping twenty years earlier had James's prospects seemed bleaker.

Even favorable news was at best mixed. In 1743, Constantine Phipps, a latecomer to the family fracas over the estate of Arthur, fifth Earl of Anglesea, had reignited the controversy. On attaining the age of majority, he brought suit against Richard, claiming a direct line of descent from his grandfather James, the third earl. Had it succeeded, the suit would have abrogated all previous claims to Arthur's titles and property—"no less than the whole Anglesea estate," reported a London newspaper. But in June 1749, the Court of Exchequer in Dublin dismissed Phipps's suit, preserving, as a consequence, Richard's inheritance and, with it, his nephew's hopes, however forlorn they may have been. Less encouraging was word that Anglesea's triumphant lawyers included Sir Dudley Ryder, the attorney-general.[57]

9

RESURRECTION

The great cause which has been so many years depending
between Lord Anglesey and Mr. Annesley is likely very
shortly to be finally determined!
Whitehall Evening Post or London Intelligencer,
December 13, 1759[1]

Patience was not in Anglesea's nature. Even when it served his interest, he was not one to mark time.

Among the ruffians Richard had enlisted in the past was Thomas Stanley, who in early 1742 had stalked Annesley outside the London home of Daniel Mackercher. Two years later, Stanley was arrested for participating in their attempted shooting in Dublin just days before the Curragh races. Assisted by six lawyers, he escaped conviction at a Court of Oyer and Terminer when one of the jurors appeared to suffer an epileptic seizure, resulting in a mistrial. So it was not altogether surprising when Stanley was apprehended yet again, on a winter evening in 1750, while lying in wait for James in a London street. Taken before Henry Fielding, the famed magistrate and novelist, he was remanded under heavy guard to Newgate prison.[2]

In truth, Anglesea, at fifty-seven years of age, had much to be thankful for. Gone were the vexations of recent years, especially his nephew's worrisome lawsuits. With judicial proceedings crippled for want of funds and Ryder's continued inaction, a resolution in either kingdom seemed, at most, a distant prospect. Then, also, upon the death of his cousin Francis in 1750, Richard became the undisputed head of the house of Annesley. His cousin Charles had died three years earlier, bringing an end, ever since 1742, to the sequestration of Richard's income.[3] If, in the past, both men had lent the earl timely support, there had always been a blunt realism to their assistance. Now, with their deaths, no longer did a danger exist that one or the other might break ranks to side with his nephew.

And, at long last, the earl and his wife could publicly acknowledge their marriage. For nine years, Juliana had masqueraded at Camolin Park as Anglesea's mistress, all but ignored by respectable women in the neighborhood and never permitted to use the family name, much less claim the title of countess. Once, when required to sign her maiden name to a legal document, she had broken down in tears, fearing that it might one day be used to contest the legacies of her children. By then, she had given birth to three daughters and a son, all of whom were considered illegitimate.[4]

In the wake of Francis's death, Richard shared the details of his marriage with close confidants. Then, in the fall of 1752, at the strong suggestion of his lawyers, he and Juliana invited several acquaintances to dinner at Camolin Park. It was an odd tableau, to be sure. Before Lawrence Neil, the same English clergyman who had married them in 1741, the couple produced their original marriage certificate and repeated their vows. Once the sparse crowd had been informed of the first wedding, no explanation was offered for the second, other than the earl's desire that their union be made public.[5]

In later years, the couple followed a secluded life, occasionally receiving small parties of friends. They rarely traveled, even to Dublin, much less abroad to England. Anglesea last attended the Irish House of Lords in January of 1746, though by then his presence had already suffered in the wake of the Exchequer trial. Intermittent bouts of gout kept him away, but, more important, he had become a social pariah outside County Wexford. Except for a handful of connections in the capital, his circle of friends had steadily shrunk. In 1753, during a fierce election in Wexford for a seat in the House of Commons, not only did the earl play a limited role—bribing at least one voter—but the victory of his favorite was overturned by a House committee.[6]

Hours with his family, for the first time, exerted greater appeal. In Julie, as he called her, Richard seems at last to have met his match. Twenty-eight years his junior, she was both bright and strong-willed, and could not be easily cowed. Over the years, he had grown increasingly dependent upon her companionship. "He could not bear the thought of being separated from her," an acquaintance acknowledged.[7]

Besides their own children, the earl had fathered five others: three daughters by Ann Simpson, his second wife (Dorothea, Caroline, and Elizabeth); a son, Richard, born to Ann Salkeld, a London mistress; and a daughter, Ann, the product of a subsequent London liaison in the early 1740s. "Was there a country in the world that did not teem with his progeny?" a lawyer later scoffed.[8]

Abandoning their mothers, Anglesea barely maintained contact with any of the five save for Richard Salkeld ("Yellow Dick"), who resided at Camolin Park before being boarded at a school on the outskirts of New Ross. As a boy, he had often scuffled with his half-brother Arthur, who once drew a knife before the two could be separated. Anglesea reserved the bulk of his affection for his three daughters by Juliana (Richarda, Juliana, and Catherine) and for Arthur, his presumptive heir, born in 1744. To Arthur's tutor, Richard urged that his son become a "good Latin scholar" and a "gentleman." "You might make a gentleman a lord," he observed to the tutor, "but the king himself could not always make a lord a gentleman."[9]

In the meantime, James had been dealt another blow, the death of his wife from consumption shortly before Christmas in 1749. She left behind a six-year-old daughter, Mary. Six days later, at St. Andrew's church in central London, her body was interred in the same vault that contained the remains of his mother, Lady Altham.[10]

On September 14, 1751, in Bidborough, Kent, Annesley wed a second time, taking for his bride Margaret I'Anson of New Bounds, the twenty-four-year-old daughter of the baronet Sir Thomas I'Anson, gentleman porter of the Tower of London, and the former Mary Bankes of Kingston Hall in Dorset. The marriage lessened the likelihood that James might return to Ireland anytime soon. Not only did the path to reclaiming his inheritance lie through Westminster, but Sir Thomas roundly welcomed him into the family fold, as did the Bankeses, one of Dorset's most powerful dynasties.[11]

Early in the following year, James drafted a lengthy will that was a singular testament to his resilience. For all of his recent misfortunes, he still trusted in his eventual vindication. The preamble immediately set forth his birthright as heir to Arthur, Baron Altham. Noting efforts to recover his lands and "a considerable personal estate" in Ireland and Great Britain, James named four executors: Caesar Colclough of Wexford, John Paterson, his longtime solicitor, and two uncles by marriage, John and Henry Bankes, descendants of the chief justice to Charles I.

The will made numerous bequests. Not only did Annesley provide for his bride (£1,000 per annum) and his daughter Mary (£1,000), but he also reserved £1,000 per annum for a son that might be born. Included were generous sums for members of his wife's family along with an annuity of £100 for his former mother-in-law, the widow Mary Chester.

One of the largest bequests was reserved for Daniel Mackercher,

£15,000 over and above the debts that James had incurred—
"as a return for the many obligations I lye under to him." Nor
did Annesley forget such stalwart allies as William Livingstone
(£2,000) and Hugh Kennedy (£1,000). Not named was the trai-
torous William Goostry or, for that matter, Joan Landy, his former wet-nurse who, his adversaries had long alleged, was his real
mother.

Surprisingly, the will entrusted the executors with £20,000
for the benefit of persons who had "been of any service" in the
"prosecution of my just rights," particularly those "most in need
of my benevolence." In later years, James envisioned the creation
of a second trust. To a close friend, he repeatedly expressed the
hope to "establish a fund for the relief of oppressed claimants, that
they may not suffer as I have done, but have a speedy access to
justice."[12]

No single calculation prompted the sudden revival of his legal
struggle. Besides the boost to his purse by his second marriage,
improved economic prospects in Ireland had increased the potential value of his inheritance. And not only had land rents risen
since the late 1740s, but numerous leases on Richard's estates
were due to expire in 1755. If James was ever to prevail against his
uncle, he had renewed reason to attempt to resuscitate the stalled
proceedings at Chancery.[13]

And new grounds for hope. In June 1751, the House of Lords
in London denied the appeal of Constantine Phipps in his suit
against Anglesea, clearing the way, as a newspaper noted, "for Mr.
Annesley to prosecute his right against his uncle, and his other
adversaries, which had been in a great measure suspended." Moreover, that same year, the Court of Exchequer in Dublin finally set
aside Richard's own appeal, on a writ of error, of the court's original ruling in 1743. Further opportunities for appeal lay open to
the earl, but the ruling amounted to a strong reaffirmation of support for James and his suit. The entire writ, complained the *Penny*

London Post, had been "an artful contrivance calculated merely to create vexations, expense, and delay."[14]

Buoyed by the decision, Mackercher arranged for additional Irish witnesses to travel to Bristol and thence by coach to London. Several had not yet met with Chancery commissioners, and all, despite the infirmities of health and age, were staunch in their support—none more so than Dr. Samuel Jemmat, who had testified to Lady Altham's pregnancy during Mary Heath's trial for perjury. In poor health at seventy-eight years of age, he resisted all attempts by his family to discourage the trip, hoping, as he put it, to "live to do justice," a desire that he was denied. He died on the night of his arrival in Bristol.[15]

Over the next two years, preparations advanced among Annesley and his small following, including old friends like Mackercher and William Livingstone, bolstered by the fresh assistance of his wife's father and two uncles. In 1755, James placed a newspaper advertisement cautioning prospective buyers against purchasing "parts of the disputed estate." In addition, the notice announced his determination to prosecute "his cause by all lawful means to a final issue, as soon as it shall please God to enable him."[16]

On the heels of this declaration, a new campaign to raise legal funds was begun, by reacquainting the public with the particulars of his plight. Unlike any peerage contest in the past, popular support, now more than ever, became critical to the successful restoration of Annesley's titles and estates. Already in 1751, Smollett in *Peregrine Pickle* had devoted the better part of a chapter to his struggle. The novel borrowed heavily from a lengthy tract, *An Abstract of the Case of the Honourable James Annesley, Esq.*, written the same year, in all likelihood, by Mackercher, who was a friend of the young Scottish author. "All their efforts," wrote Smollett of James's adversaries, "are bent to that one point of stifling, rather than suffering the merits of this cause to come to a fair and candid hearing." The sole issue, he bluntly asserted, was whether the unfortunate claimant "shall or shall not find money to bring this cause to a final determination." Just as pointed was an essay in the September 1755 issue of the *London Magazine*. Observing that money represented the "very life and soul of law," the author urged readers to rally to Annesley's cause. "If justice be on his side, what can be a greater merit than to contribute to his obtaining it."[17]

The ensuing year, to rekindle interest, Mackercher commissioned a sympathetic pamphlet, *The Case of the Honourable James Annesley, Esq; Humbly Offered to All Lovers of Truth and Justice*, whose anonymous author rejoiced that the suit, having "slept for so many years," should "once more revive." No radical manifesto, the tract, like previous appeals, invoked the rhetoric of injustice and oppression in defense of a young aristocrat's birthright—a "nobleman," it declared, "whose legitimacy has been proved before a court of judicature in Ireland . . . and whose wrongs call aloud for the united assistance of every friend of justice to vindicate, if ever private cause deserved a public commiseration." Noting the huge sums previously spent, a minimum of £20,000, the author estimated that £5,000 was the maximum amount needed to ensure success. "All delaying and expensive litigation, with which the other side have embarrassed the cause for so many years," he confidently asserted, "are now out of their power."[18]

Annesley's supporters established subscription funds in London and Kent, where the *Gentleman's Magazine* shortly reported contributions totaling £500 in the town of Tunbridge Wells. "Many great names," attested the article, "have appeared upon the [subscription]." About the same time, plans commenced to create a third fund at the popular resort of Bath. Better yet, Beau Nash, the city's flamboyant arbiter of fashion, lent invaluable credentials to the campaign by agreeing to manage the collection. A list for Bath, compiled in 1756, contains the names of 108 subscribers who either donated or pledged contributions totaling £1,885.5. Following Nash's own modest gift of five pounds, subscriptions

Bath Subscription List [1756]. The seventh of eight pages contains the largest sum, £1,000, pledged by Annesley's uncle by marriage, John Bankes.

flowed in from a cross-section of polite society, including the famed former actress Lavinia, Duchess of Bolton (£24); the Duchess of Norfolk (£52); and Frederick, Baron Baltimore (£10), a notorious rake. Far and away the largest offering, £1,000, was pledged by Margaret Annesley's uncle, John Bankes of Kingston Hall, a member of Parliament for Corfe Castle in Dorset. The succeeding year, John I'Anson, Annesley's brother-in-law, assured an acquaintance, "We are now going on with his cause as fast as we can."[19]

At long last, on Tuesday, November 21, 1758, the Court

In Forma Pauperis petition, Court of Chancery,
April 30, 1759.

of Chancery closed the examination of witnesses. Fifteen years
after the suit's inception, hearings would proceed on the basis
of the accumulated evidence. Just two days later, however, the
court granted Anglesea a continuance to the first day of the
Hilary term, early in the new year. The delay was followed by
the court's approval of another extension, all the while noting
that the postponement was "not to hinder the plaintiff's setting
down the cause in the meantime." Still a further delay ensued in
February.[20]

On April 30, his funds finally drained, Annesley petitioned
the master of the rolls to prosecute the suit *in forma pauperis* (in

the form of a pauper). In a feeble hand (shaking perhaps from the humiliation), he swore under oath to a net worth of less than five pounds, "his just debts being first paid, his necessary wearing apparel, and the matters in question in this cause only excepted." As a consequence, the case was allowed to proceed with normal fees waived, both by the court and by James's newly appointed counsel, Arthur Jones.[21]

The ruling was a mixed blessing, resulting in yet further postponements to allow Jones time to review a daunting pile of evidence. Finally, on November 6, the court declared that it would hear the suit in January on the "first day of causes." To this, Anglesea's counsel, the attorney-general Charles Pratt, consented, having exhausted all grounds for an additional continuance. "The great cause which has been so many years depending between Lord Anglesey and Mr. Annesley," reported a London newspaper in December, "is likely very shortly to be finally determined!"[22]

That day never came. On Friday, January 5, 1760, James Annesley died at his home on the outskirts of London in Blackheath, Kent. He was only forty-four. One of the many newspaper accounts of the death claimed that he had "suffered the plague and torture of the law, 'till at last he has fell a victim to a broken heart." Most obituaries reported instead that he had died from an attack of asthma, first contracted, according to the *London Evening Post*, while he labored as a servant in America. Annesley, stated the paper, "may be truely said to have died a victim to the avarice, inhumanity, and injustice of others." Among the tributes to "that remarkable and truly unfortunate gentleman," the *Pennsylvania Gazette* pointedly noted the long number of years that he had spent in America in "the most abject slavery." Of his legacy, a London correspondent observed, "Starting from the low and ignominious state of a slave, he laid claim to a coronet and estate, and at once engrossed the attention of the three kingdoms,

Old Churchyard, St. Margaret's, Lee, Kent, 2008, photograph by the Rev. David Gatliffe. The exact location of James Annesley's grave is unknown.

more, I believe, than any private man ever did." More than that, Annesley had achieved a broad measure of public vindication that would forever elude his uncle. Buried in St. Margaret's church-yard in nearby Lee, his gravestone read "James Annesley, Esq.," a title reserved for gentlemen of notable distinction.[23]

Annesley's executors, according to a newspaper report, intended "to lose no time in prosecuting the claim in favour of the orphan, for he has left a son." Born in October 1757, Bankes Annesley had been named after his mother's uncle John. (Margaret had also borne two daughters, Margaret in 1753 and Sophie, who died in infancy.)[24]

Not long after that news, Richard's own health, toward the end of 1760, seriously declined, tempering whatever satisfaction he received from his nephew's death. He was said to suffer from a

severe cold from having shaved his head just as autumn temperatures were beginning to dip.[25]

The season was one of the wettest in memory. On a raw day in
November, the earl, bedridden at Camolin Park, received a surprise visit from his eldest child, Dorothea Du Bois, who had been
born in 1728 to Ann Simpson. She had not seen her father for
years and now, learning of his condition, arrived to make peace.
Richard had adamantly disapproved of her marriage in 1752 to a
French musician and very likely perceived a mercenary purpose to
the visit.[26]

Dropping to her knees beside his bed, Dorothea begged for
Anglesea's blessing. Instantly he let loose a torrent of invective,
shouting all the while for his pistols. While Juliana made for
the firearms, servants dragged Dorothea from the chamber as she
vainly drew a small, silver-plated pistol in defense. Having cocked
a pistol of his own at the back of her head, the earl's eighteen-
year-old son, Arthur (Dorothea's half-brother), ordered a servant
to shoot her. "You may do it yourself, I have no mind for the gallows," replied the pantry-boy. Nor, it appears, did Arthur.[27]

So ended the visit of Richard's daughter, though not before an
ear was sliced from her horse at Arthur's bidding. Dorothea and
her two servants—one a boy, the other an elderly man—were left
to travel two miles to the village of Camolin, where they barely
escaped being jailed for the night on orders from the earl. An
aspiring writer, she memorialized the confrontation in her poem
"A True Tale," published in 1764 ("The cruel father imprecating
lay, / Disowning nature, order'd her away").[28]

During his confinement, Richard was nursed by Juliana and
their oldest daughter, both of whom spent nights in his bedchamber. He also passed long hours with the Reverend James Edkins,
who had joined the household in September both as a chaplain and
as Arthur's tutor. From the outset, Anglesea pointedly identified
Juliana as his lawful wife and his children as his "true and lawful

issue," as he would continue to emphasize over the coming months. He appeared peculiarly haunted by lingering rumors of Arthur's illegitimacy. To a friend, he insisted, "May I never enter into the kingdom of glory, but that is my son born in wedlock."[29]

As his health worsened over the winter, Richard often asked the chaplain to pray for him, expressing, we are told, great remorse. The end came on the night of February 14, 1761, St. Valentine's Day. Looking back, the Reverend Edkins observed, "I never attended any sick man that was more penitent."[30]

The site of Anglesea's grave remains unknown. In his will, he instructed that he be buried at a church in nearby Rossminoque "or any other church," an acknowledgment of the dilemma caused by his excommunication, following his third marriage, from the established Church of Ireland. Newspaper accounts of his death were few—the prominent *Dublin Journal* did not even report Richard's passing, as it had that of his nephew a year earlier.[31]

On learning in London of Anglesea's death, Daniel Mackercher immediately traveled to Buckinghamshire to take legal possession of the manor of Newport Pagnell for Annesley's son. From there, the Scot set out to seize estates in Warwick, Carmarthen, and Pembroke.[32] Before long, no shortage of newspapers, from London to Portsmouth, New Hampshire, assured readers that the "great cause" would soon be revived. What was more, young Bankes would be represented in court by Henry Wilmot, secretary to the lord chancellor of England—a lawyer "from whose skill and integrity a speedy issue may certainly be expected," wrote the *London Evening Post* in March 1762. Or so hoped "all lovers of justice," declared the paper.[33]

The final act was played out the following year. To judge from bills of mortality, November was one of London's cruelest months. Late fall was a particularly deadly time for victims of "fever," a catchall category including typhoid fever, typhus, and influenza. In Westminster, where Margaret resided with all three of James's children, Bankes, at age six, suddenly fell ill and died. "Fever" was the cause given for his death. Like his father, he was buried in the churchyard of St. Margaret's in Lee. "This youth," observed a paper, "being the last of the male line of the body of Arthur, the first earl of Anglesey." His death brought an abrupt and decisive close to a legal clash over the family's succession that had ground on for more than twenty years.[34]

Mackercher, Annesley's longtime champion, devoted most of his final years to defending the inheritance left to the nephew of a Scottish duke. The cause was eerily reminiscent of Annesley's legal struggle. After an unfavorable judgment in the Scottish Court of Session, the House of Lords in 1769 affirmed the nephew's claim on appeal—all in the course of just two years, as the young man had considerable legal resources. Three years afterward, Mackercher died at his London home in Cavendish Square at sixty-nine years of age—the man famous, noted an obituary, for spending "an ample fortune in the great cause of Mr. Annesley." The death received wide coverage in London newspapers. Never having married, he bequeathed his remaining estate to more than twenty heirs, with substantial portions left to a pair of godsons and two "ministers of the Gospel" in Fife and Dundee.[35]

Despite talk of resuming the suit at Chancery over Anglesea's property, James's widow, Margaret, lacked the heart, after her son's death, for another exhausting battle. In 1764, she lost her father and then the next year, to sickness, her daughter. That left only her stepdaughter, who eventually married the son of a merchant in the slave trade. Margaret Annesley spent her last years in a madhouse.[36]

REQUIEM

Revenge is a dish that is eaten cold.

French proverb,
nineteenth century[1]

In keeping with family tradition, Richard's death in 1761 set off a scramble for his titles and property. On the very day of his passing, his estranged second wife, Ann Simpson, and her three daughters, including Dorothea Du Bois, filed caveats asserting their interest in the earl's estate, with his widow, Juliana, following suit shortly afterward.[2]

Anglesea's will was a model of clarity. Drawn up during an attack of ill health in May 1752, it had been revised and registered seven years later. To Juliana, the sole executor, he bequeathed a jointure of £1,000 per annum and all his personal estate, estimated at £10,000. Most of the property in Ireland, England, and Wales was placed in trust for his son, Arthur. Each of Richard's daughters by Juliana was to receive several thousand pounds and a modest annuity should they marry with her approval. The earl's illegitimate son, Richard Salkeld, was given £1,000, whereas his four "natural" daughters received smaller sums, including a paltry five shillings to Dorothea ("my natural yet most unnatural daughter") because of her marriage to a "fiddler." Ann Simpson received £10 in order to "buy her mourning [garments] for the many abuses given me by her."[3]

That the will accurately reflected Anglesea's wishes was not in doubt. What gave Simpson and her daughters grounds for hope was the questionable legitimacy of Richard's third marriage. The union's legality rested, much as he had anticipated, on proving the bigamous nature of his marriage to Simpson while his first wife, Ann Prust, remained alive.

By the time of her death in 1765, Simpson had achieved scant progress at court. Stung by her father's rejection, Dorothea pursued the cause more aggressively, even petitioning the king to block Arthur's admission to the English House of Lords. At risk was not only Juliana's inheritance but also the titles due to her son. Even if Richard's marriage to Julie was legitimate, Arthur's birth, depending on the year of their union, might not have been.[4]

Meanwhile, yet another claimant had entered the sweepstakes. Following Anglesea's death, John Annesley of Ballysax, the nephew of Francis, petitioned in vain for the Irish honors of Viscount Valentia, Baron Mountnorris, and Baron Altham, disputing Richard's marriage to Juliana in 1741. After nearly four years of hearings, in September 1765 both the attorney-general and the solicitor-general of Ireland ruled in Arthur's favor, allowing him at last to take his seat in Dublin as Viscount Valentia.[5]

Barely had Parliament adjourned before Arthur hastened to London to petition the king for admission to the House of Lords as seventh Earl of Anglesea and Baron Annesley of Newport Pagnell. Prospects appeared promising for the new viscount. Besides the merits of his case, unprecedented numbers of Irish peers at the time were gaining English titles. As in Ireland, he received a favorable report from the attorney-general advising the king to honor the request.[6]

For all of his failings, George III was not one to shirk his royal responsibilities, taking particular interest, in fact, in legal controversies that might adversely affect the honor of the English nobility. Although a young boy in 1743 when James Annesley first took his uncle to court, George had, one senses, followed succeeding developments in the family's long-running drama. Having received Dorothea's petition in January 1766, he became skeptical of Arthur's claim. With the American colonies careening toward open rebellion over the Stamp Act, he took time to quickly write to the lord chancellor: "The enclosed is a petition I received this day from a poor woman that is daughter to the late very infamous earl of Anglesey." By November, the king had even read an impassioned pamphlet published that year by Du Bois, which he thought "better drawn up than the petition." His sympathies aroused, George instructed that the lord chancellor read the pamphlet "previous to any application he may receive from the young man who styles himself earl of Anglesey." More important, the king expressed his view that "the case be brought before the House of Lords for their decision."[7]

Not until 1770 did the Lords' Committee of Privileges take up Arthur's application. In addition, his father's old rival, Constantine Phipps—now Lord Mulgrave—stepped forward to aid Dorothea in a separate lawsuit. Should Valentia be denied his titles and estates, Phipps might be able to revive his forlorn claim, or so he hoped. "Mrs. Dubois is to be supported in her wanton persecution by the generous noble Lord Mulgrave," Arthur grumbled to his brother-in-law. Despite his inheritance, plus his sudden elopement in 1767 with Lucy, the only daughter of Thomas, Lord Lyttelton, Valentia faced daunting legal bills, much as his father had. Like his father, he decided to raise some of the necessary cash by cutting down several large stands of trees on his Wexford lands. "We must deal with those," he wrote, "that will pay best and soonest." Unlike his father, however, he showed no appetite for silencing his rivals with raw intimidation.[8]

A sign of changing times? Maybe, instead, the odds already lay in his favor, with his mother ready to testify, as she had successfully done on behalf of his Irish titles. "There is no doubt," declared a

London correspondent in May, that Valentia "will be admitted to the seat in the house of peers here as earl of Anglesea."[9]

The committee did not convene hearings until May 15. Notwithstanding the steady hand of the chairman, delays invariably arose. Increasingly, rather than the questionable legitimacy of Richard's marriage to Ann Simpson, the issue instead became whether he had married Juliana in 1741. Witnesses had to be summoned from Ireland to testify to the validity of the signatures on the original marriage certificate. In all, more than twenty persons gave testimony as the committee met sporadically over the course of the succeeding year. Arthur's chief nemesis was Mulgrave, who arrived with a train of witnesses eager to impeach the document's authenticity. Not only was counsel for Valentia forced, however haphazardly, to rebut Mulgrave's allegations, but he also had to explain Anglesea's unusual decision to conceal the marriage. It was done, testified Thomas Fitzgerald, the earl's former lawyer, "for fear of the family," whose support had been critical in the contest against his nephew James. "You can't blame me for that," Richard had reportedly told Fitzgerald, "for you know how I should have been distressed by Charles Annesley . . . He would not have left me bread to eat."[10]

On April 22, 1771, the committee assembled to announce its long-awaited decision. To widespread surprise, it ruled by a vote of seven to six that Valentia had "no right to the titles, honours, and dignities by his petition." Apparently, the slender majority, already skeptical about the clandestine wedding, had determined the marriage certificate to be forged, rendering his birth illegitimate— notwithstanding the best efforts of the distinguished jurist the Earl of Mansfield, Richard's former attorney, to sway the committee in Valentia's favor. His lawyers urged Valentia to appeal, but, riddled with bills, he was forced to abandon the claim. The warmhearted Scot Daniel Mackercher, in the final year of his life, must have smiled at the striking irony of this unexpected reversal, as did Dorothea Du Bois, notwithstanding the recent failure of her lawsuit. "Revenge," according to a French proverb, "is a dish that is eaten cold." Along with the English barony of Newport Pagnell, the Annesleys' most prized peerage, the earldom of Anglesea, first awarded by Charles II in 1661, was ruled extinct.[11]

Nor was this all. In light of the Lords' ruling, the following year saw the House of Lords in Dublin abruptly reconsider Arthur's Irish titles. Joining the fray as claimants were his half-brother, Richard Salkeld, and John Annesley of Ballysax. In language reminiscent of that employed in 1743 by Anglesea's lawyers at the Court of Exchequer, John Annesley's counselor argued that a victory for Valentia "would enable every mistress . . . to give heirs to the best blood and to the greatest honours and estates in Great Britain and Ireland."[12]

After four weeks of hearings, Valentia at last prevailed. He thus had the unique distinction of being declared legitimate in one kingdom and illegitimate in another. "The son of a w[hore] is a Lord!" disappointed opponents mocked. New evidence, not available in London, had lent credence to the original date of his parents' marriage. At the same time, his lawyer had appealed to burgeoning Irish nationalism by urging the House to ignore London's precedent. "This is a fact, in the decision of which, the Lords of Ireland naturally take the lead, because it happens at their doors." Nor, he implored, should the sins of the father be visited upon the son, of which, he readily admitted (with Arthur's consent), there had been numerous instances. "The irregular and immoral way of life of Lord Anglesey is confessed on all sides," he stated, even acknowledging, at one point, the cruelty shown to his nephew James. For what remained of the family's shattered honor, the victory came at a cost. His father's vilification, as if from Arthur's own lips, was a startling act of betrayal, though scarcely one unprecedented in the annals of the Annesleys.[13]

A NOTE ON LEGAL SOURCES

Despite the paucity of letters and other personal papers of the Annesleys that have survived from the eighteenth century, there is no shortage of legal sources, owing to the family's penchant for confrontation. These include published transcripts from the 1740s of every major trial directly or indirectly involving James Annesley, from his prosecution at the Old Bailey in 1742 for murder to Mary Heath's trial for perjury three years later. Included are transcripts for the trial at the Court of Exchequer in Dublin in 1743 and the Kildare assizes prosecution against the Earl of Anglesea et al. in 1744. Transcripts of all four trials were reprinted in volumes 17 and 18 of Thomas Bayly Howell et al., comps., *A Complete Collection of State Trials and Proceedings for High Treason and Other Crimes and Misdemeanors from the Earliest Period to the Present Time*, 34 vols. (London 1809–28), upon which I have relied extensively, though not without consulting other contemporary accounts. The climactic trial of 1743 spawned several transcripts. Although none contain substantive differences from the text in Howell's *State Trials*, at times I found the testimony in alternate transcriptions to be more detailed. In such instances, as the notes reflect, I tried to rely upon the most accurate testimony available, regardless of the transcript from which it originated. The principal alternative, in this regard, to Howell's *State Trials* was *The Trial in Ejectment between Campbell Craig, Lessee of James Annesley, Esq., and others, Plaintiffs*

*and the Right Honourable Richard, Earl of Anglesey, Defendant: Before
the Barons of His Majesty's Court of Exchequer in Ireland: Begun on
Friday, November 11th, 1743 and Continued by Several Adjournments
to Friday, the 25th of the Said Month: Containing, the Evidence at
Large as Delivered by the Witnesses, with All the Speeches and Arguments of the Judges and of the Counsel* (Dublin, 1744).

Depositions taken in Ireland between 1743 and 1745, during
the preliminary stages of the Chancery suit between Annesley
and his uncle, were another critical source of information, often
involving parties that did not testify at the Court of Exchequer in
1743 or who possessed additional information when questioned
by Chancery examiners. Out of a total of 398 depositions, the
late author Lillian de la Torre of Colorado Springs purchased 217
from a Sussex bookseller in 1965, which she later donated to the
National Library of Ireland. These form the most valuable portion
of the collection in the Manuscripts Department labeled the Anglesey Peerage Papers. Another set of 181 depositions, which de la
Torre never saw, resides in the records of the Court of Chancery
(C 12/1168/7 and C 12/1977/1) at the National Archives, Kew.
Additional Chancery records, notably the entry books of decrees
and orders (C 33), allowed me to follow the protracted path of
Annesley's suit against his uncle, whereas the pleadings (C 11,
12), combined with records in the Parliamentary Archives, contain useful information on the legal crossfire between Richard and
his cousins following the death of Arthur, fifth Earl of Anglesea,
in 1737.

Finally, of unexpected importance were the published transcripts of the investigations conducted by the English House of
Lords in 1770–71 and the Irish House of Lords in 1772 pertaining
to Arthur Annesley's peerage claims. Committees in both houses
delved deeply into the affairs of Arthur's father, the sixth Earl of
Anglesea, from the time of his reported marriage to Juliana Donovan in 1741 until his death two decades later, thereby affording

crucial information for much of his later life. See *Minutes of the Proceedings and Evidence, before the Lords Committees for Privileges in England, in the Years 1770–1771, upon the Claim of Arthur Viscount Valentia in Ireland (Late Earl of Mountnorris), to Succeed His Father, Richard Earl of Anglesey, in the Titles of Earl of Anglesey and Baron Annesley, in England* (London, n.d.); and *Minutes of the Proceedings before the Lords Committees for Privileges, upon the Several Claims to the Titles of Viscount Valentia, &c.* (Dublin, 1773).

My principal dilemma in using legal sources was the contradictory nature of much of the testimony. Perjury, I quickly realized, was a persistent problem in eighteenth-century Ireland. In the historical novel *Castle Rackrent* (1800), Maria Edgeworth contrasts the "Englishman who expects justice" at court with the "Irishman who hopes for partiality."[1] The extent of perjury during the Exchequer trial in 1743 was unusually flagrant. And while disagreements between witnesses arose over dates, places, and personalities, invariably the underlying point of contention was the same: whether or not James Annesley was the legitimate son of Lord and Lady Altham and, in turn, the rightful heir to the honors and property of the house of Annesley.

How, then, best to determine the facts of the controversy? As much as possible, I tried to shed any presuppositions, despite a natural inclination to sympathize with Annesley's plight (bastard or not, he *was* abducted by his uncle). Grasping heirs and bogus claimants are common enough in British history, if rarely on the scale alleged by Annesley's enemies. And there was always the chance, I recognized, that James himself, however sincere his protestations, might not have known the true details of his birth.

In the end, my task turned out to be less tortuous than I first imagined. Despite its inconsistencies, the totality of the evidence, I discovered, veered strongly in Annesley's favor. Independent sources, when available, almost always corroborated the claims of James and his followers. With few exceptions, their statements, in and out of court, were more apt to be accurate. One compelling example was the devastating testimony by John Giffard at the Four Courts that the Earl of Anglesea, in a fit of despair, had planned in 1742 to surrender his titles and estates to his nephew in favor of removing to France, for which he employed a French tutor, Captain Stephen Hay, at his London home. Not only did the earl's lawyers fail to rebut Giffard's testimony, but the actress Charlotte Charke, in her autobiography, subsequently recounted her brief tenure as a tutor before Hay's retention.[2]

In general, testimony favoring Annesley during the course of his lawsuits often seems more credible than that of his opponents. If his witnesses were less artful, their responses were less contrived. Natural inconsistencies, mostly of a minor nature, were more likely to crop up in their statements. As Serjeant Robert Marshall noted in his closing remarks at the Court of Exchequer, "Nay, the variations show that the evidence is not framed."[3] Nor were James's supporters as likely to conceal weaknesses in their testimony. Deborah Annesley, for one, readily volunteered during the trial that she had never visited Kinnea during Annesley's residence there as a boy, though she remained absolutely certain of his legitimacy—as was Major Richard Fitzgerald, despite his belief that James had been born in the fall of 1715 rather than the spring.

The earl, it bears repeating, alone commanded the resources and authority to suborn legal testimony, particularly in Wexford. Not only was he the most prominent member of the county's landed class, but his assets dwarfed those of his nephew, notwithstanding past quarrels with his cousins (hence, too, the earl's ability to impede legal proceedings rather than permit the law to run its course). In stark contrast, when James and his companions arrived in Ireland in 1742, they enjoyed neither personal connections nor political influence, much less the wherewithal to suborn witnesses. It was, I concluded, the merits of their cause that drew such large numbers of supporters, many of whom still recalled the young lord, Jemmy Annesley.

Finally, like Lord Mountney in his remarks from the bench at the Court of Exchequer, I decided that no explanation other than a desire to deny James's birthright could possibly explain Richard's relentless persecution, which his legal counsel never successfully disputed. Indeed, neither Anglesea nor his lawyers ever offered a consistent explanation for Jemmy's disappearance in 1728. Plainly, his arrival in London thirteen years later dispelled reports of his death. Moreover, the notion that Richard resorted to kidnapping his nephew, along with perpetrating other misdeeds, merely to avoid the nuisance of proving the boy's illegitimacy is implausible at best.

More farfetched, as an explanation for Richard's actions, is the suggestion, voiced by a lone defense witness, William Elmes, in 1743, that Lord Altham, upon the arrival of his infant son at Dunmain, decided to conceal from James his illegitimate birth. To accept such a hypothesis would be to conclude 1) that Richard never learned of his brother's subterfuge, either from him or from his servants; and 2) that the extensive body of testimony recounting Lady Altham's pregnancy and James's birth was false. In fact, no other defense witness at the Court of Exchequer corroborated Elmes's claim. According to the bulk of the defense testimony, Altham made no secret of James's alleged illegitimacy.

Such, then, were my principal reasons for believing James to have been his father's rightful heir. Arguing otherwise would ignore a small mountain of material evidence that the most prominent lawyers of Dublin and London found themselves hardpressed to refute. Of course, short of locating Annesley's remains for genetic analysis, we may never learn with absolute certainty the actual circumstances of his birth. Considering all that we already know, forgoing that final indignity seems, in the end, a small sacrifice.

NOTES

Abbreviations

Abstract	*An Abstract of the Case of the Honourable James Annesley, Esq. Humbly Submitted to the Consideration of all Disinterested Persons, and of All Lovers of Justice and Truth* (Dublin, 1754)
AC	Andrew Lang, ed., *The Annesley Case* (Edinburgh and London, 1912)
Add. Mss.	Additional Manuscripts, British Library, London
AWM	*American Weekly Mercury* (Philadelphia)
Annesley Family Pedigree	Annesley Family Pedigree, 1817, Richard Anglesey Correspondence, 1741–1766, British Library, London, Add. Mss. 31,889
APP	Anglesey Peerage Papers, 1744–1980, National Library of Ireland, Dublin, Mss. 36,084
BL	British Library, London
C	Chancery Records, National Archives, Kew
CARD	J. T. Gilbert and R. M. Gilbert, eds., *Calendar of the Ancient Records of Dublin*, 19 vols. (Dublin, 1899–1944)
Case	*The Case of the Honourable James Annesley, Esq; Humbly Offered to All Lovers of Truth and Justice* (London?, 1756)
DWJ	*Dublin Weekly Journal*
Egmont Diary	Historical Manuscripts Commission, *Report on the Manuscripts of the Earl of Egmont. Diary of Viscount Percival, Afterwards First Earl of Egmont*, vol. 1 (London, 1920)
GM	*Gentleman's Magazine* (London)

HIP	Edith Mary Johnston-Liik, *History of the Irish Parliament, 1692– 1800 Commons, Constituencies and Statutes*, 6 vols. (Belfast, 2002)
LCP	"Minutes of Proceedings and Evidence before the Lords Com- mittees for Privileges (1770–1771) Relating to the Claim of Arthur Viscount Valentia in Ireland . . . ," Parliamentary Archives, Houses of Parliament, London, HL/PO/DC/CP/3/3
LEP	*London Evening Post*
LJI	*Journals of the House of Lords of the Kingdom of Ireland*, 8 vols. (Dublin, 1779–1800)
Memoirs	*Memoirs of an Unfortunate Young Nobleman, Return'd from a Thir- teen Years Slavery in America, 'Where he had been sent by the Wicked Contrivances of his Cruel Uncle*, 2 vols. (1743; rpt. edn, New York, 1975)
MEP	*Minutes of the Proceedings and Evidence, before the Lords Committees for Privileges in England, in the Years 1770–1771, upon the Claim of Arthur Viscount Valentia in Ireland (Late Earl of Mountnorris), to Succeed His Father, Richard Earl of Anglesey, in the Titles of Earl of Anglesey and Baron Annesley, in England* (London, n.d.)
MIP	*Minutes of the Proceedings before the Lords Committees for Privileges, upon the Several Claims to the Titles of Viscount Valentia, &c.* (Dub- lin, 1773)
NA	National Archives, Kew
NAD	Depositions, 1715–1880, Court of Chancery, National Archives, Kew, C 12/1168/7; C 12/1977/1
NLD	Depositions, 1744–1747, Papers Concerning the Anglesey Peerage, 1744–1980, Ms. 36,084, with the permission of the National Library of Ireland, Dublin
NLI	National Library of Ireland, Dublin
ODNB	*Oxford Dictionary of National Biography*, 60 vols. (Oxford, 2004)
OED	*Oxford English Dictionary*, 1st edn (Oxford, 1888–1928)
OP	Countess of Cork and Orrery, ed., *The Orrery Papers*, 2 vols. (London, 1903)
OPH	Orrery Papers, Houghton Library, Harvard University, MS. Engl. 218.2 (vol. 3) [photocopies in Anglesey Peerage Papers, 1744–1980, National Library of Ireland, Dublin, Ms. 36,084]

PA	Parliamentary Archives, London
PG	*Pennsylvania Gazette* (Philadelphia)
PHA	A *Plain Historical Account of the Tryal, Between the Honourable James Annesley, Esq; Plaintiff . . . and the Right Honourable the Earl of Anglesea, Defendant . . .* (London, 1744)
PP	Tobias Smollett, *The Adventures of Peregrine Pickle*, 2 vols. (1751; rpt. edn, London, 1967)
P&P	*Past and Present* (Oxford)
PROB	Probate National Archives, Kew
PRONI	Public Record Office of Northern Ireland, Belfast
Proverbs	Morris Palmer Tilley, ed., *A Dictionary of the Proverbs in England in the Sixteenth and Seventeenth Centuries . . .* (Ann Arbor, MI, 1966)
RAC	Richard Annesley Correspondence, 1741–1766, British Library London, Add. Mss. 31,889
ST	T. B. Howell, et al., comps., *A Complete Collection of State Trials and Proceedings for High Crimes and Other Crimes and Misdemeanors from the Earliest Period to the Present Time*, 34 vols. (London, 1809–28)
TCD	Trinity College, Dublin
TE	*The Trial in Ejectment between Campbell Craig, Lessee of James Annesley, Esq., and others, Plaintiffs and the Right Honourable Richard, Earl of Anglesey, defendant: Before the Barons of His Majesty's Court of Exchequer in Ireland: begun on Friday, November 11th, 1743 and Continued by Several Adjournments to Friday, the 25th of the Said Month: Containing, the Evidence at Large as Delivered by the Witnesses, with All the Speeches and Arguments of the Judges and of the Counsel* (Dublin, 1744)
TL	*The Trial at Large Between James Annesley, Esq., and the Right Honorable the Earl of Anglesea, Before the Barons of the Court of Exchequer in Ireland: Begun on Friday, November 11, 1743, and by Adjournments Continued until the 25th of the same Month inclusive* (Newcastle-upon-Tyne, 1744)
WJ	*Westminster Journal* (London)

EPIGRAPH

1. "A.M.," *DWJ*, Oct. 16, 1725.

PREFACE

1. Nikolai Tolstoy, *Patrick O'Brian: The Making of a Novelist* (New York, 2004), 297.

2. Others have included Lady Morgan, *Florence Macarthy: An Irish Tale* (London, 1818); William Godwin, *Cloudesley: A Tale* (London, 1830); Charles Reade, *The Wandering Heir* (New York, 1873). A reviewer of *Kidnapped* wrote, "Of both 'Guy Mannering' and 'Kidnapped' the main action was suggested by the Annesley case, that marvelous romance of real life which, in 'The Wandering Heir,' not even Charles Reade could effectually vulgarize and spoil for future use. And no doubt it may be said that in [David] Balfour's struggle with old Ebenezer there is nothing so improbable as the real struggle of Annesley with *his* wicked uncle, and that Annesley's adventures in the plantations . . . surpass in wonderfulness any of the chances, escapes, and disasters that befell Balfour." *Athenaeum*, Aug. 14, 1886.

3. Diary of John Lewis, 1718–1760, MS Eng. misc. f.10, Bodleian Library, Oxford. For biographical sketches of both James and Richard Annesley, see the *ODNB*. The only book-length study of the Annesley case is an unpublished manuscript completed in 1980 by the late Lillian de la Torre, a pseudonym of Lillian McCue, a prolific mystery writer, who resided in Colorado Springs: "The Annesley Trials or, The Kidnapped Earl: An Eighteenth Century Melodrama of Disputed Birthright Shewing, How James Annesley Came Back from Bond-slavery in the American Colonies, into which he had been sold by Richard, the Rake-hell Earl of Anglesey; How He Brought Suit to Reclaim the Earldom; and What Came of It." Typescript copies are kept in the Special Collections Department of Tutt Library, Colorado College, Colorado Springs, and in the Manuscripts Department of the National Library of Ireland, Dublin. Of greater value, arguably, than the manuscript are the scholarly articles that de la Torre wrote or co-authored: L. M. Knapp and Lillian de la Torre, "Smollett, Mackercher and the Annesley Claimant," *English Language Notes* 1 (1963–64), 28–33; Lillian de la Torre, "New Light on Smollett and the Annesley Cause," *Review of English Studies*, New Ser. 22 (1971), 274–81; Lillian de la Torre, "The Melting Scot: A Postscript to Peregrine Pickle," *ELN* 10 (1972), 20–27.

4. David Luban, *Lawyers and Justice: An Ethical Study* (Princeton, 1988), 3.

5. *Hibernicus's Letters: or, a Philosophical Miscellany* (London, 1734), I, 462.

PROLOGUE

1. Sir John Fortescue, *De Laudibus Legum Anglie*, ed. S. B. Chrimes (Cambridge, 1949), 109.

2. *ST*, XVII, 1334, 1202, 1203; *AC*, 235; *Whalley's News-Letter* (Dublin), Mar. 14, 1723; *CARD*, VII, 46; Paul Ferguson, ed., *The A to Z of Georgian Dublin: John Rocques's Maps of the City in 1756 and the County in 1760* (Kent, 1998), 10–11.

3. NAD (M. O'Neal, B. Donohue).

4. *ST*, XVII, 1332–34; Clare Gittings, *Death, Burial and the Individual in Early Modern England* (London, 1984), 188–200.

5. William Wilson, *The Post-Chaise Companion: or, Traveller's Directory Though Ireland . . .* (Dublin, 1786), xxvii; J. T. Gilbert, *A History of the City of Dublin* (Dublin, 1854), I, 124.

6. *ST*, XVII, 1332, 1203; *TE*, 274; Raymond Refaussé and Colm Lennon, eds., *The Registers of Christ Church Cathedral, Dublin* (Dublin, 1998), 29, 122.

7. [John Bush], *Hibernia Curiosa: A Letter from a Gentleman in Dublin, to his Friend at Dover in Kent . . .* (London, 1769), 10, 11, 12; Constantia Elizabeth Maxwell, *Dublin Under the Georges, 1714–1830* (London, 1946), 85; Thomas and Valerie Pakenham, eds., *Dublin: A Travelers' Companion* (New York, 1988), 314; S. J. Connolly, *Religion, Law and Power: The Making of Protestant Ireland 1660–1760* (Oxford, 1992), 44; T. C. Barnard, *A New Anatomy of Ireland: The Irish Protestants 1649–1770* (New Haven, 2003), 2.

8. *TE*, 25; *ST*, XVII, 1180, 1189, 1191.

9. *AC*, 136–37; *ST*, XVII, 1198, 1190, 1196–97; *Some Considerations for the Promoting of Agriculture, and Employing the Poor* (Dublin, 1723), 41; NAD (C. Byrn).

10. NLD (T. Maxwell); *ST*, XVII, 1198; NAD (C. Purcell). One of the baron's servants later testified, "Miss Gregory had as much power . . . as any woman could have over a husband." NAD (B. Walsh).

11. *ST*, XVII, 1198–99; *TE*, 103.

12. NAD (C. Purcell); *TE*, 103; *ST*, XVII, 1199–1201; NAD (J. Purcell); *AC*, 138.

13. Connolly, *Religion, Law, and Power*, 126; James Kelly, *The Liberty and Ormond Boys: Factional Riot in Eighteenth-Century Dublin* (Dublin, 2005).

14. *ST*, XVII, 1201; *TE*, 106; *AC*, 141.

15. *ST*, XVII, 1201, 1216; NAD (J. Purcell); *TE*, 106, 111.

16. *TE*, 109; *ST*, XVII, 1201–02; NAD (J. Purcell).

17. *ST*, XVII, 1206, 1202; NLD (T. Power); NAD (R. Bayly).

18. *ST*, XVII, 1202; *AC*, 142; "Diary of the Weather at Dublin 1716–34," Gilbert Manuscripts 132, 263, Pearse Street Library, Dublin; NAD (W. Jones).

19. *ST*, XVII, 1202–03; NAD (J. Purcell, C. Purcell).

20. *AC*, 146, 143; *ST*, XVII, 1203.

21. "Diary of the Weather," 269–71; *AWM*, July 4, 1728; *ST*, XVII, 1207, 1209; *TE*, 114–5; *AC*, 150.

22. NAD (J. Field); *ST*, XVII, 1207–08; Kelly, *Liberty and Ormond Boys*.

23. *ST*, XVII, 1210, 1208–09; *CARD*, VII, 453.

24. *ST*, XVII, 1209; Jonathan Swift, *Gulliver's Travels and a Modest Proposal*, ed. Jesse Gale (New York, 2005), 341–53; James Kelly, "Harvests and Hardship: Famine and Scarcity in Ireland in the Late 1720s," *Studia Hibernica* 26 (1991–92), 65–105. A Dublin resident reported on April 2, "We hear that 40 or 50 houses have been broke open and robb'd within this week past in the city, and that several persons have been knock'd down and robb'd in the by-streets." *New-England Weekly Journal* (Boston), July 1, 1728.

25. *ST*, XVII, 1209–12; Patrick Fagan, *The Second City: Portrait of Dublin, 1700–1760* (Dublin, 1986), 19.

1: FAMILY

1. *ST*, XVII, 1323.

2. *Egmont Diary*, 387. The value of £10,000 was adjusted according to the retail price index at http://www.measuringworth.com/index.html.

3. Anne Somerset, *Elizabeth I* (New York, 1991), 525; Nicholas Canny, *Making Ireland British, 1580–1650* (Oxford, 2001).

4. Michael MacCarthy-Morrogh, *The Munster Plantation: English Migration to Southern Ireland, 1583–1641* (Oxford, 1986), 69, 291–92; John Lodge, *The Peerage of Ireland, or, a Genealogical History of the Present Nobility of that Kingdom . . .* (London, 1754), II, 273.

5. Lodge, *Peerage of Ireland*, II, 274–81, 285–89; *ODNB*, s.v. "Francis Annesley, second Viscount Valentia," "Arthur Annesley, first earl of Anglesey"; Rebecca Kathern Hayes-Steuck, "Emerging from the Shadows: The Life and Career of Arthur Annesley, earl of Anglesey, 1614–1686" (PhD diss., Florida State University, 2005).

6. Francis Nichols, *The English Compendium: or, Rudiments of Honour, Containing the Genealogies of All the Nobility of England . . .* (London, 1769), II, 152; Hayes-Steuck, "Arthur Annesley"; *Independent Reflector* (New York), Oct. 25, 1753; Annabel Pat-

terson and Martin Dzelzainis, "Marvell and the Earl of Anglesey: A Chapter in the History of Reading," *Historical Journal* 44 (2001), 703–26.

7. *ST*, XVII, 1257. Despite an estimated income of £11,360 in the late 1660s, he complained late in life of insufficient funds due to estates already bestowed on his children. *ODNB*, s.v. "Arthur Annesley"; Hayes-Steuck, "Arthur Annesley," 11, 122, 124, 186.

8. F. G. James, "The Active Irish Peers in the Early Eighteenth Century," *Journal of British Studies* 18 (1979), 55–56; Barnard, *New Anatomy of Ireland*, 21–22.

9. Charles R. Mayes, "The Early Stuarts and the Irish Peerage," *English Historical Review* 73 (1958), 245, 238; Barnard, *New Anatomy of Ireland*, 23.

10. Connolly, *Religion, Law, and Power*, 64, 178–79; Barnard, *New Anatomy of Ireland*, 30–34: R. M. Foster, *Modern Ireland, 1600–1972* (London, 1988), 170–73; *ODNB*, s.v. "John Perceval, first earl of Egmont"; J. L. McCracken, "The Social Structure and Social Life, 1714–60," in T. W. Moody and W. E. Vaughan, eds., *A New History of Ireland* (Oxford, 1986), IV, 36.

11. *OP*, I, 280; Connolly, *Religion, Law, and Power*, 178, 66.

12. "Hibernicus," *DWJ*, Apr. 10, 1725; *Tribune* (Dublin, 1729), 69; Connolly, *Religion, Law, and Power*, 66–67; McCracken, "Social Structure," 36.

13. John Loveday, *Diary of a Tour in 1732 Through Parts of England, Wales, Ireland and Scotland* (Edinburgh, 1740), 58; *Letters from an Armenian in Ireland, to his Friends at Trebisond, &c.* (London, 1757), 9.

14. Jim Smyth, "'Like Amphibious Animals': Irish Protestants, Ancient Britons, 1691–1707," *HJ* 36 (1993), 785–95; "Hibernicus," *DWJ*, Nov. 6, 1725; *HIP*, II, 94–96; David Hayton, "Anglo-Irish Attitudes: Changing Perceptions of National Identity Among the Protestant Ascendancy in Ireland, ca. 1690–1750," *Studies in Eighteenth-Century Culture* 17 (1987), 148; Samuel Madden, *Reflections and Resolutions Proper for the Gentlemen of Ireland . . .* (Dublin, 1738), 84; Connolly, *Religion, Law, and Power*, 109–25; James Kelly, *'That Damn'd Thing Called Honour': Duelling in Ireland, 1570–1860* (Cork, 1995), 64.

15. *OP*, I, 280; Samuel Derrick, *Letters Written from Leverpoole, Chester, Corke, the Lake of Killarney, Dublin, Tunbridge-Wells, Bath* (London, 1767), 80, 86; Connolly, *Religion, Law, and Power*, 71; Neal Garnham, "How Violent Was Eighteenth-Century Ireland," *Irish Historical Studies* 30 (1997), 377–92.

16. S. J. Connolly, "Violence and Order in the Eighteenth Century," in Patrick O'Flanagan, et al., eds., *Rural Ireland: Modernization and Change* (Cork, 1985), 49; Derrick, *Letters*, 59; James Kelly, "The Abduction of Women of Fortune in Eighteenth-Century Ireland," *Eighteenth-Century Ireland* 9 (1994), 7–43; Toby Barnard, *The Abduction of a Limerick Heiress: Social and Political Relations in Mid-Eighteenth-Century Ireland* (Dublin, 1998). For the decline of swords worn in public in London

by the 1720s and 1730s, except at night, see Robert B. Shoemaker, "Male Honour and the Decline of Public Violence in Eighteenth-Century London," *Social History* 26 (2001), 205.

17. Madden, *Reflections*, 152; Kelly, *"That Damn'd Thing."*

18. Connolly, *Religion, Law, and Power*, 59; Barnard, *New Anatomy of Ireland*, 67; Lawrence Stone and Jeanne C. Fawtier Stone, *An Open Elite: England, 1540–1880* (Oxford, 1984), 69–70, 90.

19. Sandy Bardsley, *Women's Roles in the Middle Ages* (New York, 2007), 83; William Wenman Seward, *The Hibernian Gazetteer* . . . (Dublin, 1789), xxiv–xxv; Stone and Stone, *Open Elite*, 86, 106.

20. Annesley Family Pedigree.

21. Stone and Stone, *Open Elite*, 93–104.

22. Annesley Family Pedigree; Valerie Rumbold, *Women's Place in Pope's World* (Cambridge, 1989), 169–71.

23. Annesley Family Pedigree; Nichols, *English Compendium*, II, 150; *ODNB*, s.v. "Arthur Annesley"; Barnard, *New Anatomy of Ireland*, 26; Eveline Cruickshanks, et al., eds., *The House of Commons, 1690–1715* (Cambridge, 2002), III, 27–34; Daniel Gahan, "The Estate System of County Wexford, 1641–1876," in Kevin Whelan and William Nolan, eds., *Wexford: History and Society: Interdisciplinary Essays on the History of an Irish County* (Dublin, 1987), 212.

24. Stone and Stone, *Open Elite*, 109, 144–45.

25. Lodge, *Peerage of Ireland*, II, 292.

26. Lodge, *Peerage of Ireland*, II, 292–93; Robert Beddard, "The Commission for Ecclesiastical Promotions, 1681–84: An Instrument of Tory Reaction," *HJ* 10 (1967), 15–16.

27. Ralph A. Houlbrooke, *The English Family, 1450–1700* (London, 1984), 216; Annesley Family Pedigree.

28. Stone and Stone, *Open Elite*, 102–3.

29. G. E. Cokayne, et al., eds., *The Complete Peerage of England, Scotland, Ireland, Great Britain and the United Kingdom, Extant, Extinct or Dormant* (Gloucester, 2000), I, 115; Houlbrooke, *English Family*, 65; *ST*, XVII, 1151, 1182, 1186.

30. *Proverbs*, 399; *Abstract*, 1; *ODNB*, s.v. "John Sheffield, first duke of Buckingham and Normanby"; Geoffrey Holmes, *British Politics in the Age of Anne* (rev. edn, London, 1987).

31. OPH, 308–9; *ST*, XVII, 1330; Annesley Will, n.d., PROB 11/534/107–1100.

32. NAD (T. Rolph); OED, s.v. "basset"; *ST*, XVII, 1318.

33. *Johnsoniana: A Collection of Miscellaneous Anecdotes and Sayings of Dr. Samuel Johnson* (London, 1845); Indenture, Mar. 14, 1708, OPH, 308–9; *Abstract*, 1–2; Stone and Stone, *Open Elite*, 22, 268.

34. Toby Barnard, *Making the Grand Figure: Lives and Possessions in Ireland, 1641–1770* (New Haven, 2004), 285; "Extracts from the Journals of the House of Lords," Apr. 2, 1744, APP; Annesley Family Pedigree.

35. Geraldine Stout, "Wexford in Prehistory, 5000 B.C. to 300 A.D.," in Whelan and Nolan, eds., *Wexford*, 1–2; Arthur Young, *A Tour in Ireland, 1776–1779*, ed. A. W. Hutton (1780; rpt. edn, Shannon, 1970), I, 84–85; II, 11, 14; L. C. Cullen, *An Economic History of Ireland since 1660* (London, 1972), 70. A detailed topographical map can be found in Robert Fraser, *Statistical Survey of the County of Wexford . . .* (Dublin, 1807).

36. *Abstract*, 50; *A Tour Through Ireland in Several Entertaining Letters . . .* (Dublin, 1746), I, 164, 166; Seward, *Hibernian Gazetteer*, s.v. "New Ross."

37. *Tour Through Ireland*, I, 167; John F. Ainsworth and Edward MacLysaght, *Analecta Hibernica: Including the Report of the Commission Survey of Documents in Private Keeping* (Dublin, 1958), 13; David Rowe and Eithne Scallan, *Historical Genealogical Architectural Notes on Some Houses of Wexford* (Whitegate, Ireland, 2004), s.v. "Dunmain House"; *ST*, XVII, 1267.

38. *ST*, XVII, 1262, 1323; Joseph P. Swan, "The Justices of the Peace for the County of Wexford," *The Journal of the Royal Society of Antiquaries of Ireland*, 5th Ser., 4 (1894), 69; *HIP*, II, 354–55.

39. Art Ó Maolfabhail, *Camán: Two Thousand Years of Hurling in Ireland* (Dundalk, 1973), 42; Kevin Whelan, "The Geography of Hurling," *History Ireland*, 1 (1993), 27–28; *ST*, XVII, 1282, 1285–86; NAD (E. Fisher, C. Holbrook, M. Keating, D. Murphy); Billy Coffer, *The Hook Peninsula, County Wexford* (Cork, 2004), 116–17; Barnard, *Making the Grand Figure*, 235–36; Connolly, *Religion, Law, and Power*, 132.

40. *Abstract*, 3; *TE*, 79, 194; *ST*, XVII, 1223, 1319.

41. *Abstract*, 1–2; Lawrence Stone, *The Family, Sex and Marriage in England, 1500–1800* (New York, 1977), 37–38.

42. *Abstract*, 2; Annesley Family Pedigree.

43. *ST*, XVII, 1149–51; NAD (H. Coles); *Abstract*, 2–3; *PHA*, 123; *TL*, 43.

44. Stone, *Family*, 325–74.

45. *ST*, XVII, 1282; *TE*, 160; Stone, *Family*, 372–74.

46. *ST*, XVII, 1149–50.

47. *ST*, XVII, 1149–50, 1300; NAD (H. Coles).

48. *ST*, XVII, 1152, 1150, 1151, 1304; *TL*, 6; AC, 89; NLD (H. Lawler).

49. *PHA*, 14, 23; NLD (A. O'Connor, E. Murphy, T. Higginson); *ST*, XVII, 1155; *ST*, XVIII, 111; Roy Porter, *The Greatest Benefit to Mankind: A Medical History of Humanity* (New York, 1997), 189–90.

50. NAD (P. Closey, T. Barron, T. Conway, L. Howlett, M. Morgan, D. Murphy, D. Redmond, J. Redmond, P. Rourke); *ST*, XVII, 1155; NLD (G. Cavenagh, E. Conway, H. Reynolds).

51. *ST*, XVII, 1155–56, 1163–64; NLD (A. Moore, T. Barron, M. Moran); *TE*, 31; *PHA*, 17.

52. Dorothy McLaren, "Marital Fertility and Lactation, 1570–1720," in Mary Prior, ed., *Women in English Society* (London, 1985), 22–46; Houlbrooke, *English Family*, 132–33.

53. NAD (H. Monfriffe, A. Roony); NLD (B. Furlong); Stone, *Family*, 424–25.

54. NAD (A. Roony, J. Wheedon, M. Doyle); NLD (D. Redmonds); *ST*, XVII, 1155–57; *Abstract*, 6; *TL*, 8, 20.

2: BETRAYAL

1. *Proverbs*, 145.

2. Stone, *Family*, 530, 519–45 passim; Robert Halsband, ed., *The Complete Letters of Lady Mary Wortley Montagu* (Oxford, 1966), II, 51–52.

3. *ST*, XVII, 1159; NAD (T. Barns); *Letters from an Armenian*, 120; [Jonathan Swift], *A Humorous Description of the Manners and Fashions of the Inhabitants of the City of Dublin* . . . (Dublin, 1734), 4–5; Stone, *Family*, 501–7, 543–45; Houlbrooke, *English Family*, 115–17.

4. *ST*, XVII, 1278–81, 1294; *TE*, 194–96; *Abstract*, 8; NLD (W. Bolton, T. Palliser, Jr.).

5. *ST*, XVII, 1278–81, 1294; *TE*, 194–96; *AC*, 193; *Abstract*, 8.

6. OPH, 313–14, 316–17.

7. NLD (S. Jemmatt); *Abstract*, 7–8.

8. NLD (T. Rawson); Jonathan Swift, *Letters Written by the Late Jonathan Swift* . . . (London, 1766), II, 233; *ODNB*, s.v. "Arthur Annesley, fifth earl of Anglesey."

9. *ST*, XVII, 1234, 1278; NLD (E. Power).

10. *DWJ*, Nov. 28, 1739; Barnard, *New Anatomy of Ireland*, 60–61.

11. Madden, *Reflections*, 35, 73, 128–29.

12. Thomas P. Power, *Land, Politics and Society in Eighteenth-Century Tipperary* (Oxford, 1993), 148; Kevin Whelan, "An Underground Gentry?: Catholic

Middlemen in Eighteenth-Century Ireland," *Eighteenth-Century Ireland* 10 (1995), 8–17; Connolly, *Religion, Law, and Power*, 50.

13. Young, *Tour in Ireland*, ed. Hutton, II, 26; *Letters from an Armenian*, 60, 78; Peter Roebuck, "Landlord Indebtedness in Ulster in the Seventeenth and Eighteenth Centuries," in J. M. Goldstrom and L. A. Clarkson, eds., *Irish Population, Economy, and Society: Essays in Honour of the Late K. H. Connell* (Oxford, 1981), 135–54; Power, *Land, Politics, and Society*, 159; L. M. Cullen, *An Economic History of Ireland since 1660* (London, 1972), 78; Barnard, *New Anatomy of Ireland*, 61.

14. Tichborn West to Ward, June 10, 1724, Castleward Papers, D2092/1/1/132, PRONI.

15. *ST*, XVII, 1281.

16. OPH, 322; NLD (M. Kavenagh, E. Lutwidge); *ST*, XVII, 1175, 1297; *Abstract*, 9.

17. NAD (D. Annesley); *Abstact*, 9; NLD (C. Murphy).

18. NAD (G. Cavenagh); NLD (M. Fitz Henry); *Abstact*, 9–10; Art Kavanagh and Rory Murphy, *The Wexford Gentry* (Enniscorthy, Ireland, 1994), 13; http://www.irelandbyways.com/ireland-routes/byroute-4/2/.

19. McCracken, "Social Structure," 49; Barnard, *New Anatomy of Ireland*, 37; NAD (D. Annesley); NLD (J. Wheeden); *TE*, 166.

20. NLD (D. Farrell, J. Cavanagh, J. McCormick); Stone, *Family*, 405–7; Houlbrooke, *English Family*, 134–36, 140–45.

21. *AC*, 116; NAD (J. Dempsey, F. Stone); NLD (A. Cowman, J. Kavenagh, C. Murphy, T. Rawson, E. Wheeden); *ST*, XVII, 1176–77. It is unknown whether father and son attended a church.

22. NAD (B. O'Neal, J. Carroll); *PHA*, 33.

23. NAD (B. O'Neal).

24. *Abstract*, 10; NAD (A. O'Neal, P. Costello); NLD (T. Freeman, J. Nowland, E. Wheeden); *AC*, 228. See also NLD (B. Harford, J. Scadden, E. Storey).

25. Cullen, *Economic History*, 25; Connolly, *Religion, Law, and Power*, 48.

26. *LJI*, II, 691–97; Philip Perceval to Lord Perceval, Oct. 5, 1721, Egmont Papers, Add. Mss. 47029, f. 71; A. S. Turberville, "The 'Protection' of the Servants of Members of Parliament," *EHR* 42 (1927), 590–600.

27. *LJI*, II, 697–98, 700, 714; *Whalley's News-Letter*, Mar. 14, 1723.

28. King to Francis Annesley, Mar. 24, 1719, and Mar. 15, 1722, King Papers, Mss. 750/5/143, 750/7/84–85, TCD.

29. *ST*, XVII, 1194–95; *TE*, 262; *Abstract*, 10–12.

30. NAD (D. Farrell); NLD (A. Purcell); *Abstract*, 12–13.

31. *AC*, 138; *TE*, 82; Houlbrooke, *English Family*, 150–53; Stone, *Family*, 451–52.

32. NAD (M. Terrell); NLD (T. Rawson, N. Reeves).

33. *ST*, XVII, 1188, 1181; NLD (B. O'Neill); NAD (C. O'Neal); *TE*, 83.

34. *Egmont Diary*, 387; *Abstract*, 13–14; J. H. Baker, *An Introduction to English Legal History* (London, 2002), 274–76.

35. *Abstract*, 14–15; *ST*, XVII, 1258; "The Trial between James Annesley, Esq. and Richard, Earl of Anglesey," *GM* 14 (1744), 26.

36. NAD (R. Bayly).

37. *ST*, XVII, 1392–93; *Abstract*, 14.

38. John Brydall, *Lex Spuriorum: or The Law Relating to Bastardy* (1703; rpt. edn, New York, 1978), 21; Stone, *Family*, 532–34; Nicholas Rogers, "Carnal Knowledge: Illegitimacy in Eighteenth-Century Westminster," *Journal of Social History* 32 (1989), 361.

39. Stone and Stone, *Open Elite*, 229.

40. *MEP*, 13; *ODNB*, s.v. "Richard Annesley, sixth earl of Anglesey"; *An Apology for the Life of Mr. Bampfylde-Moore Carew . . .* (London, 1758), 229.

41. *Proverbs*, 665; *ODNB*, s.v. "Richard Annesley, sixth earl of Anglesey."

42. "Case of the Right Honourable George, Earl of Mountnorris . . . ," LCP; "The Answer of John Giffard, Gentleman, Deft. to the Bill of Complaint of the Right Honorable Richard Earl of Anglesey Complt.," [1742], Giffard Family Papers, 7107, Devon Record Office, Exeter; *General Evening Post* (London), May 17, 1770; Annesley Will, n.d., PROB 11/534/107–1100; Stone and Stone, *Open Elite*, 228–39; *ODNB*, s.v. "Richard Annesley."

43. Stone, *Family*, 34–37.

44. *TE*, 166; *ST*, XVII, 1269; Stone and Stone, *Open Elite*, 144–45; Houlbrooke, *English Family*, 41, 234–37; Linda Pollock, "Younger Sons in Tudor and Stuart England," *History Today* 39 (1989), 23–29. Although the exact date of Dorothy Annesley's death is uncertain, her will, drawn in 1715, was probated on Feb. 18, 1718. http://the peerage.com/p549.htm i 1581.

45. *ST*, XVII, 1187; *AC*, 178, 106.

46. *ST*, XVII, 1266; *TE*, 166, 168. For a similar conflict, albeit between father and

son, over the sale of reversionary leases, see "Autobiography of Pole Cosby, of Stradbally, Queens County," *Journal of the County Kildare Archaeological Society* 5 (1907), 170.

47. NAD (W. Milton, A. Bath).

48. *ST*, XVII, 1223; NAD (R. Halpen, R. Bayly, W. Milton, P. Plunkett).

49. King to [?] Annesley, Mar. 4, 1725, King Papers, Mss. 750/14/224, TCD; *Egmont Diary*, 387.

50. King to Francis Annesley, May 22, 1725, King Papers, Mss. 750/14/247–48, TCD.

51. NAD (R. Bayly).

52. NAD (R. Bayly).

53. NAD (M. O'Neal, B. Donohue); Francis G. James, *Lords of the Ascendancy: The Irish House of Lords and its Members, 1600–1800* (Washington, DC, 1995), 105.

54. NAD (M. O'Neal, B. Donohue).

55. NAD (D. Farrell); NLD (D. Farrell).

56. Carol Turkington, *The Poisons and Antidotes Sourcebook* (New York, 1999), 32–33, 35–37, 176, 240–42.

57. *Proverbs*, 145.

58. NAD (M. O'Neal, B. Donohue); NLD (A. Purcell, M. Wilkinson).

3: EXILE

1. Marianne Sophia Wokeck, "A Tide of Alien Tongues: The Flow and Ebb of German Immigration to Pennsylvania, 1683–1776" (PhD diss., Temple University, 1983), 69.

2. *Proverbs*, 589; *ST*, XVII, 1212–13; J. W. De Courcy, *The Liffey in Dublin* (Dublin, 1996), 22–25, 372; Donal T. Flood, "Dublin Bay in the 18th Century," *Dublin Historical Review* 31 (1978), 139.

3. John Wareing, "Preventive and Punitive Regulation in Seventeenth-Century Social Policy; Conflicts of Interest and the Failure to Make 'Stealing and Transporting Children, and other Persons' a Felony, 1645–73," *SH* 27 (2002), 288–308; Richard B. Morris, *Government and Labor in Early America* (New York, 1946), 337–43; Don Jordan and Michael Walsh, *White Cargo: The Forgotten History of Britain's White Slaves in America* (New York, 2007), 75–87, 127–36.

4. Penelope Aubin, *The Life of Charlotta du Pont, An English Lady* (London, 1723);

Thomas M. Truxes, *Irish–American Trade, 1660–1783* (Cambridge, 1988), 129–30, 140; Marianne Sophia Wokeck, *Trade in Strangers: The Beginnings of Mass Migration to North America* (University Park, PA, 1999), 176; Kerby A. Miller, *Emigrants and Exiles: Ireland and the Irish Exodus to North America* (New York, 1985), 137–68.

5. Joseph W. Hammond, "George's Quay and Rogerson's Quay in the Eighteenth Century," *Dublin Historical Record* 5 (1942–43), 46, 48–49; Truxes, *Irish–American Trade*, 135; Wokeck, *Trade in Strangers*, 169, 192; Michael Brown, *Francis Hutcheson in Dublin, 1719–30: The Crucible of His Thought* (Dublin, 2002), 97.

6. *Boston Gazette*, May 20, 1728; A. C. Elias, Jr., ed., *Memoirs of Laetitia Pilkington* (Athens, GA, 559); Morris, *Government and Labor*, 343.

7. A. Roger Ekirch, *Bound for America: The Transportation of British Convicts to the Colonies, 1718–1777* (Oxford, 1987), 20, 24–25, 46–47, 83–85.

8. NAD (R. Bayly); *ST*, XVII, 1212–15.

9. Susan E. Klepp and Billy G. Smith, eds., *The Infortunate: The Voyage and Adventures of William Moraley, an Indentured Servant* (University Park, PA, 1992) 53; Wokeck, *Trade in Strangers*, 200; *ST*, XVII, 1213.

10. Cox, *A Charge Delivered to the Grand-Jury . . .* (Dublin, 1748), 22; Neal Garnham, *The Courts, Crime, and the Criminal Law in Ireland, 1692–1760* (Dublin, 1996), 263; *AC*, 16. See also *Dublin Gazette*, Oct. 11, 1729.

11. *ST*, XVII, 1213; *TE*, 127; David Noel Doyle, *Ireland, Irishmen and Revolutionary America, 1760–1820* (Dublin, 1981), 68; Truxes, *Irish–American Trade*, 132, 134, 139.

12. *AWM*, July 4, 1728; Truxes, *Irish–American Trade*, 132–33; Wokeck, *Trade in Strangers*, 197–98.

13. *TE*, 129–30; *Boston News-Letter*, Feb. 6, 1724; *AWM*, Mar. 17, 1720; Wokeck, *Trade in Strangers*, 199, 208.

14. *ST*, XVII, 1213; Henry B. Culver, *The Book of Old Ships . . .* (Garden City, NY, 1935), 234–36; Angus Konstam, *Pirates, 1660–1730* (Botley, England, 1998), 48.

15. Kerby A. Miller, et al., eds., *Irish Immigrants in the Land of Canaan: Letters and Memoirs from Colonial and Revolutionary America, 1675–1815* (Oxford, 2003), 53–54, 24–27; *DWJ*, June 7, 1729; Bernard Bailyn, *The Peopling of British North America: An Introduction* (New York, 1986), 112–13.

16. Miller, et al, eds., *Irish Immigrants*, 69; Ekirch, *Bound for America*, 63.

17. Ian K. Steele, *The English Atlantic, 1675–1740: An Exploration of Communication and Community* (New York, 1986), 11–18, 274.

18. Klepp and Smith, eds., *Infortunate*, 60; *ST*, XVII, 1393; Sharon V. Salinger, *"To*

Serve Well and Faithfully": Labor and Indentured Servants in Pennsylvania, 1682–1800 (Cambridge, 1987), 87; Wokeck, *Trade in Strangers*, 208.

19. "Journal of the Voyage of Charles Clinton from Ireland to America, 1729," *Old Ulster; An Historical and Genealogical Magazine* 4 (1908), 175–83; Truxes, *Irish–American Trade*, 132; *Old Dublin Intelligencer*, Feb. 8, 1729.

20. *Memoirs*, 56–59.

21. William Stevens Perry, ed., *Historical Collections Relating to the American Colonial Church* (1878; rpt. edn, New York, 1969), 43–44; Harold B. Hancock, "Descriptions and Travel Accounts of Delaware, 1700–1740," *Delaware History* 10 (1962), 119–20; Wokeck, *Trade in Strangers*, 176–77, 208; Anthony Higgins, ed., *New Castle on the Delaware* (Newark, DE, 1973), 34–35.

22. *PG*, Jan. 13, 1730; Wokeck, *Trade in Strangers*, 174; Abbot Emerson Smith, *Colonists in Bondage: White Servitude and Convict Labor in America, 1607–1776* (New York, 1971), 220.

23. Wokeck, "Tide of Alien Tongues," 69; *Rind's Virginia Gazette* (Williamsburg), July 26, 1770; Truxes, *Irish–American Trade*, 134–35, 139.

24. Salinger, *"To Serve Well and Faithfully,"* 112, 73; Wokeck, *Trade in Strangers*, 200–1, 211–13.

25. *Memoirs*, 61; *AWM*, July 25, 1728; John A. Munroe, *Colonial Delaware: A History* (Millwood, NY, 1978), 197.

26. Klepp and Smith, eds., *Infortunate*, 106; Adolph B. Benson, ed., *Peter Kalm's Travels in North America* (New York, 1964), I, 79.

27. Benson, ed., *Kalm's Travels*, I, 224, 78, 94, 306–7; Klepp and Smith, eds., *Infortunate*, 89, 106–7; Young, *Tour in Ireland*, ed. Hutton, II, 8; William R. Cario, "Anglicization in a 'Frenchified, Scotchified, Dutchified Place': New Castle, Delaware, 1690–1750" (PhD diss., 1994, New York University). See also Fintan O'Toole, *White Savage: William Johnson and the Invention of America* (New York, 2005), 39–40.

28. R. W. Kelsey, ed., "An Early Description of Pennsylvania: Letters of Christopher Sower, Written in 1724, Describing Conditions in Philadelphia and Vicinity, and the Sea Voyage from Europe," *Pennsylvania Magazine of History and Biography* 45 (1921), 249; Perry, ed., *Historical Collections*, 46; Klepp and Smith, eds., *Infortunate*, 89.

29. Klepp and Smith, eds., *Infortunate*, 96; *Old Dublin Intelligencer*, June 3, 1729; William H. Williams, *Slavery and Freedom in Delaware, 1639–1865* (Wilmington, 1996), 40–41; Doyle, *Ireland, Irishmen*, 102; Edmund S. Morgan, *American Slavery, American Freedom: The Ordeal of Colonial Virginia* (New York, 1975), 126–27.

30. Munroe, *Colonial Delaware*, 167; Carol J. Garrett, ed., *New Castle County, Delaware Land Records, 1728–1738* (Lewes, DE, 2001), 76, 141; Thomas J. Scharf, *History of Delaware, 1609–1888* (Philadelphia, 1888), II, 914; Carol J. Garrett, ed., *New Castle County, Delaware County Land Records, 1762–1765* (Lewes, DE, 2003), 94.

31. *Memoirs*, 74–76; Hancock, "Descriptions," 130.

32. Gottlieb Mittelberger, *Journey to Pennsylvania*, ed. and trans. Oscar Handlin and John Clive (Cambridge, MA, 1960), 20; *Memoirs*, 92; Truxes, *Irish–American Trade*, 220–22.

33. *Memoirs*, 62–63, 69, 92; Klepp and Smith, eds., *Infortunate*, 88, 71, 107; Ekirch, *Bound for America*, 159; *PG*, Jan. 5, 1731; Doyle, *Ireland, Irishmen*, 94.

34. *PG*, July 24, 1735, Apr. 6, 1738, June 5, 1740, Nov.27, 1731; Daniel Meaders, comp., *Eighteenth-Century White Slaves: Fugitive Notices* (Westport, CT, 1993), I, passim; Kenneth Scott, comp., *Genealogical Abstracts from the American Weekly Mercury, 1719–1746* (Baltimore, 1974), passim; Simon P. Newman, *Embodied History: The Lives of the Poor in Early Philadelphia* (Philadelphia, 2003), 94–97.

35. NAD (T. Walker); Salinger, *"To Serve Well and Faithfully,"* 101–2; Carl Bridenbaugh, ed., *Gentleman's Progress: The Itinerarium of Dr. Alexander Hamilton, 1744* (Chapel Hill, NC, 1948), 12, 209; Klepp and Smith, eds., *Infortunate*, 105; A. Roger Ekirch, *At Day's Close: Night in Times Past* (New York, 2005), 236–37, 233–34; Miller, et al., eds., *Irish Immigrants*, 78.

36. *Memoirs*, 72, 64–67; Kenneth Morgan, *Slavery and Servitude in Colonial North America* (New York, 2001), 61. For a compelling biography of the legendary Irish adventurer William Johnson, which argues that Ireland's multicultural society rendered his identity in the New World more malleable, see O'Toole, *White Savage*, passim.

37. NAD (J. Deacon); *Memoirs*, 78, 72, 92, 110–11.

4: FLIGHT

1. Klepp and Smith, eds., *Infortunate*, 97.

2. NLD (H. Perry); *LEP*, May 31, 1770.

3. *ST*, XVII, 1206; NAD (R. Murray); *Abstract*, 18–20.

4. NAD (T. Byrne, M. Hughes); *ST*, XVII, 1210; *AC*, 151; NLD (L. Feighery, E. Handley); *Abstract*, 23.

5. *AC*, 146; *TE*, 112.

6. Mar. 13, 1729, and Apr. 22, 1734, *LJI*, III, 126, 289; Hugh Boulter, *Letters Written by His Excellency Hugh Boulter . . .* (Oxford, 1770), II, 87, 123–24, 125;

[Dorothea Du Bois], *The Case of Ann Countess of Anglesey, Lately Deceased: Lawful Wife of Richard Annesley, Late Earl of Anglesey, and of Her Three Surviving Daughters* (London, 1766). 10–11.

7. Apr. 14, 1737, *Egmont Diary*, 387; *Grub Street Journal* (London), Oct. 17, 1734; Marmaduke Coghill to Edward Southwell, Jr., Feb. 4, 1735, in D. W. Hayton, ed., *Letters of Marmaduke Coghill, 1722–1738* (Dublin, 2001), 155.

8. *Read's Weekly Journal or British Gazetteer* (London), Sept. 10, 1737; Apr. 14, 1737, *Egmont Diary*, 388; *OBNB*, s.v. "Arthur Annesley, fifth earl of Anglesey"; Earl of Anglesey v. Annesley, Apr. 7, 1741, June 15, 1742, HL/PO/JO/10/3/239/10, 30, PA; Rowe and Scallan, *Historical Genealogical Architectural Notes*, s.v. "Camolin Park."

9. Apr. 14, 1737, *Egmont Diary*, 387–88; *Abstract*, 21–22.

10. *Weekly Miscellany* (London), Apr. 15, 1737; *London Evening-Post*, Apr. 2 and 5, 1737.

11. *Daily Post* (London), Apr. 12, 1737.

12. Will of Arthur, Earl of Anglesey, Feb. 18, 1735, PROB 11/683/10–11; *HIP*, III, 94–96.

13. *Proverbs*, 102; Apr. 14, 1737, *Egmont Diary*, 387–88; Anglesey Will, Feb. 18, 1735, PROB 11/683/10–11.

14. *Proverbs*, 550; NAD (R. Bayly); NLD (P. Doyle); *Daily Gazetteer*, Apr. 18, 1737.

15. Connolly, *Religion, Law, and Power*, 43; Earl of Anglesey v. Annesley, Apr. 7, 1741, HL/PO/JO/10/3/239/10, PA; Peter Roebuck, "Landlord Indebtedness in Ulster in the Seventeenth and Eighteenth Centuries," in Goldstrom and Clarkson, eds., *Irish Population, Economy, and Society*, 150; Ekirch, *At Day's Close*, 241.

16. *Read's Weekly Journal or British Gazetteer*, Sept. 10, 1737; *DG*, May 25 and Sept. 7, 1737; Earl of Anglesey v. Annesley, Apr. 7, 1741, HL/PO/JO/10/3/239/10, PA; Josiah Brown, *Reports of Cases upon Appeals and Writs of Error, in the High Court of Parliament, from the Year 1701, to the Year 1779* (Dublin, 1785), IV, 425. According to William Blackstone, the justice selected for *custos rotulorum* in English counties was "a man for the most part especially picked out, either for wisdom, countenance, or credit." William Blackstone, *Commentaries on the Laws of England* (Chicago, 1979), IV, 269.

17. Earl of Anglesey v. Annesley, Apr. 7, 1741, and June 15, 1742, HL/PO/JO/10/3/239/10, 30, PA; Earl of Anglesey Papers, 1770–72, 1819, HL/PODC/CP/3/3, PA; *MIP*, 153; John Tracy Atkyns, comp., *Reports of Cases Argued and Determined in the High Court of Chancery . . .* (London, 1768), II, 57–58; "The Answer of John Giffard, Gentleman, Deft. to the Bill of Complaint of the Right Honorable

Richard Earl of Anglesey Complt.," [1742], Giffard Family Papers, 7107, Devon Record Office, Exeter; Cruickshanks, et al., eds., *The House of Commons*, III, 36; Answer of Constantine Phipps, 1738, C 11/2701/8. The petitions and responses at the Court of Chancery may be read in full in C 11/2701/8/1–4, passim.

18. NLD (E. Power).

19. Bernard de Mandeville, *An Enquiry into the Causes of the Frequent Executions at Tyburn . . .* (1725; rpt. edn, Millwood, NY, 1975), 47; Salinger, *"To Serve Well and Faithfully"* 103–7; Morgan, *Slavery and Servitude*, 95–97; Ekirch, *Bound for America*, 209–12.

20. J. A. Leo Lemay and P. M. Zall, eds., *Benjamin Franklin's Autobiography* (New York, 1986), 19; Klepp and Smith, eds., *Infortunate*, 97; Salinger, *"To Serve Well and Faithfully,"* 103–7; Barry Levy, "Born to Run: White Runaway Servants and the New England and Delaware Valley Labor Systems, 1700–1780," a paper presented to the McNeil Center for Early American Studies, Sept. 9, 2005, 7.

21. Meaders, comp., *Eighteenth-Century White Slaves* I, 1–85 passim; Scott, comp., *Genealogical Abstracts*, 45–108 passim.

22. *Memoirs*, 78–87. Not until 1739 did the Delaware assembly codify past practice by the courts. "An Act for the Better Regulation of Servants and Slaves . . . ," 1739, in John D. Cushing, ed., *The Earliest Printed Laws of Delaware, 1704–1741* (Wilmington, 1978), 133.

23. Miller, et al., eds., *Irish Immigrants in the Land of Canaan*, 253–67; *Memoirs*, 87–88.

24. Perry, ed., *Historical Collections*, 22; *Memoirs*, 91–99, 118; Timothy J. Shannon, "King of the Indians: The Hard Fate and Curious Career of Peter Williamson," *William and Mary Quarterly*, 3rd. Ser., 66 (2009), 7.

25. *Memoirs*, 125–37; *PG*, June 4 and Sept. 2 and 23, 1731.

26. *Memoirs*, 139; *Daily Post*, Feb. 12, 1741.

27. Mittelberger, *Journey to Pennsylvania*, eds. and trans. Handlin and Clive; 36; Carl Bridenbaugh, *Cities in the Wilderness: The First Century of Urban Life in America, 1625–1742* (Oxford, 1971), 327, 408–66 passim; Klepp and Smith, eds., *Infortunate*, 70.

28. *PG*, July 2, 1752; Salinger, *"To Serve Well and Faithfully,"* 102–3.

29. *DP*, Feb. 12, 1741; *Abstract*, 26; Richard S. Dunn, *Sugar and Slaves: The Rise of the Planter Class in the English West Indies, 1624–1713* (New York, 1972) 21,43–44, 149–50, 186–87; Maxine Van de Wetering, "Moralizing in Puritan Natural Science: Mysteriousness in Earthquake Sermons," *Journal of the History of Ideas* 43 (1982), 417–38.

30. *ODNB*, s.v. "Robert Jenkins"; Thomas McGeary, "Farinelli in Madrid: Opera, Politics, and the War of Jenkins' Ear," *Musical Quarterly* 82 (1998), 62.

31. *ODNB*, s.v. "Edward Vernon"; William Kennon Kay, "An Expedition for King and Country," *Virginia Cavalcade* 15 (1966), 30–37; Maurice Craig, *Dublin, 1660–1860* (London, 1952), 152.

32. N. A. M. Rodger, *The Wooden World: An Anatomy of the Georgian Navy* (New York, 1986), 40, 113–18; de la Torre, "New Light," 275; J. J. Colledge, *Ships of the Royal Navy* (Annapolis, 1987), 131; *PG*, July 29, 1742; Robert Beatson, *Naval and Military Memoirs of Great Britain from 1727 to 1783* (Boston, 1972), III, 26.

33. *Abstract*, 26–27; NLD (R. Collier).

34. *Abstract*, 26–27; Rodger, *Wooden World*, 24–25.

35. *DP*, Feb. 12, 1741; "Extract of Letters from the West Indies," *GM* 11 (1741), 110; Steele, *English Atlantic*, 273–75.

36. B. McL. Ranft, ed., *The Vernon Papers* (London, 1958), 181; Richard Harding, *Amphibious Warfare in the Eighteenth Century: The British Expedition to the West Indies, 1740–1742* (Woodbridge, England, 1991).

37. *PG*, Aug. 13, 1741; ADM 106/948/159, ADM 106/949/151, ADM 354/117/215, NA; Colledge, *Ships*, 33; N. A. M. Rodger, *The Command of the Ocean: A Naval History of Britain, 1649–1815* (New York, 2005), 303.

5: DELIVERANCE

1. *ST*, XVII, 1112.

2. Frederick A. Pottle, ed., *Boswell's London Journal, 1762–1763* (New York, 1950), 153–54; Roy Porter, *London: A Social History* (Cambridge, MA, 1995), 98, 93–184.

3. de la Torre, "New Light," 14; Cokayne, et al., eds., *Complete Peerage*, VI, 411; *Abstract*, 28–29.

4. *Abstract*, 29; *LJI*, II, 700; *PP*, 710, 719.

5. *PP*, 692–710; Jacob M. Price, "The French Farmers-General in the Chesapeake: The MacKercher-Huber Mission," *William and Mary Quarterly*, 3rd Ser., 14 (1957), 128–29.

6. *PP*, 709; Price, "French Farmers-General in the Chesapeake," 125–53.

7. *Proverbs*, 431; *Abstract*, 30; *PP*, 710, 719.

8. *Abstract*, 30; *PP*, 719.

9. Alison Findlay, *Illegitimate Power: Bastards in Renaissance Drama* (Manchester,

1994), 15–19; *ODNB*, s.v. "William Knollys"; *The Parallel: or a Collection of Extraordinary Cases, Relating to Concealed Births, and Disputed Successions* (London, 1744).

10. *ST*, XVII, 1222, 1319, 1321; *Abstract*, 65–67.

11. *ST*, XVII, 1156.

12. NAD (B. O'Neal, D. Leary).

13. Porter, *London*, 105; *Abstract*, 30–31.

14. *Abstract*, 31–32.

15. *Abstract*, 34–35.

16. Response of Earl of Anglesea, June 10, 1751, Earl of Anglesey Papers, 1770–72, 1819, HL/PODC/CP/3/3, PA.

17. *MEP*, 4; [Du Bois], *Countess of Anglesey*, 12–13.

18. *MIP*, 219, 44; [Dubois], *Countess of Anglesey*, 13–18; Petition of Ann Countess of Anglesey, Dec. 2, 1747, HL/PO/JO/10/6/5333, PA.

19. *MIP*, 42; [Dubois], *Countess of Anglesey*, 17.

20. *MEP*, 7; *MIP*, 20, 42, 218, 219; Case of Earl of Mountnorris, 1819, Earl of Anglesey Papers, 1770–72, 1819, HL/PODC/CP/3/3, PA.

21. *MIP*, 18–20, 79, 218, 223; Case of Mountnorris, 1819, Earl of Anglesey Papers, 1770–72, 1819, HL/PODC/CP/3/3, PA; Josiah Brown, *Reports of Cases*, IV, 421–35.

22. *ST*, XVII, 1245, 1246; "The Answer of John Giffard, Gentleman, Deft. to the Bill of Complaint of the Right Honorable Richard Earl of Anglesey Complt.," [1742], Giffard Family Papers, 7107, Devon Record Office, Exeter; Fidelis Morgan and Charlotte Charke, *The Well-Known Troublemaker: A Life of Charlotte Charke* (London, 1988), 99–100, 123–24.

23. *ST*, XVII, 1096, 1100, 1107, 1112, 1121–24.

24. *ST*, XVII, 1113, 1115.

25. *ST*, XVII, 1100–1, 1105, 1107, 1108.

26. Frank McLynn, *Crime and Punishment in Eighteenth-Century England* (London, 1989), 262; J. M. Beattie, *Crime and the Courts in England, 1660–1800* (Princeton, 1986), 77–81; Ekirch, *Bound for America*, 32–40.

27. *ST*, XVII, 1245–46, 1247, 1252–53.

28. Beattie, *Crime and the Courts*, 35–42, 352–56.

29. *Abstract*, 37–38, 44; *ST*, XVII, 1125.

30. Robert B. Shoemaker, *Prosecution and Punishment: Petty Crime and the Law in London and Rural Middlesex, c. 1660–1725* (Cambridge, 1991), 119; *Abstract*, 38–40.

31. Beattie, *Crime and the Courts*, 298–309; W. J. Sheehan, "Finding Solace in Eighteenth-Century Newgate," in J. S. Cockburn, ed., *Crime in England, 1550–1800* (Princeton, 1977), 229–45; *Abstract*, 39–40; *ST*, XVII, 1120.

32. *The Oxford Dictionary of Quotations* (Oxford, 1980), 381; Beattie, *Crime and the Courts*, 309; Baker, *English Legal History*, 510.

33. "History of the Old Bailey Courthouse," http://www.oldbaileyonline.org/ history/the-old-bailey; Gerald Howson, *Thief-Taker General: The Rise and Fall of Jonathan Wild* (London, 1970), 27; Peter Linebaugh, *The London Hanged: Crime and Civil Society in the Eighteenth Century* (Cambridge, 1992), 75–76.

34. *ST*, XVII, 1093–95; "History of the Old Bailey Courthouse."

35. *ST*, XVII, 1094–95.

36. *ST*, XVII, 1095.

37. *ST*, XVII, 1095–97; *Abstract*, 41.

38. *ST*, XVII, 1097, 1093–94; *Universal Spectator and Weekly Journal* (London), July 17, 1742; Beattie, *Crime and the Courts*, 356–62; John H. Langbein, *The Origins of Adversary Criminal Trial* (Oxford, 2003), 106–15.

39. *ST*, XVII, 1098–105; Beattie, *Crime and the Courts*, 76.

40. *ST*, XVII, 1109.

41. *ST*, XVII, 1112.

42. *ST*, XVII, 1112–21.

43. *ST*, XVII, 1121–22; Stephan Landsman, "One Hundred Years of Rectitude: Medical Witnesses at the Old Bailey, 1717–1817," *Law and History Review* 16 (1998), 445–56.

44. *ST*, XVII, 1124–25.

45. *ST*, XVII, 1126–33.

46. *ST*, XVII, 1133–40.

47. *The Proceedings at the Sessions of Peace, Oyer and Terminer, for the City of London, and County of Middlesex*, June 14–17, 1742 [London, 1742]; *The Trial of James Annesley and Joseph Redding* [London, 1742].

48. *Abstract*, 43–44.

6: HOME

1. *ST*, XVIII, 209.

2. *Memoirs*, 212; *PP*, 719.

3. Petition of James Annesley to the Duchess of Marlborough, Sept. 14, 1742, C.G.Y. Vol. 218, f. 1, College of Arms, London.

4. NLD (J. Cavanagh); César de Saussure, *A Foreign View of England in the Reigns of George I & George II: The Letters of Monsieur César de Saussure to his Family*, trans. Van Muyden (London, 1902), 162; *Abstract*, 46; *LEP*, Sept. 2, 1742; ST, XVII, 1170–71.

5. *Abstract*, 46–47; Charles G. Harper, *The Holyhead Road: The Mail-Coach Road to Dublin* (London, 1902), 308, 309, passim; W. T. Jackman, *The Development of Transportation in Modern England* (New York, 1968), 271–72; http://www.sacred-texts.com/earth/za/za14.htm.

6. Connolly, *Religion, Law, and Power*, 44; David Dickson, *Arctic Ireland* (Dublin, 1997); *ST*, XVII, 1191.

7. *ST*, XVII, 1195, 1191; *TL*, 20; *Abstract*, 47–48; *PHA*, 47–48.

8. Madden, *Reflections*, 104; *Abstract*, 48–49; Connolly, *Religion, Law, and Power*, 138–40.

9. Young, *Tour in Ireland*, ed. Hutton, II, 54; Connolly, *Religion, Law, and Power*, 140–41.

10. Coffer, *Hook Peninsula*, 116, 119–20; Kavanagh and Murphy, *Wexford Gentry*, 83–85; *HIP*, V, 109–10; II, 354–57; *MIP*, 87; *Abstract*, 27–28.

11. *Abstract*, 49; *LEP*, Aug. 20, 1737; *Daily Gazetteer*, Feb. 7 and July 25, 1738; Connolly, *Religion, Law, and Power*, 135; Jonathan Powis, *Aristocracy* (Oxford, 1984), 48.

12. *Abstract*, 49.

13. NLD (R. Murphy); *Abstract*, 51.

14. NAD (A. O'Connor). See also NLD (G. Harford).

15. Barry to Orrery, Jan. 14, 1743, *OP*, I, 283.

16. Martin Stephen Flaherty, "The Empire Strikes Back: Annesley v. Sherlock and the Triumph of Imperial Parliamentary Supremacy," *Columbia Law Review* 87 (1987), 593–622; Baker, *English Legal History*, 31–33.

17. *Abstract*, 52.

18. Blackstone, *Commentaries*, I, 161; *Abstract*, 52; Badford E. Biegon, "Presidential

Immunity in Civil Actions: An Analysis Based upon Text, History and Blackstone's Commentaries," *Virginia Law Review* 82 (1996), 684–85.

19. *ST*, XVII, 1141–43; Baker, *English Legal History*, 301–2; *Pue's Occurrences* (Dublin), Dec. 3, 1743.

20. Blackstone, *Commentaries*, III, 45; Harold Wurzel, "The Origin and Development of Quo Minus," *Yale Law Journal* 49 (1939), 39–64; Baker, *English Legal History*, 47–49.

21. Mackercher to Standish, Jan. 27, 1743, Standish of Duxbury Muniments, DP 397/7, Lancashire Record Office, Preston.

22. *ST*, XVII, 1143; *LEP*, June 28, 1743; *Abstract*, 52–53.

23. Henry Horwitz and Patrick Polden, "Continuity or Change in the Court of Chancery in the Seventeenth and Eighteenth Centuries?" *JBS* 35 (1996), 24–57; Baker, *English Legal History*, 39–40, 108–13.

24. Complaint of James Annesley, July 15, 1743, C 11/2267/4.

25. *LEP*, June 4, Sept. 10, 1743.

26. *Daily Advertiser* (London), Jan. 3, 1743; *MIP*, 19; Response of Earl of Anglesea, June 10, 1751, Earl of Anglesey Papers, 1770–72, 1819, HL/PODC/CP/3/3, PA.

27. *MIP*, 154; *Abstract*, 25; NAD (D. Annesley); *MIP*, 192.

28. Charles Richardson, *Racing at Home and Abroad: British Flat Racing and Breeding, Racecourses, & the Evolution of the Racehorse* (London, 1922), 197; John Dunton, *The Dublin Scuffle* (Dublin, 2000), 228.

29. *A Tour Through Ireland* I, 235; Barnard, *Making the Grand Figure* 228–29; Brian Lalor, ed., *The Encyclopedia of Ireland* (New Haven, 2003), 502.

30. *ST*, XVIII, 206; John Rutty, *A Chronological History of the Weather and Seasons, and of the Prevailing Diseases in Dublin . . .* (London, 1770), 106; *Abstract*, 56.

31. *ST*, XVIII, 214, 206–7, 239; *London Daily Post and General Advertiser*, Oct. 4, 1743; Henry B. Wheatley, *London Past and Present: A Dictionary of Its History, Associations, and Traditions* (London, 1891), II, 554.

32. *ST*, XVIII, 201, 207, 220, 239–40.

33. *ST*, XVIII, 207–8, 217, 230, 240.

34. *ST*, XVIII, 208–9, 221–22, 240–41.

35. *ST*, XVIII, 232, 203, 231, 209–10, 222, 226–27, 233–34, 241.

36. *ST*, XVIII, 211–12, 223, 241–42.

37. *ST*, XVIII, 212–13, 242.

38. *ST*, XVIII, 213–14, 242–43.

39. *ST*, XVIII, 248–49, 223.

7: REDEMPTION

1. "Extract of a Letter from Dublin," Nov. 26, 1743, *WJ*, Dec. 10, 1743.

2. [Swift], *Humorous Description*, 6; Colum Kenny, "The Four Courts at Christ Church, 1608–1796," in W. N. Osborough, ed., *Explorations in Law and History: Irish Legal History Society Discourses, 1988–1994* (Blackrock, Ireland, 1995), 122, 107–32 passim; Edward McParland, "The Old Four Courts, at Christ Church," in Caroline Costello, ed., *The Four Courts: 200 Years* (Dublin, 1996), 23–32.

3. Kenny, "Four Courts," 127, 130.

4. McParland, "Old Four Courts," 30; Kenny, "Four Courts," 122; *Whalley's News-Letter*, June 17, 1721.

5. *ST*, XVII, 1339; Barry to Orrery, Jan. 14, 1743, *OP*, I, 284; *WJ*, Nov. 5, 1743; Rutty, *Chronological History of the Weather*, 106–7.

6. *Case*, 9; Éamonn Ó Ciardha, *Ireland and the Jacobite Cause, 1685–1766* (Dublin, 2004), 271.

7. Perceval to Egmont, Nov. 26, 1743, Egmont Papers, Add. Mss. 47008, 28–30; Apr. 14, 1737, *Egmont Diary*, 387.

8. *An Authentic Journal of the Proceedings in the Great Cause Tried at Dublin, between the Honourable James Annesley, Plaintiff and a Noble Person, Defendant . . .* (London, 1743), 3; *LEP*, Nov. 3, 1743; *ST*, XVII, 1139; *Abstract*, 72.

9. James Roderick O'Flanagan, *The Lives of the Lord Chancellors and Keepers of the Great Seal of Ireland: From the Earliest Times to the Reign of Queen Victoria* (London, 1870) II, 71; *ODNB*, s.v. "John Bowes."

10. *ODNB*, s.v. "Richard Mountney"; *HIP*, IV, 19–20; O'Flanagan, *Lord Chancellors*, II, 92–93.

11. Garnham, *Courts*, 99; *Abstract*, 68; A. R. Hart, *A History of the King's Serjeants at Law in Ireland: Honour rather than Advantage* (Dublin, 2000), 72; Barnard, *New Anatomy of Ireland*, 118.

12. "Letter from Dublin," Nov. 26, 1743, *WJ*, Dec. 10, 1743; R. Tighe to Orrery, Dec. 22. 1743, *OP*, I, 284; *ST*, XVII, 1139–41; *Abstract*, 72.

13. *ST*, XVII, 1141–43.

14. *ST*, XVII, 1143–48; *HIP*, V, 194–96.

15. *ST*, XVII, 1149–64: Thomas Welburn Hughes, *An Illustrated Treatise on the Law of Evidence* (Chicago, 1905), 320–21; *PHA*, 139.

16. *ST*, XVII, 1157–58, 1164; *Authentic Journal of the Proceedings*, 6.

17. *TE*, 60; *ST*, XVII, 1164–72; *Authentic Journal of the Proceedings*, passim.

18. *ST*, XVII, 1177–78.

19. *ST*, XVII, 1180–81; *AC*, 119–21; *Authentic Journal of the Proceedings*, 8.

20. *TE*, 88; *ST*, XVII, 1185–86.

21. *TE*, 108–11; Tighe to Orrery, Dec. 22, 1743, *OP*, I, 285; *ST*, XVII, 1200–1205.

22. *AC*, 151; *ST*, XVII, 1207–12.

23. "To the Right Honorable Samuel Sandys Esquire, Chancellor and Undertreasurer of His Majestys Court of Exchequer at Westminster . . .," [1742], "The Answer of John Giffard, Gentleman, Deft. to the Bill of Complaint of the Right Honorable Richard Earl of Anglesey Complt.," [1742], Giffard Family Papers, 7107, Devon Record Office, Exeter; *ST*, XVII, 1251–54.

24. *HIP*, IV, 164; *ST*, XVII, 1217–19.

25. *ST*, XVII, 1220–22; *Pue's Occurrences*, Nov. 15, 1743.

26. *ST*, XVII, 1223–24.

27. Geoffrey C. Hazard, Jr., "An Historical Perspective on the Attorney–Client Privilege," *California Law Review* 66 (1978), 1061–80.

28. *ST*, XVII, 1223–39; Hazard, "Attorney-Client Privilege," 1075–78.

29. *ST*, XVII, 1239–44; Hazard, "Attorney-Client Privilege," 1073–80.

30. *ST*, XVII, 1244–54; Tighe to Orrery, Dec. 22, 1743, *OP*, I, 286; Hazard, "Attorney-Client Privilege," 1080. For the modern implications of Giffard's participation in Annesley's prosecution, see Luban, *Lawyers and Justice*, 3–10.

31. *ST*, XVII, 1254–62; W. N. Hargreaves-Mawdsley, *A History of Legal Dress in Europe until the End of the Eighteenth Century* (Oxford, 1963), 86, 102; *Abstract*, 104.

32. *ST*, XVII, 1262–65; *Authentic Journal of the Proceedings*, 15, 16.

33. *ST*, XVII, 1156, 1265–74; *TE*, 179–80, 193.

34. *ST*, XVII, 1274–75 passim; *Authentic Journal of the Proceedings*, 18–19; *A Letter from Ireland Giving a Short Narrative of the Trial betwixt the Right Honourable the Earl of A___y, and the Honourable J___s A___y* (London, [1743]), 7.

35. *ST*, XVII, 1277–1345.

36. *TE,* 283; *ST*, XVII, 1338–39.

37. *ST*, XVII, 1339–43; *TE*, 287–88.

38. *AC*, 246; *ST*, XVII, 1343–54; *TE*, 297–99; *PHA*, 169–70.

39. *ST*, XVII, 1354–83; *TE*, 338; *Authentic Journal of the Proceedings*, 29.

40. *ST*, XVII, 1383–1406; *Authentic Journal of the Proceedings*, 29.

41. *ST*, XVII, 1285, 1406–42; Blackstone, *Commentaries*, III, 372; Alexander Welsh, "Burke and Bentham on the Narrative Potential of Circumstantial Evidence," *New Literary History* 21 (1990), 611; *PHA*, 139.

42. *ST*, XVII, 1442–43; "Letter from Dublin," Nov. 26, 1743, *WJ,* Dec. 10, 1743; *Authentic Journal of the Proceedings*, 30; *Abstract*, 72–73; Rutty, *Chronological History of the Weather*, 107.

8: EQUITY

1. *Proverbs*, 371.

2. *WJ*, Dec. 3, 1743; *Daily Gazetteer*, Dec. 1, 1743; *Old England or the Constitutional Journal* (London), Dec. 10, 1743. For accounts of the trial's progress, see, for example, *Pue's Occurrences*, Nov. 15 and 19, 1743; *WJ*, Nov. 26, 1743; *Dublin Journal*, Nov. 19 and 22, 1743; *GM,* 13 (1743), 612. An advertisement for a portion of the transcript in the *Daily Advertiser* (London) of January 4, 1744 touted "the great desire of the publick to see this remarkable tryal."

3. "Letter from Dublin," Nov. 26, 1743, *WJ*, Dec. 10, 1743; Perceval to Egmont, Nov. 26, 1743, Egmont Papers, Add. Mss. 47008, 28–30; Tighe to Orrery, Dec. 22, 1743, Jan. 26, 1744, *OP*, I, 285, 287.

4. *Boston News-Letter*, June 21, 1744; *ODNB*, s.v. "John Brooks."

5. R. Tighe to Orrery, Jan. 26, 1744, *OP*, I, 288; Petition of Elizabeth, Lady Harversham to the King, [Dec. 1743], State Papers, Ireland (PRONI transcripts, T/1017/1/7); *Daily Post*, Dec. 17, 1743; Perceval to Egmont, Nov. 26, 1743, Egmont Papers, Add. Mss. 47008, 30–3; *MIP*, 46; *Abstract*, 74.

6. "Britannicus," *LEP*, Nov. 8, 1759; "Extract of a Letter from Dublin," Nov. 26, 1743, *WJ*, Dec. 10, 1743; *Abstract*, 72.

7. Tighe to Orrery, Dec. 22, 1743, *OP*, I, 286; Devonshire to [Duke of Newcastle], Nov. 28, 1743, SPI (PRONI transcripts, T/1016/1/22); John Loveday, *Diary of a Tour in 1732 . . .* (Edinburgh, 1890), 55.

8. Duncannon to Devonshire, Dec. 1, 1743, Chatsworth Papers, T3158/257,

PRONI; King to Francis Annesley, Jan. 28, 1725, King Papers, 750/14/209, TCD; Lords Justices to Devonshire, May 23, 1736, D2707/A/1/8/7, PRONI; Connolly, *Religion, Law, and Power*, 217.

9. Connolly, *Religion, Law, and Power*, 72–73, 314; *Universal London Morning Advertiser*, Dec. 12, 1743; Dickson, *Arctic Ireland*.

10. Orrery to Rev. Birch, May 26, 1747, *OP*, I, 320; Neal Garnham, "The Trials of James Cotter and Henry, Baron Barry of Santry: Two Case Studies in the Administration of Criminal Justice in early Eighteenth-Century Ireland," *IHS* 31 (1999), 328–42.

11. *Journals of the House of Commons of the Kingdom of Ireland* (Dublin, 1782), VII, 873, 875, 884, 886, 905; James Kelly, *Poynings' Law and the Making of Law in Ireland, 1660–1800* (Dublin, 2007), 206–7; *The Statutes at Large Passed in the Parliaments Held in Ireland* (Dublin, 1765), VI, 654–55.

12. *DJ*, Jan. 21, 1743; "Extract of a Letter from Ireland," Mar. 27, 1744, *Old England or the Constitutional Journal*, Apr. 7, 1744.

13. *Dublin Gazette*, Jan. 14, 1744; *Boston News-Letter*, June 21, 1744; *Abstract*, 50.

14. Duncannon to Devonshire, Dec. 6, 1743, Chatsworth Papers, PRONI, T3158/261; Devonshire to Duke of Newcastle, Dec. 8, 9, 1743, SPI (PRONI microfilm, MIC223, 169); *Abstract*, 79–80.

15. Devonshire to Newcastle, Dec. 22, 1743, SPI (PRONI microfilm, MIC223, 169).

16. Duncannon to Devonshire, Dec. 29, 1743, Chatsworth Papers, T3158/272; Arthur Malone, et al., to Devonshire, Jan. 12, 1743 (PRONI microfilm, MIC223, 169); Devonshire to Newcastle, Jan. 28, 1744, SPI, (PRONI transcripts, T/1017/1/7/11–12).

17. *ST*, XVII, 1443; *Abstract*, 73.

18. *LEP*, Mar. 27, 1744; *ODNB*, s.v. "Sir Dudley Ryder"; Anglesey v. C. Annesley, June 15, 1742, HL/PO/JO/10/3/239/3, PA; *Abstract*, 81.

19. OPH, 308–23; *Abstract*, 8–9, 88–90; James Oldham, "The Work of Ryder and Murray as Law Officers of the Crown," in Thomas G. Watkin, *Legal Record and Historical Reality* (London, 1989), 157–73.

20. Answer of Richard, Earl of Anglesey, Nov. 15, 1742 [*sic*], C 11/2267/4; *Abstract*, 83–84.

21. Henry Horwitz and Patrick Polden, "Continuity or Change in the Court of Chancery in the Seventeenth and Eighteenth Centuries?" *JBS* 35 (1996), 24–57; Baker, *English Legal History*, 112; Henry Horwitz, *Chancery Equity Records and*

Proceedings, 1600–1800: A Guide to Documents in the Public Record Office (London, 1995), 11–12.

22. *Abstract*, 90, 87–88; C 33/381/218a, 287a–b, 504a, 512b, 546a–b; C 33/383/57a, 420a; C 33/385/71b; Horowitz, *Chancery Equity Records*, 11; C 33/379/508b; C 33/381/218a, 287a–b; C 33/385/59b, 71b; Christopher W. Brooks, *Lawyers, Litigation and English Society Since 1450* (London, 1988), 47.

23. Saussure, *A Foreign View of England*, 162; Dror Wahrman, "National Society, Communal Culture: An Argument about the Recent Historiography of Eighteenth-Century Britain," *SH* 17 (1992), 45; T. C. W. Blanning, *The Culture of Power and the Power of Culture: Old Regime Europe, 1660–1789* (Oxford, 2002), 156, 103–82 passim.

24. *Daily Advertiser*, Feb. 15, 1743; *General Evening Post* (London), Feb. 10, 1743; Charles Kinian Cosner, Jr., "'Neither *Lye* Nor *Romance*': Narrativity in the *Old Bailey Sessions Papers*" (PHD diss., Vanderbilt University, 2007), 275. For an edition published in Italian, see *Memoire d'un Giovane Nobile Sventurato . . .* (n.p., 1745).

25. *The Trial in Ejectment (at large) Between Campbell Craig, Lessee of James Annesley, Esq., and Others, Plaintiffs, and the Right Honourable Richard, Earl of Anglesey, Defendant . . .* (London, 1744); *The Trial in Ejectment (at large) Between Campbell Craig, Lessee of James Annesley, Esq., and Others, Plaintiffs, and the Right Honourable Richard, Earl of Anglesey, Defendant . . .* (Dublin, 1744); *The Trial at Large Between James Annesley, Esq., and the Right Honourable the Earl of Anglesea . . .* (London and Reading, 1744); *The Trial at Large Between James Annesley, Esq., and the Right Honourable the Earl of Anglesea . . .* (Newcastle-upon-Tyne, 1744). For newspaper serializations, see, for example, *Sherborne Mercury*; *Bristol Oracle and Country Intelligencer*; *London Journal and Country Craftsman*.

26. C 33/379/508b, 523a–b; C 33/381/218a, 287a–b; NAD; *Abstract*, 69.

27. NLD; NAD.

28. Laurence Flanagan, comp., *Irish Proverbs* (Dublin, 1995), 15; NLD (J. Green).

29. NLD (A. Moore); *Abstract*, 91–99; Connolly, *Religion, Law, and Power*, 224–27.

30. NLD.

31. *LEP*, July 31, 1744; *ST*, XVIII, 198.

32. *ST*, XVIII, 198; Beattie, *Crime and the Courts*, 76.

33. *A Tour Through Ireland*, I, 236–37; Garnham, *Courts*, 104–5.

34. Garnham, *Courts*, 78–79, 105.

35. *ST*, XVIII, 198–256.

36. *ST*, XVIII, 267–80; *Abstract*, 110.

37. *ST*, XVIII, 287–90.

38. *ST*, XVIII, 288.

39. *A Narrative of the Proceedings of the Court of King's-Bench, in Ireland, Relating to the Trial of Mary Heath for Perjury* . . . (London, 1745), 5; Blackstone, *Commentaries*, IV, 137–38.

40. *Boston News-Letter*, Mar. 28, 1745; *Abstract*, 49–50, 107.

41. *ST*, XVIII, 6; Garnham, *Courts*, 72.

42. J. L. McCracken, "The Political Structure, 1714–60," in Moody and Vaughan, eds., *A New History of Ireland*, IV, 66–67; *ST*, XVIII, 7; *Trial of Mary Heath*, 8–11.

43. *Abstract*, 36; *Trial of Mary Heath*, 5–7, 19; *AC*, 83; F. Elrington Ball, *The Judges in Ireland, 1221–1921* (New York, 1927), II, 200–1, 207–8; *HIP*, 191–93; Garnham, *Courts*, 88; e-mail from Neal Garnham, Oct. 31, 2008.

44. *ST*, XVIII, 8–31, 34–45; *Trial of Mary Heath*, 22–23.

45. *ST*, XVIII, 88, 133, 45–136 passim.

46. *ST*, XVIII, 66–74, 45–136 passim.

47. *ST*, XVIII, 136–96; *Trial of Mary Heath*, 76; *Daily Post*, Feb. 19, 1745. See also *Penny London Post or the Morning Advertiser*, Feb. 18, 1745.

48. Christopher Duffy, *The '45* (London, 2003).

49. *Proverbs*, 371; *Abstract*, 84, 88, 113–14.

50. *Old England or the Constitutional Journal*, Apr. 27, 1745; *LEP*, June 15, 1745; *Abstract*, 105.

51. Livingstone to Stone, Sept. 30, 1745, State Papers, Domestic, 36/69/288, NA; *Old England or the Constitutional Journal*, Oct. 5, 1745.

52. *PP*, 728–30.

53. Hay to Anglesea, Aug. 5, 1746, RAC.

54. *PP*, 728–30.

55. Complaint of James Annesley, Nov. [?], 1747, C 12/756/3; *PP*, 730.

56. *PP*, 731.

57. *Penny London Post or the Morning Advertiser*, Sept. 22, 1749; Response of Earl of Anglesea, June 10, 1751, Earl of Anglesey Papers, 1770–72, 1819, HL/PODC/CP/3/3, PA.

9: RESURRECTION

1. *Whitehall Evening Post or London Intelligencer*, Dec. 13, 1759.

2. *Abstract*, 34–36, 54–56; *General Advertiser* (London), Nov. 13, 1744; *LEP*, Feb. 13, 1750; *Penny London Post or the Morning Advertiser*, Feb. 16, 1750.

3. *Whitehall Evening Post or London Intelligencer*, Apr. 7, 1750; *MEP*, 7.

4. *MEP*, 9, 13; *MIP*, 105.

5. *MEP*, 9.

6. *LJI*, III, IV, passim; Anglesey to Earl of Hardwicke, Feb. 17, 1747, Hardwicke Papers, Add. Mss., 35589/180; *MEP*, 13; *A Report from the Committee of Privileges and Elections, Touching the Election for the County of Wexford . . .* (Dublin, 1755).

7. *MIP*, 217, 106.

8. *MIP*, 180; *ODNB*, s.v. "Richard Annesley."

9. *MEP*, 8; *MIP*, 100, 3, 25, 44, 100–1; *ODNB*, s.v. "Richard Annesley."

10. *LEP*, Dec. 23, 1749; *ODNB*, s.v. "James Annesley."

11. http://www.ianson-international.org.uk/transcript2.htm; Viola Bankes, *A Dorset Heritage: The Story of Kingston Lacy* (London, 1953).

12. Will of James Annesley, Feb. 15, 1752, PROB 11/865/25; *Public Ledger or, Daily Register of Commerce and Intelligence*, Feb. 1, 1760.

13. L. M. Cullen, "Economic Development, 1750–1800," in Moody and Vaughan, eds., *A New History of Ireland*, IV, 178–80; *A Letter to a Nobleman in the Country, on the Affairs of Mr. Annesley . . .* (London, 1744), 6; *Egmont Diary*, 387.

14. *London Morning Penny Post*, June 19 and Feb. 20, 1751.

15. "Abstract of a Letter from Bristol," *LEP*, Nov. 25, 1752; *Read's Weekly Journal or British Gazetteer* (London), Nov. 18, 1752; *Abstract*, 3.

16. "From the Inspector," *London Magazine*, Sept. 1755, 437.

17. *PP*, 692–732; "From the Inspector," *London Magazine*, Sept. 1755, 436–37.

18. *Case*, 3–4; William Strahan, "Small Business Record Book," Add. Mss. 48802, f. 19.

19. *GM*, Sept. 1756, 8; Oliver Goldsmith, *The Life of Richard Nash of Bath* (Dublin, 1762), 93–95; *ODNB*, s.v. "Richard Nash." I'Anson's letter of January 7 to George Scott, together with the subscription list and additional correspondence, is contained in the copy of *The Case of the Honorable James Annesley* at the British Library.

20. *GM*, Nov. 1758, 552; C 33/411/93a, 159a.

21. C 31/132.

22. C 33/413/13b; *Whitehall Evening Post or London Intelligencer,* Dec. 13, 1759.

23. *Boston News-Letter,* Apr. 24, 1760; *LEP,* Jan. 8, 1760; *PG,* Apr. 24, 1760; M. L. Bush, *The English Aristocracy: A Comparative Synthesis* (Manchester, 1984), 24–25. See also, for example, *Dublin Journal* Jan. 26, 1760; *London Chronicle,* Jan. 8, 1760; *WEP,* Jan. 8, 1760; *Annual Register,* 1760, 65.

24. *Boston News-Letter,* Apr. 24, 1760; *LC,* Nov. 12, 1757.

25. *MIP,* 90.

26. Rutty, *Chronological History of the Weather,* 251; [Du Bois], *Countess of Anglesey,* 4; *ODNB,* s.v. "Lady Dorothea Du Bois"; *MEP,* 6.

27. [Du Bois], *Countess of Anglesey,* 5–6.

28. *Poems on Several Occasions by a Lady of Quality* (Dublin, 1764), 12; [Du Bois], *Countess of Anglesey,* 6.

29. *MEP,* 8; *MIP,* 88, 90; 53.

30. *MIP,* 90, 88; *WEP,* Feb. 28, 1761.

31. Will of Richard, Earl of Anglesey, Apr. 7, 1759, BK 211, 550–7 (#141447), Registry of Deeds, Dublin.

32. *PA,* Mar. 9, 1761.

33. *Lloyd's Evening Post and British Chronicle* (London), Oct. 30, 1761; *LEP,* Mar. 23, 1762. See also, for example, *St. James's Chronicle or the British Evening Post* (London), Oct. 31, 1761; *New-Hampshire Gazette,* Feb. 26, 1762; *London Chronicle,* Mar. 23, 1762.

34. *LEP,* Nov. 8, 1763; John Landers and Anastasia Mouzas, "Burial Seasonality and Causes of Death in London, 1670–1819," *Population Studies* 42 (1988), 61, 67.

35. *General Evening Post* (London), Mar. 7, 1772; F. B. Maggs, "The Annesley Case," 20–22 (paper read before the Radlett Literary Society, Nov. 15, 1954), APP; PROB 11/997. See also, for example, *London Chronicle,* Mar. 7, 1772, *Middlesex Journal: or, Chronicle of Liberty,* Mar. 7, 1772, *Westminster Journal and London Political Miscellany,* Mar. 14, 1772; *GM* 42 (1772), 151.

36. *PA,* Nov. 8, 1763; *Anonymiana; or, Ten Centuries of Observations on Various Authors and Subjects* (London, 1809), 413–14.

REQUIEM

1. Claude Duneton, *Le Bouquet des Expressions Imagées: Encyclopédie Thématiqiue des Locutions Figurées de la Langue Française* (n.p., 1990), 833.

2. Countess of Anglesey v. Ann Simpson, Dec. 9, 1762, HL/PO/JO/10/3/254/28, PA.

3. Draft of Earl of Anglesey's Will, 1752, RAC; Will of Richard, Earl of Anglesey, Apr. 7, 1759, BK 211, 550–57 (#141447), Registry of Deeds, Dublin; *MEP*, 6. Not included in the earl's will was his sister, Lady Elizabeth Haversham, who resided in Lincoln, England. A decade later, on receiving a request for her influence from Salkeld, her nephew, she replied that her brother Richard "had not mentioned her in his will" and that she "thought £1,000 was a genteel compliment to a natural son." "I detest you," Salkeld wrote back. Salkeld to Haversham [176?], Summary of Haversham to Salkeld [176?], RAC.

4. George III to Lord Chancellor, Jan. 12, 1766, in Sir John Fortescue, ed., *The Correspondence of King George the Third* (London, 1967), I, 220.

5. *MIP*, 23.

6. *MIP*, 24; A. P. Malcomson, "The Irish Peerage and the Act of Union, 1800–1971," *Transactions of the Royal Historical Society*, 6th Ser., 10 (2000), 302.

7. George III to Lord Chancellor, Jan. 12, 1766, George III to Earl of Northampton, [Nov. 24], 1766, in Fortescue, ed., *Correspondence of George the Third*, I, 220, 416; William C. Lowe, "George III, Peerage Creations and Politics, 1760–1784," *HJ* 35 (1992), 589; [Du Bois], *Countess of Anglesey*.

8. [Valentia] to Frederick Flood, Feb. 15, 1770, Add. Mss. 19349; Reginald Blunt, *Thomas Lord Lyttelton: The Portrait of a Rake, with a Brief Memoir of his Sister, Lucy Lady Valentia* (London, 1936), 223–24, 232, 272.

9. *Dublin Mercury*, May 22, 1770. Less certain was a London paper that rightly remarked, "If the proof comes out in favour of the claimant, then he enjoys the honours and barony [*sic*] in dispute; if not, the whole falls to the ground." *Lloyd's Evening Post*, May 16, 1770.

10. *MEP*, 7, 6, 154, passim.

11. *MEP*, 22; Duneton, *Bouquet des Expressions Imagées*, 833; Case of Earl of Mountnorris, 1819, Earl of Anglesey Papers, 1770–72, 1819, HL/PODC/CP/3/3; Blunt, *Lord Lyttelton*, 273.

12. *MIP*, 146.

13. "Abstract of a Letter from Dublin," *Middlesex Journal or Chronicle of Liberty* (London), June 13, 1772; *MIP*, 226, 174, passim; Connolly, *Religion, Law, and Power*, 121–24.

A NOTE ON LEGAL SOURCES

1. Maria Edgeworth, *Castle Rackrent*, ed. Bruce Teets (Coral Gables, FL, 1964), 112; Garnham, *Courts*, 272.

2. On the issue of evidence and its veracity, see also Knapp and de la Torre, "Smollett, Mackercher," 28–33; de la Torre, "New Light," 274–81.

3. *ST*, XVII, 1388.

INDEX

Page numbers in *italics* refer to illustrations.